The New Warlords:
from the G
to the reco
of the Mid

EDITED BY
EDDIE ABRAHAMS

M. D. Odusanya
april 2002

First Published 1994

Larkin Publications
BCM Box 5909 London WCIN 3XX

© Larkin Publications

British Library Cataloguing in Publication Data
A catalogue record for this book is available from the British Library

ISBN 0 905400 17 8

Typeset in Bembo and Univers
by Boldface Typesetting & Design

Printed in Great Britain by BPCC Wheatons Ltd, Exeter

Contents

PART THREE
Kurdistan: the struggle for national liberation

PART FOUR
The United Nations and the New Colonialism

Acknowledgements

Most of the material in this book first appeared in *Fight Racism! Fight Imperialism!*, the newspaper of the Revolutionary Communist Group. The original publication dates for the material are identified at the head of each article. A number of the articles have been edited and some amalgamated to avoid unnecessary repetition. Other articles have been updated. While this book has been the work of many authors, particular thanks to Jenny Sutton for all her hard editoral and organisational work.

EDDIE ABRAHAMS, DECEMBER 1993

This is the third in the 'Counterattack' series. Details of Counterattack One, 'The Legacy of the Bolshevik Revolution' and Counterattack Two, 'Labour, a Party fit for Imperialism' can be found at the back of this book.

INTRODUCTION

Imperialism, socialism and the recolonisation of the Middle East

Humanity is paying a high price for capitalism's victories in the 1980s over the Soviet Union, the socialist bloc and Third World anti-imperialist movements. Thousands of unscrupulous hired pens promised that the 'New World Order' would inaugurate an era of peace, democracy, economic prosperity and social progress. Yet since the collapse of the socialist bloc in 1989, all these triumphal claims have been buried beneath the rubble of economic crisis, political disintegration and war.

Far from a new democratic dispensation assuring the world's peoples and nations self-determination, sovereignty and progress, the post-Cold War era is witnessing the emergence of a new colonialism. It may not resemble the old British Empire, but it is just as barbaric and disastrous in its results. That the new colonialism is no myth is shown by any examination of Iraq's fate after the 1991 Gulf War or developments in Palestine during the 1990s.

When brass bands play outside the White House and the world's imperialist warmongers gather to celebrate 'peace', the Palestinian masses, veterans in the fight against overwhelming odds, know they face their biggest test. The Declaration of Principles agreed by the Israeli government and the PLO in September 1993 was a clear move to impose a neo-colonial settlement on the Palestinian people. This 'peace' does nothing to address the most elementary requirements of the Palestinian masses for self-determination, democracy and independent economic development. On the contrary, it strengthens the position of Israel – a settler colonial state in the region. The earlier redrawing of Iraq's borders after the Gulf War, the establishment of 'exclusion zones' and the maintenance of rigorous sanctions against Iraq already heralded the shameless return of colonial-style domination of the Third World by the major powers.

Today all the main features of world imperialism are evident in the Middle East – escalating imperialist militarism; an unashamed drive by the major powers to carve out new spheres of influence and recolonise the Third World; their attempts to subordinate small nations to the global profit requirements of their multi-nationals; and the increasingly fierce rivalries between the major powers. Furthermore on the political level, the retreat of national democratic and communist movements and the rise of reactionary populism as a political force within the working class and mass movements are nowhere more dramatic and more disastrous for the progressive movement than in the Middle East. The articles included in this book form a preliminary discussion of some of the main features and main forces shaping world politics since the collapse of the socialist bloc and the 1991 Gulf War.

Oil, the Gulf War and the new colonialism

' . . . a place where the oil resources constitute a stupendous source of strategic power and one of the greatest prizes in world history'
(1945 State Department Memorandum)

The Gulf War of 1991 inaugurated a new phase of Great Power militarism in world politics. The devastation of Iraq demonstrated their readiness to use unprecedented military force to defend their strategic economic interests (See Chapter One: The Gulf War: imperialism and militarism). Imperialism has never tolerated challenges to its domination of the Middle East. Even after the collapse of the Soviet Union, the region remains critical to the capitalist system. It contains 66 per cent of the world's oil reserves. Whoever controls the Middle East not only secures massive profits but wields enormous power against rival imperialist nations dependent on the area's oil.

Ever since the discovery of oil, the region has been a site of combat between British, German, French and more recently US imperialism, as each sought to assert dominant influence. During the height of British influence, the British state played a decisive part in securing imperialist domination (see Appendix One and Two and 2.9 British Labour and Zionism). The Labour Party's own odious role in this history merely demonstrates that its enthusiastic participation in the 1991 Gulf War against Iraq was but a continuation of its old imperialist history.

The pulverisation of Iraq was a warning to Third World nations. Woe betide them if they dare challenge their servile status as suppliers of cheap labour and raw materials. For the major powers democracy, national self-determination and independence are thoroughly dispensable concepts. Boutros Boutros-Ghali, UN Secretary General and puppet of the UN's real master, the US, says that 'The time of absolute and exclusive sovereignty has passed.' For whom? The US, for Europe, for Japan? Certainly not. It has passed for Third World nations. The United Nations, supposedly a forum for international peace and co-operation, is becoming an instrument of the new colonialism. It was under UN auspices that Iraq was devastated, and under UN authority that Somalia was occupied (see Chapter Four: The United Nations and the New Colonialism).

Defended as a legitimate humanitarian operation, the crude, barbaric, colonial character of the December 1992 invasion of Somalia is evident even in bourgeois press reports. Having first cultivated and then fallen out with General Aideed under the pretext of searching for him, US and UN troops unleashed an onslaught against Somali civilians. Hundreds of unarmed civilians have been gunned down in demonstrations against the occupation. In racist and colonial language reminiscent of the Vietnam war the slaughter is justified with claims that unarmed men, women and children are in fact 'hostile combatants.'

Imperialism, Zionism and the colonisation of Palestine

Imperialism cannot oppress, colonise and plunder the Third World through direct military intervention alone. It must of necessity seek out social and political agents for its domination – a local dependent and pliant ruling class. In the Middle East, besides its alliance with the Arab ruling class, imperialism has cultivated Israel. Zionism in fact conceived itself as an outpost of imperialism in the region. Long before the foundation of Israel, Theodor Herzel, the father of Zionism, said:

> 'For Europe we shall create there in Palestine an outpost against Asia, we shall be the vanguard of the civilised world against barbarism.'

British ruling class support for the formation of Israel was explicitly designed to secure imperialism a social/political prop in the area. Sir Ronald Storr, British Colonial Governor of Palestine in the 1930s, put it aptly when he said:

> 'A Jewish state ... could be for England "a little loyal Jewish Ulster" in a sea of potentially hostile Arabism.'

Lord Melchett, a leading capitalist and contemporary, said in 1937:

> 'The advantages to the British empire [of a Zionist state] are obvious. The security of ... imperial interests can be better assured by a large European [Zionist] population than by the few battalions that can be spared.'

Indeed the British state, and the Labour Party in particular, was in large part responsible for the birth of the Israeli state (see 2.9 British Labour and Zionism). That today the US is the main financier of and main beneficiary of Zionism does not alter this fundamental political reality. A massive infusion of US funding has enabled Zionism to offer its Jewish citizens a standard of living equivalent to that of the privileged, labour aristocratic sections of the working class in the imperialist countries. It has thus created a powerful counter-revolutionary social base for imperialist operations in the area (see 2.1 Zionism: the second apartheid).

Despite the collapse of the Soviet Union, Israel remains a 'strategic ally' of US imperialism (see 2.6 The colonisation of Palestine). While the US ruling class may reconsider the extent of its funding and the conditions of its support for Israel, it remains fully committed to subsidising this racist state. In supporting Israel's relentless and brutal colonisation of Palestine, the US is helping to consolidate and fortify this outpost for its new colonial designs.

The Kurdish revolution

Imperialist opposition to Kurdish national unity and independence also has a long history (see 3.1 Imperialism and the colonisation of Kurdistan) and is also motivated by its strategic need to retain control of the Middle East. For generations the Kurdish people have been divided and oppressed by Turkey, Iran, Iraq and Syria. Despite the Kurdish people's demand for national self-determination, neither the UN nor any of the major powers support the formation of an independent Kurdish state.

On the contrary, they are instrumental in securing Kurdistan's continued-carve up. Like a liberated Palestine, a united and independent Kurdistan would present a threat to imperialist interests in the region. It could spark a new round of revolutionary upheaval in the area and help lift the isolation of the Palestinian revolution. It would seriously jeopardise the stability of four countries, and in particular would seriously undermine the Turkish state, a firm ally of US imperialism. An independent Kurdistan would be an obstacle to imperialism's new colonial designs. Imperialism therefore willingly endorses the Turkish state's brutal struggle against the PKK and Kurdish independence (see 3.4 The Turkish state, the Turkish working class and the Kurdish revolution).

The retreat of the working class and national liberation movements

Today the working class movement, both in the imperialist countries, the Middle East and internationally is ill-equipped to resist the new imperialist onslaught. In the major European nations the working class remains in the grip of the most reactionary forces – those of social democracy, of the Labour Party – ready to mobilise behind the banner of the new colonialism.

In the Middle East the Gulf War marked the final demise of Arab nationalism. Nationalist regimes with previous anti-imperialist pretensions such as Syria have openly joined the imperialist camp along with Egypt and Saudi Arabia. Iraq, once the most powerful of Arab nationalist states, has been devastated. The disintegration of Arab nationalism and the defeats suffered by the left and working class movements have led to reactary Muslim fundamentalism securing a following among large sections of the working class, peasantry and impoverished urban petit-bourgeoisie (see 2.7 Communism, fundamentalism and the question of Palestine).

Since the collapse of the socialist bloc many anti-imperialist, revolutionary and self-proclaimed socialist movements have made a rapid accommodation to imperialism and a transition to liberal, social democratic reformism. Marxist forces have been easily and speedily isolated and temporarily marginalised. The driving forces in this transition have been the political representatives of the nationalist bourgeoisie, the privileged petit-bourgeoisie and the intelligentsia. The latter forces, the petit-bourgeoisie in particular, had previously sought to advance their interests through an alliance with the working class and socialist movement.

With the collapse of the Soviet Union and the retreat of the working class, the privileged petit-bourgeoisie has opted for compromise with imperialism and capitalism as the best means of securing its own narrow privileges. The right-wing and petit-bourgeois forces have abandoned revolutionary struggle and have been drawn into the trap of 'negotiated', 'political' settlements dictated by imperialism and the interests of capitalism. In so doing they act as agents of the bourgeoisie and the imperialists to prevent popular revolutionary struggles against imperialism and capitalism. The September 1993 agreement between the Israeli government and the PLO highlights the reactionary role of these forces as they reveal themselves in Palestine and the Palestinian liberation movement (see 2.8 The great betrayal). Similar forces are also organising with the Kurdish revolution and being nurtured by imperialism and the Turkish state (see 3.5 Kurdistan: revolution at a critical juncture.

Preparing for the future

Since the collapse of the socialist bloc, the capitalist system has been plunged into a major economic crisis. To resolve it, the ruling classes of the USA, the EC and Japan are seeking new ways to squeeze more profits out of the working class and peasantry – whether in the Third World or in the heartlands of imperialism. Imperialism is preparing for the working class and oppressed of this world a veritable hell of colonial oppression.

Imperialism never reconciled itself to the independence of oppressed nations achieved during the post-World War Two tide of anti-colonial struggles. The prosperity of the imperialist/capitalist economy was and remains dependent on its ability to plunder and exploit the Third World. Therefore throughout the 1960s, '70s and '80s imperialism sought to reassert its control through an alliance with reactionary sections of the dependent ruling class and army. It waged bloody, brutal and destructive wars directly or via proxies (Vietnam, Cambodia, Laos, Guatemala, Lebanon, Panama, Grenada, Angola, Mozambique, El Salvador, Nicaragua) organised or fostered brutal military coups (Chile, Brazil, Argentina), aided the massacre of working class and communist movements (Indonesia, Sudan, Afghanistan) and imposed pro-imperialist regimes in many parts of the world.

With the collapse of the socialist bloc and the defeats of national liberation movements the US, EC and Japan are seeking once more to reassert and consolidate their grip over Third World states in order to better control and plunder cheap natural resources and cheap labour. Simultaneously, these three major power blocs are engaged in a determined struggle amongst themselves to carve out new colonial spheres of influence.

The EC, under German leadership, is attempting to transform Russia and Eastern Europe into a 'Third World on its doorstep'. Germany is already the leading lender and investor in an area where today 'wages are comparable to the Far East' (*Financial Times*). Japanese capital is taking over from the US as the dominant force in South East Asia, which today accounts for 41 per cent of its trade. Japanese sales get a five per cent return in the area in contrast to 3.2 per cent in Europe and 0.9 per cent in the USA. The USA is meanwhile tightening its noose over Latin America, Central America and Mexico where average farm wages are 35 cents per hour compared to $9.50 in the USA, while the average wage of a car worker is $4.00 per hour compared to $20.00 in the USA.

Today's new colonialism is being sustained and reinforced by the economic policies of the major powers and by international financial institutions such as the International Monetary Fund and the World Bank. Under the guise of neo-liberal 'reforms' or 'structural adjustment programmes' to encourage 'economic growth' they are forcing Third World states to abandon all policies which secured them a degree of economic independence from imperialism. Massive privatisation, a main feature of neo-liberalism, by eliminating state control over Third World economies renders these nations powerless before imperialist multi-nationals, and will block any prospect of independent development. The economics of the new colonialism are also being felt sharply by the working class and peasantry in what was the socialist bloc. The Adam Smith Institute, an enthusiastic proponent of neo-liberalism in Eastern Europe, was frank about developments there:

'Three years after their anti-communist revolutions, the countries of eastern Europe face economic catastrophe, mass unemployment and social and economic breakdown.'

(*The Guardian* 19 October 1992)

While plundering and attacking the nations of the Third World, the major capitalist powers are also carrying out sweeping attacks on the working class in Europe, America and Japan. Under the impact of the capitalist crisis, social benefits, medical welfare, education, pension rights, trade union rights and living standards are all being slashed.

Today, competition among the major powers remains, for the moment, 'peaceful'. However, for the Third World the experience of the Middle East demonstrates that if the Great Powers fail to dominate by 'peaceful' means, or if they meet resistance of any sort, they can readily resort to war and devastation with no fear of effective reprisal.

To rescue humanity from such barbarism the democratic and socialist movement will have to reaffirm and develop all the fundamental principles of the communist, working class and progressive movement. A revolt by the overwhelming majority of humanity against the unbearable and intolerable conditions imposed by imperialism and capitalism is inevitable. To give this movement political clarity and direction, and to prevent it from being destroyed by forces prepared to compromise with capitalism, the age-old socialist principles of internationalism, democracy and the right of nations to self-determination remain as necessary as ever. Only the revival of a truly international working class movement and an internationalist communist movement, committed to democracy, national self-determination and socialism, can successfully resist the tide of reaction imperialism is unleashing.

This book is part of our contribution to the ideological and theoretical debate which will be necessary to clarify and develop the outlook and standpoint of the inevitable mass opposition to imperialism and its new colonial designs.

EDDIE ABRAHAMS, DECEMBER 1993

RCG contingent on anti-Gulf War demonstration

PART ONE

The Gulf War: imperialism and militarism

1.1 OIL IMPERIALISM AND THE CLASS STRUGGLE
EDDIE ABRAHAMS/DAVID REED
FRFI 97 · 15 SEPTEMBER/15 NOVEMBER 1990

'. . . one can say that the revolutionary movement in the advanced capitalist countries will remain a myth as long as the struggles of the workers in Europe and in North America against the capitalist system are not closely united against imperialism and world capitalism with those of the hundreds of millions of oppressed people in the colonies.'   (Statement from the Popular Front for the Liberation of the Occupied Arab Gulf, May 1969)

The recent developments in the Arab Gulf have settled one decisive question of world politics. They have swiftly demolished the claim that the defeat of the socialist bloc and the end of the Cold War would inaugurate an era of democracy and peace between nation states. The massive build up of the US war machine in the Gulf shows how militarism and war are necessary characteristics of imperialism's defence of its interests all over the world. It shows that the capitalist system cannot survive without neo-colonial oppression to safeguard imperialist access to cheap sources of fuel and raw materials.

It is no accident that the first major development after the collapse of the socialist bloc has seen the biggest US military operation since the

Vietnam war, to secure control of the world's largest oil reserves in the Middle East. Far from moderating imperialism's predatory character, the collapse of the socialist bloc has now removed all restraints on its drive to carve up and redivide the world.

A second fundamental characteristic of imperialism emerging from war preparations in the Gulf is the growing clash of interests between the major imperialist powers. The lukewarm Japanese and German response to US requests for financial help with its military costs indicates their resistance to accepting unqualified US control of the Middle East and its oil. The current President of the EC Council of Ministers, Gianni De Michelis, reflected this position when he said '... there should be no taxation without representation.'

As we argued in FRFI 96 (August/September 1990), the London and Houston summits of the major imperialist powers forced the US to acknowledge the emergence of a world in which Japan and Europe, led by a united Germany, would become a challenge to the US and carve out their own sphere of influence throughout the world.

Already the new Europe's GDP is over 90 per cent, and Japan's 60 per cent, of that of the USA. Of the largest hundred companies in the world, 40 are from the EC, 39 from the USA and 15 from Japan. Of the 200 leading world banks, 65 are from the EC, 51 from Japan and 36 from the USA. The emergence of three more equally matched imperialist blocs makes new conflicts inevitable.

Under imperialism, the control of the world's oil supplies has always reflected the relative strength of the contending imperialist powers. British domination over Middle East oil began to be challenged in the inter-war years by US imperialism which by then was emerging as the major imperialist power. By the 1960s the US had achieved a dominant position in the Middle East. To safeguard their positions, Britain and the US created a system of puppet regimes throughout the region through military intervention in the Arab world: Iran (1953), Jordan and Lebanon (1958), Oman (1957-59 and 1965 onwards), Kuwait (1961), Bahrain (1956 and 1965), North Yemen (1962 and 1970), Saudi Arabia (1963).

In different periods, Zionism, Iran under the Shah, Saudi Arabia,

Jordan and Syria, after its defeat in the 1967 Arab-Israeli war, have all played a critical role in defeating movements which challenged imperialism's hegemony in the region. Through repression and calculated handouts of a portion of oil wealth imperialism has succeeded in undermining the anti-imperialist movement in the Arab world.

Saddam Hussein's invasion of Kuwait threatened to upset this strategic system of alliances in a period when the US economy, with an unprecedented foreign debt of some $600bn, was entering a recession while facing a challenge to its economic supremacy. It seized the opportunity to use its immense military might, built up in the Cold War years, to reassert its dominant international position.

The third and frequently ignored fundamental feature of imperialism exposed by the Gulf crisis is that the prosperity of the imperialist nations, embracing a significant section of the working class, is only possible through the plunder and exploitation of the oppressed nations. The resulting containment of the class struggle in the imperialist countries is dependent on this plunder and exploitation. Where labour and social democratic parties have emerged, they represent the interests of the more privileged layers of the working class. They have proved to be wholly dependent on imperialism and have been just as ready as the capitalist class to carry out imperialism's predatory actions.

In Britain, the Labour Party is continuing its long historical role as a loyal servant and agent of imperialism in the Middle East and the Gulf. When Iranian nationalist Prime Minister Mohammad Mossadeq nationalised the oil industry in 1951, it was the Labour government under Attlee which organised a world-wide embargo of Iranian oil and conspired to bring down the Mossadeq government. This was accomplished in 1953 by the CIA with British complicity. The brutality of the British intervention in the Gulf under Labour governments in Oman (1964 and 1974) and South Yemen (Aden, 1964-1967) is well documented.

In keeping with this record and its class interests the Labour Party has adopted a position as warlike and as militaristic as the Tory Party. The United Nations cover for Labour militarism should deceive no one. Labour's emphasis on a UN role expresses only its leaning towards an alliance with European imperialism rather than harbouring, as Thatcher does, illusions of an independent British imperialism allied to the US. Like the US and the Tory Party, the Labour Party is determined to destroy any challenge to imperialism's strategic control of the region.

The miniscule Labour left's pacifism is in reality a fig leaf for imperialist intervention against the Arab people. They want to starve Iraq into submission, to subjugate it by 'peaceful UN sanctions' instead of a war which would see 'the Arab nations solidly united against the West.'

The abject failure of the British left to build a united opposition to imperialism's war drive is comprehensible only in the context of its subservience to the interests of the official Labour and Trade Union Movement.

The British left have refused to place demands for Kurdish and Palestinian self-determination at the centre of their work even though this would enable them to build alliances with the tens of thousands of Palestinian, Kurdish, Arab and Turkish workers in this country. Such unity could become a focus for drawing oppressed workers in Britain into organised political struggle. Instead they still harbour the illusion that the Labour Party and the official Trade Union movement are the instruments for political change in Britain. This reflects the petit bourgeois class character of these organisations which have always unequivocally refused to take the side of the oppressed in Britain or internationally.

The economic and political consequences of US imperialism's intervention in the Gulf will exacerbate inter-imperialist tensions. The near doubling of the price of oil and the cost of this military adventure threatens to send the world into a severe recession with devastating consequences for the oppressed nations.

Political opposition to imperialism in the Arab nations will become a focus for opposition elsewhere, especially in the Third World. The social and economic consequences of a recession in the imperialist countries offer the prospect for a renewal of class struggle. The opportunity exists to unite the struggles of workers in Europe and North America with the hundreds of millions of oppressed peoples opposing imperialism. It has to be seized. Without it, as the PFLOAG statement concludes, 'the revolutionary movement in the advanced capitalist countries will remain a myth.'

All revolutionary and democratic forces in the Middle East are opposing imperialism's war drive and the puppet governments which have welcomed and aided US forces. Communists in Britain should have no hesitation in joining these revolutionary and democratic forces. That is why the Revolutionary Communist Group advances the demands:

> *British hands off the Middle East!*
> *Imperialist troops out of the Gulf!*
> *Self-determination for Kurdistan!*
> *Victory to the Palestinian revolution!*

1.2 IMPERIALISM PLANS WAR
EDDIE ABRAHAMS
FRFI 97/98 · SEPTEMBER 1990/JANUARY 1991

The imperialist war preparations in the Gulf have nothing to do with the 'defence of small nations', 'Kuwaiti sovereignty' or with principles of democracy and national self-determination. US imperialism is mounting its biggest military operation since the Vietnam war for one purpose only – to ensure its control over Gulf oil reserves which represent a 'stupendous source of strategic power'.

The 2 August 1990 Iraqi invasion and subsequent annexation of Kuwait has upset a carefully constructed arrangement of imperialist domination. With one blow, Iraq became the possessor of 20 per cent of the world's oil reserves. With this wealth and its 900,000 strong battle-trained army it posed a threat to the staunchly pro-imperialist Saudi Arabia, the other major oil producer in the Gulf. This the imperialist powers are not prepared to accept.

Under the guise of liberating Kuwait and defending Saudi Arabia from Iraqi 'aggression' the US is commencing military operations of which the real aim is to cut the Iraqi regime down to size. A US Administration official declared that 'any withdrawal that left the Iraqi war machine intact would be unnaceptable.' Thatcher chipped in to assert that Iraqi withdrawal from Kuwait was not enough, claiming that it was also necessary to destroy its capacity for nuclear and chemical warfare. While Saddam Hussein remains a vicious anti-working class tyrant and one-time partner of imperialism, he is not a reliable ally. He represents a faction of the Iraqi ruling class which displays independent and imperialistic ambitions. He must therefore be crushed.

That the whole affair is about the defence of imperialist privilege and wealth was expressed frankly by President Bush:

'our jobs, our way of life, our own freedom and the freedom of friendly countries (would) all suffer if the control of the world's great oil reserves fell into the hands of Saddam Hussein.'

On 13 November Secretary of State Baker, defending the US's military mobilisation, said:

'The economic lifeline of the industrial (ie imperialist) world runs from the Gulf. If you want to sum it up in one word it is jobs.'

Imperialism and Gulf oil

Current imperialist intervention in the Middle East is only the latest in a long line of interventions. Indeed the history of the region this century has to a large degree been shaped by imperialism's efforts to suppress the Arab nationalist movement and working class in order to control the region's oil reserves which constitute a critical political and economic foundation for imperialism. The Middle East and the Gulf contain at least 66.3 per cent of these reserves! In comparison the US has only 4 per cent. Saudi Arabia has estimated reserves of 252,000m barrels. The US has 35,000m.

The major imperialist powers consume 49.1 per cent of all oil produced, the United States alone guzzling a massive 25.6 per cent of world output. Without a constant supply of Gulf oil, their economies and profits would suffer heavy blows. The United States imports more than 45 per cent of its oil, 25 per cent of it from the Gulf with 10 per cent from Iraq and Kuwait. Japan imports all its oil, 45 per cent of it from the Gulf with 10 per cent from Iraq and Kuwait. Germany, the other major imperialist power, imports 97 per cent of its oil with at least 40 per cent from the Gulf.

Is it any wonder then that imperialism willingly spends between $2-3bn a month and deploys anything up to 700,000 troops in the Gulf, in addition to 45 warships and hundreds of its most modern and deadly fighter and bomber planes, anti-tank and anti-aircraft missiles and a massive arsenal of other lethal weaponry? Such money imperialism never spends on democracy. Democracy is not profitable. But Gulf oil is. And in more ways than immediately meet the eye.

The international significance of Gulf oil

The Iraqi invasion of Kuwait threatened to undermine Gulf regimes which play a critical role in enabling imperialism to extend its influence and power throughout the Middle East, the Muslim world and Asia. The role of Saudi Arabia is a case in point. Saudi Arabia willingly does imperialism's dirty work. It was responsible for financing the Afghan counter-revolutionaries to the tune of billions of pounds; it was a conduit for money and arms to the Contras in Nicaragua and it is the main financier of reactionary Muslim fundamentalist movements devoted to the eradication of communism and socialism in the Arab world.

Saudi Arabia and the Gulf states have also tried to subvert the revolutionary character of the Palestinian liberation movement by pouring millions into the coffers of the Palestine Liberation Organisation (PLO). Such funding was designed and to a certain extent has succeeded in strengthening the compromising and vacillating bourgeois wing of the Palestinian national movement and consolidating its domination of the PLO at the expense of the working class and oppressed.

The political and economic influence of Gulf oil extends well beyond the Middle East to Turkey, Pakistan, India, Bangladesh, Malaysia,

Thailand, Sri Lanka, the Philippines, South Korea and elsewhere. Nearly four million migrant workers from these countries are employed in the Gulf forming 69.8 per cent of the labour force in the Gulf states. Working as servants (20 per cent), unskilled labourers in the oil and construction industry and in the public services, they enjoy none of the political and social rights of local people. In Kuwait alone there are 100,000 Sri Lankan and Filipino maids.

These workers each year send home up to $10bn in remittances. By no means sufficient to raise the mass of the population out of poverty, these sums nevertheless help keep the wheel of imperialist exploitation turning. Egyptian workers send nearly $3bn, Jordanians $1bn, Pakistanis and Indians $2.2bn and $2.5bn respectively. Sri Lanka depends on remittances for 40 per cent of its income. These remittances play a crucial role in stabilising the imperialist-controlled economies of these countries and serve to weaken the anti-imperialist movements by buying off a tiny section of the working class and the petit-bourgeoisie.

It is in defence of this vast structure of imperialist exploitation that the US's awesome military machine is being augmented by imperialist forces from Britain, France, Denmark, Italy, Canada, Netherlands, Australia and Belgium. West Germany and Japan respectively are substituting for some US forces in the Mediterranean and offering financial assistance. The bourgeois ruling classes of Egypt, Syria, Turkey, Morocco, Pakistan and Bangladesh are all committing forces too, independently or under the auspices of the Arab League.

The global context of the imperialist attack on the Gulf

However, beneath the apparent imperialist united front there are serious tensions and divisions. They are all united on the need to subjugate Third World nationalism in general and Saddam Hussein in particular. But this is where unity ends. The Gulf is emerging as a sphere for inter-imperialist conflict as each power fights for a bigger and better slice of the Gulf cake.

On 15 August 1990 George Bush declared that:

'there is no substitute for American leadership and American leadership cannot be effective in the absence of American strength.'

Japanese and German imperialism however, are not willing to accept unqualified US military domination which would allow the US an enormous lever over Japan and Germany. Despite US protests they both refuse to share a significant part of the enormous financial burden of the war. Sections of the Japanese and German ruling class go even further. Sensing the danger of US military strength, they are expressing discontent with constitutional restrictions on their own international military role. A Japanese Self-Defence Force lieutenant complained that Japan was 'being left outside the international political scene while other major industrialised countries are forming united forces to prevent the Iraq-Kuwait crisis from further escalating.' Meanwhile a German general stated: 'The whole of society needs to be prepared, not just to accept that its troops might have to intervene in a regional crisis but also to support them. Germans have to learn that such an action is respectable.'

European and Japanese imperialism are using the hostages issue, aid and various 'peace initiatives' to distance themselves from the US stand. Adopting a less bellicose posture the French, German and Japanese ruling class are sounding out the possibilities of a new post-crisis Gulf order in which their interests will be served better by their 'moderate stand'.

Japan has committed $2bn in aid for Arab regimes suffering as a result of sanctions against Iraq. It has offered Egypt a $400m loan at 1 per cent interest. Germany too offered aid and has even sent medicines to Iraq! Senior German, French and Japanese politicians, with the full backing of their governments, are visiting Baghdad not just to release hostages but to explore possibilities of a settlement without war. The only senior politician not to receive such backing was ex-Tory Prime Minister Edward Heath who visited Baghdad and returned to popular, but not governmental, acclaim with 33 freed hostages.

German and Japanese imperialism are using the Gulf crisis as a first step in preparing for a long term challenge to the US's worldwide superiority. The only imperialist government to give unqualified support to the Bush Administration is the British. Also representing a weak and declining imperialist power, it hopes that by clinging to US military coat-tails, it too can defend its international position and its share of the Gulf cake against economically better-equipped competitors. This is why Thatcher took the initiative in imposing a military blockade of Iraq which she insisted include food and medicine.

British imperialism's 'no negotiation', 'Saddam Hussein must unconditionally surrender or be fought' position has been fully endorsed by the Labour Party. Displaying its subservience to imperialism and hoping to harvest the chauvinist vote in the next election, the Labour Party has been outflanked on the left by Tory Heath. Heath urged negotiations and warned against the 'madness of war'; the Labour Party loudly endorsed war preparations. When James Baker visited Europe to firm up a fractured imperialist alliance and get support for the use of force, he was welcomed by Gerald Kaufman, the Shadow Foreign Secretary. Simultaneously the Labour Party disassociated itself from Tony Benn's visit to Baghdad in search of a peaceful solution.

Imperialist troops out of the Gulf

The imperialist intervention in the Gulf is not directed exclusively against Saddam Hussein. It is designed as a blow against all forces capable of challenging its control of the Gulf. Understanding well what imperialism is planning for the region, the poorest sections of the Arab masses and particularly the Palestinians are rallying in defence of Iraq. The Arab masses also justifiably harbour burning hatred for the ruling classes of Gulf states. A Jordanian expressed a widely held view when he said:

> 'The oil rich Gulf states have allowed the US a free hand with their wealth and oil while their poor stricken Arab brethren had to go on their knees for Arab aid.'

Like the Arab masses, the British and international working class has no interest in supporting any imperialist intervention against Iraq. It is the duty of all British communists and democrats to uncompromisingly expose and oppose the Labour Party imperialists, left and right, who are supporting the imperialist campaign against Iraq and the Arab people. Unlike the reactionary imperialists of the Labour Party, we call on all working class militants, on all socialists, democrats and progressives to demand the immediate withdrawal of all imperialist troops from the Gulf.

1.3 OPERATION DESERT STORM – IMPERIALISM GOES TO WAR
EDDIE ABRAHAMS/MAXINE WILLIAMS
FRFI 99 · FEBRUARY/MARCH 1991

The attempted demolition of Iraq began under the cloak of darkness at 3am on 17 January 1991. By the end of just the first day of Operation Desert Storm Iraq had been subjected to a bombardment one and a half times more powerful than Hiroshima and double that which flattened Dresden. Days of unrelenting bombing, the biggest in history, will be followed by the use of ground forces against shell-shocked Iraqi troops.

For the first time we are witnessing the full range of modern high-tech conventional imperialist warfare. Overwhelming force is the key phrase. A massive technically superior military machine is being used against Iraq's 18 million people. To ensure against the remotest possibility of defeat or heavy imperialist casualties nothing must be left to chance. Hence the over 700,000 imperialist and allied troops, the 1,650 fighter and bomber aircraft, the 3,800 tanks and 129 battleships carrying cruise missiles, and the 1,000 US nuclear warheads with British and Israeli additions held in reserve. Hence on day one the dropping of 18,000 tons of explosives in 1,300 sorties and the firing of 1,000 plus cruise missiles (each costing £1m). This onslaught was designed to rapidly and completely destroy Iraq's capacity to retaliate. It failed – US and British aircraft have been destroyed and Iraqi Scud missiles have hit targets in Israel.

The obscenity of this war is cloaked behind the computer war games jargon of 'taking out' and 'pinpoint bombing'. They have reduced the horrors of war to a carefully censored 24-hour TV spectacle without a shred of honest information. Government ministers, armchair generals and Labour hacks blandly assess the success of 'our war'. We will not see the blood, the bones, the charred bodies. The extent of devastation, injuries and deaths is not and, if the imperialists have their way, never will be, known. But we do know that Britain's role in this bloody slaughter has been second only to the USA.

What is this war about? Only fools would believe that the international gangsters of US and British imperialism have suddenly become converts to the cause of self-determination. If the Kuwaitis had no oil they could weep until the deserts bloomed before the imperialists would aid them.

This war is about imperialist power, profit and oil. When they talk of 'stability in the Middle East' they mean the subordination of the Arab masses and Arab oil to the imperialists and their obscenely rich hireling Kuwaiti and Saudi sheiks. They mean the permanently enforced balance of power that keeps their only stable and reliable ally – their ghastly offspring Israel – stronger than any other nation in the region.

The rumble of bombs in Iraq may be the prelude of greater storms to come. If the rivalry between the USA, Europe and Japan continues to grow, we or our children will see a war to redivide the world. And then those who live in imperialist countries and previously only watched wars on TV will come to understand the meaning of the term 'taking out' for themselves.

Whatever happened to the anti-war movement?

Never has there been a greater need for a massive anti-war movement. But where are the voices raised against war? Day one of Operation Desert Storm saw a packed House of Commons rallying behind 'our boys'. Hundreds of comfortable old men talked about the need for 'courage' and 'sacrifice'.

What is there left to say about Kinnock and co? Wanting to safeguard British imperialism, wanting to court votes, terrified of being deemed unpatriotic if they so much as coughed during the war debate: 'Our forces are engaged in pursuing legitimate objectives and should enjoy full support across the political spectrum . . . Dictators don't withdraw, they have to be defeated.' Thus said Kinnock, the grammar schoolboy who knows his place, looks up to his betters, and glows warmly when they let him into their club.

In the USA, where they are fortunate enough not to have a large social democratic party, the Senate and House of Representatives were deeply divided. With black people and other oppressed layers playing a far more significant role politically, a serious anti-war movement is developing. Not in Britain.

Yet it cannot be said that it is the Labour leadership that has prevented a significant anti-war movement. They are not contenders for the leadership of anti-war sentiment, they are explicitly leading the war party. The culprits must be sought amongst those who have taken the leadership of the anti-war trends, primarily Tony Benn and the Labour left. It may seem churlish to focus on Tony Benn given that he is one of the few politicians to oppose the war. But it must be said – he and his trend have prevented the building of an enduring and effective anti-war movement.

Through the five months leading to war the Labour left's position, expressed by large CND demonstrations, was to give sanctions a chance. To starve the Iraqis rather than bomb them. A week before the war the CND, calling for more time for sanctions, organised a demonstration of 100,000. And when war came and the bombs fell, what could they say? They led the anti-war movement into a blind alley.

What does Benn's position represent? 'The consequences of the war in the Gulf could be . . . the Arab nations solidly united against the West.' He wants to oppose the war – for the good of imperialism! Hence his grotesque illusions in the United Nation's ability to secure a just solution. A UN which since the collapse of the socialist bloc has become an instrument of imperialist policy, and under whose flag the blitzkrieg on Iraq is being waged. With his call for sanctions and UN action what is Benn actually saying? – that the oppressed can be kept down by peaceful means rather than war, that the current world order can be defended by becoming a little more just.

29

This tired old rubbish persists because it has a purpose. People in the imperialist nations are faced with a choice. Many of them do not approve of the war, poverty and starvation which imperialism creates. To do something about it they would have to ally with those who directly suffer at the hands of imperialism. Or they could become silent accomplices to imperialist oppression. The choice is there. Today it is summed up in the question: 'Are you for or against imperialist intervention in the Gulf?' Benn invents a comfortable third option: a peaceful solution via the UN. At the same time he gives the Labour Party the entirely spurious appearance of being worthy of support from those opposed to this war.

In the Gulf war there is only one position which reflects both the interests of the Arab masses and of those sections of the British population who desire peace: Stop the War! Imperialist Troops Out of the Gulf! It won't build a mass movement tomorrow. But then a mass movement that disappears when war is declared is not a great deal of use. It will however start to attract to its ranks the most consistent and enduring forces. It will provide a means of allying with and defending Arabic, Turkish and Kurdish people in Britain now under chauvinist attack. It will be the beginning of a new trend in Britain. If it is not born now, in the midst of this slaughter, the future is bleak indeed.

1.4 PREMEDITATED MURDER OF A NATION
EDDIE ABRAHAMS/MAXINE WILLIAMS
FRFI 100 · APRIL/MAY 1991

'Then this civilisation and justice stand forth as undisguised savagery and lawless revenge ... A glorious civilisation, indeed, the great problem of which is how to get rid of the heaps of corpses it made after the battle was over'

(Karl Marx, *The Civil War in France*)

After 40 days of war there are not heaps but mountains of Iraqi corpses. 200,000 Iraqi people are dead or mutilated. The imperialists lost just 157. In this statistic is starkly revealed the one-sided savagery of the war. 1,000 Iraqi lives for each Western one. 28 countries, including the richest and most powerful, against one nation of 18 million people. An imperialist army of terrifying technological killing power against a conscript army equipped with second rate weaponry. An air force that could pound Iraqi towns and troops without fear of airborne challenge until pilots complained there was nothing left to bomb. Minds that are not shamed and disgusted by this spectacle have forfeited their humanity.

US soldiers dig pits that are filled with the mangled remains of the numberless retreating Iraqis burned and dismembered in that final holocaust on the Kuwait–Basra highway. Iraqi families await the return of sons, brothers, husbands and lovers who will never come back. They wait for them in devastated cities where cholera, typhoid and hepatitis seep out of the ground to kill the young. The work of decades has been reduced to rubble. 'They have bombed us back to the stone age.'

What words are adequate to describe this crime in an era when language itself has been polluted by the doublespeak of war? The frying alive of men inside a metal tank coffin is a 'surgical strike'. The systematic pulverisation of thousands of men in cars and lorries is 'a turkey shoot'. A shelter for men, women and children is a 'command and control centre'. The bombing of trucks of soldiers as they bent in prayer at the roadside is a 'fun mission'.

Military theorist Clausewitz wrote: ' The invention of gunpowder, the constant progress of improvements in the construction of firearms, are sufficient proof that the tendency to destroy the adversary which lies at the bottom of the conception of War is in no way changed or modified through the progess of civilization.' The day by day destruction of Iraq certainly revealed the limits of civilization in the West.

British bishops searched their theological vaults to discover means of calling this carnage 'justifiable'. Journalists acted as pimps and propagandists for the war machine. Warm, safe, well-fed politicians and intellectuals blithely called for sacrifice from young British men too poor, stupid or amoral to find any other trade than killing. And the Labour Movement, whose 'progressive' nature is talked of only amongst small groups of Trotskyist visionaries, clapped its hands and counted up the new jobs to be had in arms production.

Few questioned the right of imperialist nations to impose their will by force on the Arab world.

The murder of a nation

And what was the imperialist will? General Norman Schwarzkopf said: 'There is a lot more purpose to this war than getting the Iraqis out of Kuwait.' Indeed so. Saddam Hussein is the type of vicious anti-working class and anti-communist tyrant usually lovingly nurtured by the USA. But he made the fatal error of displaying independent bourgeois ambitions in a region which the USA believes it alone should control. Oil wealth and a massive army threatened to allow the realisation of these ambitions. The USA was not prepared even to contemplate an Iraq capable of dictating terms about oil prices and regional power. So on 17 January they began the demolition of Iraqi economic and military power in order to eliminate this threat. In the process they hoped to unseat Hussein himself if a safe alternative could be found.

Proof that this, rather than the liberation of Kuwait, was their aim came on at least three occasions. On the eve of war, Saddam Hussein told UN Secretary General Perez de Cuellar that withdrawal from Kuwait was negotiable. This being the last thing the USA wanted to hear, it was kept secret by the UN and the bombing began. On the eve of the ground war the Soviet government negotiated a peace plan committing Iraq to withdraw from Kuwait. The US answer was the thunder of artillery. And even after the Iraqi government accepted all UN resolutions and the decimated Iraqi forces were fleeing Kuwait, the US response was to bomb the helpless retreating men, occupy parts of Iraq and step up the bombing.

The reconquest of Kuwait did not demand the destruction of Iraq's industrial and social infrastructure. But Iraq's roads, railways, bridges, airports, electricity generating plants, water pumping and purification plants, telecommunications, oil refineries, factories, schools, health services, research institutions and government buildings lie in ruins. The estimated material damage amounts to $200bn. Reconstruction will take decades.

Also in ruins is the Iraqi army, first armed and now destroyed by the imperialists. It has lost 3,500 of its 4,200 tanks, 2,000 of its 3,000 artillery guns and 2,000 of its 2,700 troop carriers. Just as the imperialists willed at the beginning of this conflict, the costs of reconstruction and the threat of reparations will ensure that for years to come Iraq will be unable to challenge imperialism.

The outcome of this war is a devastating setback for human progress, socialism and communism. For in the murder of Iraq, the US-led imperialists have issued a warning to all the poor and oppressed nations of the world: the wealth of the world belongs only to us, dare to question this and you will be cut down as Iraq was.

The tide of reaction

Now we see the reality of the world in which the socialist bloc has collapsed. The Soviet Union under Gorbachev's pro-imperialist leadership cannot stay the hand of rich and powerful nations as they plunder the world. Our Nobel Peace prize winner, who has brought the Soviet Union to the brink of political collapse, was bribed by the imperialists to support the war. His peace effort was merely a cynical response to internal anti-imperialist pressure. Nor will the UN, however much Tony Benn et al pretend, act as anything other than the rubber stamp for the US. Although the war was fought under its auspices, the UN Security Council did not even meet during hostilities. In this war the United Nations has been the hand-wringing archbishop of imperialist diplomacy.

The new world order to which Bush and Major plan to subject the world is the bloody dictatorship of imperialist capital. It will be the world order of rich nations who live at the expense of those who have nothing. Already the imperialist plans for the Middle East are unfolding and they are grim indeed.

The spoils of war

The post-war Gulf is being shaped. The first US priority was to restore the feudal al-Sabah family in Kuwait. After kissing the soil its next act was to start shooting its democratic opponents. Palestinians in Kuwait are being tortured and terrorised. The second priority for the US is to engineer a satisfactory outcome to the violent contest for power taking place in Iraq. The US is carefully weighing its options but it is clear already from its actions around Basra and its silence on the Kurdish uprising that it would prefer a tame Baathi/army alliance without Saddam Hussein to an altogether unpredictable outcome.

And what of the Middle East as a whole? The major Middle East governments are to be compliant client regimes. Syria, clutching Lebanon as its war booty, needs US and Saudi money to survive. Egypt has long been on the US payroll. Saudi Arabia is the payroll. At a meeting of the Gulf states, Syria and Egypt agreed to provide the Arab cover for US policing of the Gulf. In return they will receive a large part of a $15bn development fund to fend off the threat of economic disintegration and revolution.

As ever, these political arrangements are designed to safeguard and multiply the mighty dollar. Hundreds of foreign firms have converged like vultures expecting to reap enormous profits from Kuwaiti reconstruction estimated at $50bn. British capital also expects a cut for services rendered. 'Prizes are still to come as far as British industry is concerned' said one businessman, especially as Kuwaiti officials 'know who their friends are.' The oil companies are now plotting to reverse the process of nationalisation of the oil industry in Arab countries and thus enhance their already giant profits.

The table is laid for the victory feast but the guests are already fighting over the choicest dishes. A French proposal for a UN conference to discuss a new world order for the next 10-15 years has been shunned by the US. It hopes to use its military ascendancy to fashion a world in which its interests reign supreme. However the Japanese and Germans are resisting these designs and threatening to withold billions of dollars of subsidies they promised to the US. The Japanese want to use some of this money to make profits for themselves out of reconstruction contracts. With the recession biting deeper in the US and economic complications mounting in Germany and Japan there will be no easy ride for imperialism.

Palestinian and Kurdish self-determination – a different story

In his post-war speech a triumphal Bush pledged to resolve the Arab-Israeli conflict. Such words sent a cold shiver down the spines of all Palestinians. The threat is that another generation's hopes for self-determination and statehood are to be buried. For occupying Kuwait, Iraq suffered death and destruction. For occupying the West Bank and Gaza Israel receives unwavering support. During the war it kept all the West Bank Palestinians under a five week 24-hour curfew. Human rights, like self-determination are a very flexible concept. Israel has now been advanced another $650m with another $10bn being negotiated. These funds will be used to settle hundreds of thousands of Soviet Jews and will be the first step in the displacement of all Palestinians from the Occupied Territories.

During the war much was said about Saddam Hussein's suppression of the Kurds. Afterwards a deathly silence fell. Kurdistan was not to be on the agenda for the post-war settlement. As the first uprisings began in Turkish and Iraqi Kurdistan, the imperialists kept a cool distance, confident that their fascist ally, the Ozal regime in Turkey, was ready to crush any potential independent Kurdish state.

Can anything stem the tide?

As the imperialist victory parade marches around the world it faces obstacles and challenges. US military dominance in the area by no means secures it against social and political upheavals whipped to exploding point by poverty and humiliation. Foremost amongst these are the decades-long struggles of the Palestinian and Kurdish peoples. They have shown a will to continue the struggle that surmounts setbacks and defeats. As the Intifada continues a new Kurdish uprising breaks out.

But isolated they face a terrible situation. The crushing of Iraq has increased the odds against them enormously. Communist and revolutionary nationalist forces have been gravely weakened. Muslim fundamentalism, funded primarily by Saudi and Kuwaiti money and cloaking its bourgeois and petit-bourgeois ambitions in the language of the poor, is poised to exploit and manipulate the mass movement to its own ends. Today more than ever, the Palestinian people, like all oppressed nations fighting for freedom, need the solidarity and support of an international anti-imperialist movement. These exist amongst movements in oppressed nations. In contrast, the working class in the imperialist countries has demonstrated no independent political existence from its imperialist masters.

In the face of the most massive assault on an oppressed nation the British working class proved itself either impotent or, worse, an enthusiastic accomplice to the imperialist crime. At all stages the Labour Party stood solidly behind the war effort. Colonel Kinnock shamelessly defended the Basra-Kuwait City Highway slaughter. Like the Conservative Party, the Labour Party is committed to destroying any challenge to imperialism's control of region.

Seventy years ago Lenin said that the choice facing humanity was socialism or barbarism. Imperialism has inflicted barbarism on most of the world's population with the passive or active acquiescence of large sections of the imperialist nations' working class. How and under what conditions any forces in imperialist countries can begin to forge a movement to undermine imperialism from within remains the great unanswered question of the epoch. Only if anti-imperialists address this question can there be a way forward.

1.5 IMPERIALISM'S 'NEW WORLD ORDER'
EDDIE ABRAHAMS
FRFI 101 · JUNE/JULY 1991

The Gulf War was waged to stop Iraq from ever again challenging imperialist interests in the Middle East and Gulf region. It was an integral element of US strategy as expressed in a National Security Review on 'Third World Threats':

'In cases where the US confronts much weaker enemies, our challenge will be not simply to defeat them, but to defeat them decisively and rapidly.'

Oppressed nations who dare resist imperialist plunder will suffer Iraq's fate, a fate vividly described in a post-Gulf War UN report on Iraq:

'The recent conflict has wrought near apocalyptic results upon the economic infrastructure of what had been, until January 1991, a rather highly urbanised and mechanised society. Now most means of modern life support have been destroyed or rendered tenuous. Iraq has, for some time to come, been relegated to a pre-industrial age, but with all the disabilities of post-industrial dependency on an intensive use of energy and technology.'

The report then outlines the consequences. Approximately 90 per cent of industrial workers are inactive as the 109,876 US and British air sorties dropped 88,500 tons of bombs and destroyed factories, power plants, oil refineries, water-related pumps and chemical factories, communications systems, railways, roads and bridges.

As a result hunger, disease, unemployment and lack of shelter are now features in what was one of the Third World's more developed countries. Iraq imports 70 per cent of its food. With virtually no foreign exchange and the continued enforcement of most sanctions it cannot obtain enough food. Prices have risen nearly 1,000 per cent and there are serious shortages of sugar, rice, tea, vegetable oil, powdered milk and other essentials. Livestock farming has been devastated by sanctions and the destruction of the sole laboratory producing vaccines against cattle disease.

The report predicts massive health problems as:

'. . . Iraqi rivers are heavily polluted by raw sewage, and water levels are unusually low. All sewage treatment and pumping plants have been brought to a standstill by the lack of power supply and the lack of spare parts. Pools of sewage lie in the streets and villages. Health hazards will build in the weeks to come.'

Famine and disease are stalking the country. A Harvard University team of doctors warned that in 1991 alone, 'at least 170,000 children under five years of age will die' because of sanctions. Dr Eric Hoskins of the Gulf Peace Team commented:

'Iraq's civilians have been dying of starvation and disease in their thousands because of lack of basic food and medicine. Never before in history has a government been prohibited from purchasing and importing food and medicines for its own people.'

An Oxfam/Save the Children Fund report noted:

'The unavailability of powdered milk spells nutritional disaster for children . . . the spread of disease such as cholera and typhoid in the present conditions are inevitable.'

Deaths among children under five have quintupled. Close to a million children are malnourished and 100,000 are starving. With production in public and private industry down by anything between 50-90 per cent and real wages down by 90 per cent the situation can only grow worse. Nearly one year after the war the situation continues to deteriorate. The imperialists are well on the way to reducing Iraq to one of the most impoverished of Third World countries. Already, in real terms, Iraqi workers now earn less than agricultural workers in rural India.

The new colonialism

The post-war UN ceasefire resolution accepted by Iraq on 6 April 1991 was but the judicial expression, on an international level, of the essentially colonial character of the much trumpeted 'new world order'.

By means of this resolution, which only Cuba voted against, Iraq's sub-jugation by and dependence on imperialism was affirmed. Described as the most punitive since the Versailles Treaty, the UN, for the first time, imposed border demarcations and extended Kuwait's borders 7 miles into Iraq. This now allows the emirate to steal even more of Iraq's oil from its Rumallah fields.

To ensure that Iraq never again presents a military threat to imperialism, it is now compelled to hand over for destruction all its chemical and biological weapons, all its ballistic missiles with a range beyond 90 miles and all materials for building nuclear weapons. The Security Council has also banned all sales of conventional weapons to Iraq. Meanwhile, of course, the major imperialist powers continue to arm themselves to the hilt with even more deadly and sophisticated weapons. And they continue to supply such weapons to their clients in Israel and other reliable ruling classes. But then the Gulf War was but the first of a new round of essentially colonial wars.

Imperialism uses the Iraqi ruling class

On the anvil of imperialism's predatory and reactionary designs in the Middle East the Kurdish people and Shiites in southern Iraq are being forced to pay a deadly price. During the war Bush urged 'the Iraqi people to take matters into their own hands', authorised CIA aid to 'rebel factions inside Iraq' and organised the 'Voice of Free Iraq Radio'.

A multitude of liberals, professorial socialists and media hacks who had supported the war were subsequently 'outraged' and 'horrified' that the US and British forces watched passively as Saddam Hussein turned with deadly effect against mass uprisings in Kurdistan and southern Iraq. Hussein's Republican Guards wreaked revenge, killing tens of thousands in the South and forcing millions to flee for their lives into the Kurdish mountains on Turkish and Iranian borders.

But of course imperialism had its own agenda unrelated to the sentimental and hopeless proposals from liberal and 'socialist' warmongers. Whilst destroying Iraq's capacity to challenge imperialism, its ruling class was needed to deal with internal and Kurdish democratic forces.

An independent Kurdish government in Iraqi-occupied south Kurdistan could spark uprisings in Turkish, Iranian and Syrian-occupied Kurdistan and as a result gravely destabilise a region critical to imperialism.

Imperialism therefore intervened to establish 'safe havens' only after the Kurdish national uprising had been crushed and hundreds of thousands of Kurdish refugees were facing death by cold, starvation and disease in the mountains. However, not one iota of humanitarian sentiment animated this intervention. It was a cynically calculated political move made necessary first and foremost by the flood of refugees into Turkish-occupied Kurdistan which was seriously undermining political stability in Turkey.

Despite impressions, John Major was not the humane and wise father of the 'safe havens' concept. Turkish President Ozal, eager to find ways of keeping Kurdish refugees out of Turkish-occupied Kurdistan, was the first to suggest the plan. John Major, with the acumen inherited from the British ruling class's long colonial history, recognised more rapidly than the US its potential political benefits.

With millions of Kurdish refugees reduced to total destitution imperialist 'safe havens', food, medical and other aid appeared like godsends to avert massive tragedy. With this programme Bush and Major hope to cultivate pro-imperialist sentiment among sections of the Kurdish population. These schemes were also designed to strengthen the position of the bourgeois Patriotic Union of Kurdistan (PUK) and the Kurdish Democratic Party (KDP). Both oppose Kurdish independence and are presently engaged in negotiations with Saddam Hussein for 'autonomy'.

The imperialists hope that such trends, buttressed by safe havens and aid will act as an effective counter-weight to revolutionary developments in other parts of Kurdistan and to Kurdish organisations such as the Kurdistan Workers' Party (PKK) who fight for the independence and unity of the whole of Kurdistan. Additionally, they expect a somewhat strengthened Kurdish bourgeois force within Iraq to act as a dampener on future Iraqi ruling class ambitions.

1.6 IMPERIALISM, WAR AND THE SOCIALIST MOVEMENT
ROBERT CLOUGH
FRFI 100 · APRIL/MAY 1991

The brief span of the imperialist war against Iraq rekindled some interest in the Marxist position on war, especially as it was developed by Lenin during the first imperialist war. An understanding of the Marxist standpoint is a necessary condition for communists responding to the new wave of imperialist assault on the Third World.

The position of revolutionaries vis-à-vis any war depends on a concrete analysis of the political content or substance of that war. How do we disclose and define the substance of a war?

> 'War is the continuation of policy. Consequently, we must examine the policy pursued prior to the war, the policy that led to and brought about the war . . . The philistine does not realise that war is "the continuation of policy", and consequently limits himself to the formula that "the enemy has attacked us", "the enemy has invaded my country", without stopping to think what issues are at stake in the war, which classes are waging it, and with what political objects.'
>
> (*Collected Works (CW)* Vol 23, p33)

In other words, Marxism requires

> '. . . an historical analysis of each war in order to determine whether or not that particular war can be considered progressive, whether it serves the interests of democracy and the proletariat and, in that sense, is legitimate, just, etc.'
>
> (*CW* Vol 23, p32)

Lenin often quoted Clausewitz's famous dictum that war is the continuation of politics by other means. In fact, he took it a step further, saying 'War is not only a continuation of politics, it is the epitome of politics' (*CW* Vol 30, p224), to emphasise that it was not a break from the norm of political struggle, but quite the opposite, especially in the imperialist epoch.

Second, in analysing the substance of any war, communists need to determine what class aims are at stake.

'The social character of the war, its true meaning, is not determined
by the position of the enemy troops . . . What determines this
character is the policy of which the war is the continuation ("war is
the continuation of politics"), the class that is waging the war, and
the aims for which it is waging this war.'

(*CW* Vol 25, p362)

In other words, the military and political issues involved cannot be
separated.

Third, such analysis would establish that some wars – those for
national liberation, for instance – were completely justifiable, and had
to be supported by socialists. Lenin particularly dealt with the slogan of
'defence of the fatherland' advanced by the open opportunists of the
warring imperialist powers during 1914–18. Concrete analysis determined that 'the war is being waged for the partitioning of colonies and
for the plunder of other lands' (*CW* Vol 21, p185). Further, applying
Clausewitz's dictum on war as the continuation of politics:

'You will see that for decades, for almost half a century, the governments and the ruling classes of Britain and France, Germany
and Italy, Austria and Russia have pursued a policy of plundering
colonies, oppressing other nations, and suppressing the working
class movement. It is this, and only this, policy that is being
pursued in the current war.'

(*CW* Vol 21, p304.)

Hence the war was an 'unjust' war, since it was a war for the continued
enslavement of the working class and oppressed nations. 'Defence of
the fatherland' in this context meant the defence of the right of one
imperialist power to oppress colonies at the expense of another
imperialist power. However, socialists recognise the existence of just,
legitimate wars, wars to overthrow feudalism, absolutism and alien
oppression. Lenin again:

'I am not at all opposed to wars waged in defence of democracy or
against national oppression, nor do I fear such words as "defence of
the fatherland" in reference to these wars or insurrections. Socialists

always side with the oppressed, and, consequently, cannot be opposed to wars whose purpose is democratic or socialist struggle against oppression. It would therefore be absurd . . . not to recognise the legitimacy of wars of oppressed nations against their oppressors, wars that might break out today – rebellion of the Irish against England, for instance, rebellion of Morocco against France, or the Ukraine against Russia, etc . . . '

(CW Vol 23, p196)

Such wars, of the colonial, oppressed nations against their imperialist oppressors, would be completely legitimate:

'irrespective of who would be the first to attack; any socialist would wish the oppressed, dependent and unequal states victory over the oppressor, slave-holding and predatory "Great" Powers.'

(CW Vol 21, p301)

Lastly, socialists in the oppressor nation, in siding with the oppressed, would have to fight those who supported that oppression, in particular, the privileged labour aristocracy and its political representative, the bourgeois labour party:

'The fact is that "bourgeois labour parties", as a political phenomenon, have already been formed in all the foremost capitalist countries, and that unless a determined and relentless struggle is waged all along the line against these parties – or groups, trends etc, it is all the same – there can be no question of a struggle against imperialism, or of Marxism, or of a socialist labour movement.'

(CW Vol 23, p118)

These then are some of the relevant principles for socialists to understand if they are to adopt a principled approach to any war that 'their' imperialist power carries on.

The war against Iraq

The trigger for the war against Iraq was the latter's invasion of Kuwait. This was a dispute between two factions of the Arab bourgeoisie over the price of oil. Iraq needed a high price to rescue its economy from complete collapse, while the al Sabah family in Kuwait wanted a lower price so as not to upset the imperialist economies in which it had enormous investments. In this dispute, the war aims of either party were entirely reactionary.

However, the Iraqi invasion upset the network of alliances which US and British imperialism had established to sustain their control of the Gulf and its oil in the post-colonial era. A greater Iraq could be a threat to the Zionist state. It might provide an avenue through which Japanese or German imperialism could obtain a foothold in the Gulf and undermine the stranglehold of the US and Britain.

Hence the war aims of Britain and the US were very simple: destroy the Iraqi war machine, re-establish the al Sabah family, and use this position to reassert complete supremacy over the Arab people. To these ends, they were quite happy to bribe the Egyptian bourgeoisie and allow Syria a free hand in northern Lebanon in order to co-opt them into their designs. Democracy in Kuwait, Syria, Turkey, or freedom in Palestine or Kurdistan were completely irrelevant to their designs.

Hence socialists supported a defeat for British and US imperialism for a very concrete reason. Yet they could not by the same token extend that to a call for a victory for Iraq, because its war aims were also reactionary. Some sects fought to distinguish between a military victory for Iraq (which socialists could support) and a political victory (which socialists couldn't). But this distinction is sophistry. A military victory for Iraq was always an impossibility: even if it were not, it could only mean a political victory for Saddam, with the continued enslavement of the Kurdish people and the Iraqi working class as its consequences.

The Iraqi war aims were then the war aims of the Iraqi bourgeoisie alone. And the turn the war took proved that beyond doubt. The Iraqi army collapsed, not just because of the terrible pounding it took from the imperialist forces, but because the conscripts that made it up did not want to fight a war in whose outcome they saw no interest. 'Victory to Iraq' sounds very hollow when we see that the hatred of the Iraqi army for Saddam was much greater than for the imperialists Saddam had summoned them to fight.

As we have shown, there is another aspect to the struggle against imperialist war, and that is the fight to expose those in the working class of the oppressor nation who support the imperialist war aims – the 'bourgeois labour party' Lenin referred to.

From the outset, Labour declared its support for British war aims. They needed no encouragement; indeed, Kaufman as Shadow Foreign Secretary boasted at the Labour Party conference that he had called for Iraqi reparations fully one month before Thatcher took it up. As the economic war turned into military war, and the wider war aims of imperialism were made public, Kinnock and Kaufman did not hesitate to support them. Most despicable of all, in the slaughter of the last 24 hours, not one word of protest was uttered, as Kinnock echoed the call for an unconditional Iraqi surrender.

If Labour fulfilled its role as defender of imperialism to perfection, we must not forget the part played by the Labour left and its admirers, Lenin argued that in a period of revolutionary crisis, when the working class becomes disaffected with the 'bourgeois labour party', a trend appears which seeks to reconcile the working class to that bourgeois labour party. During the first imperialist war, Karl Kautsky, a prominent leader of the pre-war international socialist movement, was such a conciliator. Kautsky argued that socialists should oppose the war by calling for a democratic peace: that since the war was in his view was an interruption to normal politics, the fact that German Social Democrats openly defended German war aims should not be held against them, and they should not be expelled from the movement. Lenin wrote:

'Kautskyism is not an independent trend, because it has no roots either in the masses or in the privileged stratum which has deserted to the bourgeoisie. But the danger of Kautskyism lies in the fact that utilising the ideology of the past, it endeavours to reconcile the proletariat with the "bourgeois labour party", to preserve the unity of the proletariat with that party and thereby enhance the latter's prestige. The masses no longer follow the avowed social

45

chauvinists . . . The Kautskyists' masked defence of the social
chauvinists is far more dangerous.'

(*CW* Vol 23, p119)

The Labour and Trotskyist left in their own small ways played this part
to perfection. No matter how indignant Benn, Bernie Grant and other
'opponents' of Kinnock were, they were never going to break with the
butcher's assistant. To the left, the SWP made sure that its formal commitment to 'troops out' never upset its friends in CND. As Lenin said:

'One of the common sophistries of Kautskyism is its reference to
the "masses". We do not want, they say, to break away from the
masses and mass organisations!'

(*CW* Vol 23, p119)

How many times did the SWP plead that the Committee to Stop War in
the Gulf and its associated organisations were the 'broad left forces' that
were the only way to a mass movement? But as Lenin argued:

' . . . it is not so much a question of the size of an organisation, as of
the real, objective significance of its policy; does its policy represent the masses, does it serve them, does it aim at their liberation
from capitalism, or does it represent the interests of the minority,
the minority's reconciliation with capitalism?'

(*CW* Vol 23, p119)

The Committee, with its support for sanctions against Iraq and its
opposition to the withdrawal of the imperialist troops, expressed the
'minority's reconciliation with capitalism'. And the SWP? Its 'masked
defence' of the Committee was no more than a pale imitation of
Kautskyism. Truly the one point on which the left puts no condition is
its support for the Labour butchers.

The peace is a continuation of the war. The al Sabah family has re-
gained control of its private fiefdom. The Palestinian population of
Kuwait who make up the labour force are being subjected to a reign of
terror. Even the tame 'democratic' opposition is persecuted: within
days of the end of the war, one had been shot dead and another
wounded. Within Iraq, whilst imperialism hopes for a coup organised

from within the Republican Guard to topple Saddam, the Kurds fight on for liberation.

As we have explained, the issue for US and British imperialism was how best to reassert their domination of the Arab people. They could only have been defeated by the people of the Middle East as a whole acting to prevent their rulers from supporting the war. 'Victory to Iraq' could not express this standpoint; by pretending a military victory for Saddam was not a political victory it sacrificed the interests of the Kurdish and Iraqi people. 'Victory to the workers and oppressed peoples of the Middle East', the slogan of FRFI, was and still is the only legitimate standpoint of communists, since it alone states what is the case – that it is the united mass of the oppressed who can defeat imperialism, not the unwilling conscripts of a bourgeois dictator.

APPENDIX: The Historical Background

1.7 HOW BRITAIN AND THE US PLUNDER THE GULF
TREVOR RAYNE
FRFI 97 · APRIL/MAY 1991

For 170 years the peoples of Arabia and the Gulf were slaughtered and suppressed in the interests of British imperial power. The British fleet shelled along the entire coastline of the Peninsula; British troops have poisoned wells, burnt crops, tortured and murdered Arab resistance; the Royal Air Force has bombed villages into oblivion. All of this accomplished by Conservative, Liberal and Labour governments alike with the connivance of Arab ruling classes prepared to sell their people's blood and land for gold.

Initial British interest in the Gulf stemmed from the conquest of India. For strategic purposes the frontiers of India were deemed to extend from the Red Sea to the Straits of Malacca off Malaya. Before the opening of the Suez Canal in 1869 there were three routes to India: around the Cape and into the Indian Ocean; overland via the north Syrian desert , the Euphrates valley and the Gulf; or via Alexandria, the town of Suez and the Red Sea. The nineteenth century British ruling class feared French, then Russian and eventually German encroachment onto these routes and the Indian colony itself. By the 1880s India contained a fifth of Britain's overseas investment and took a fifth of its exports. Lord Curzon and later Winston Churchill maintained that India made the difference between Britain being a first and a third-rate power. To maintain Britain's control over the trade routes required a combination of brute force and financial inducements – bribes.

During 1819-20 British naval forces burned down a string of coastal towns along the Arabian peninsula and sank local fleets, calling them 'pirates' for attempting to retain control over their traditional waters. Trade was seen as a threat and destroyed, along with the Omani Empire that stretched to Zanzibar. Local leaders were forced to sign a 'General Treaty of Peace with the Arab Tribes'. The effect was to secure assurances that Britain could exclude all other foreign powers from the region. Scores of similar treaties were imposed across the region over the next hundred years. In 1839 British troops sent from Bombay attacked and occupied Aden. The following year Hong Kong was taken and the Peninsular and Oriental (P and O) Steam Navigation Company was established. It rapidly became the most successful steamship company in the world converting the Red Sea into a British lake and tying together British trading operations throughout Asia. Disruptions were handled severely: when it was reported that 20 'Christians' had been killed in Jedda in 1858 the Royal Navy bombarded the town for two days until 11 Moslems were yielded up. They were beheaded. The Annual Register recorded the hope that Moslems had been given a lesson 'of the irresistible power of England, which they are not likely soon to forget'.

By the 1870s Britain controlled two-thirds of the Arabian Peninsular's coastline: from Aden, north-eastward to Muscat and Oman, Dubai, Abu Dhabi, Qatar, Bahrain and up to Kuwait. The hinterlands were scarcely developed, there was no colonisation. Apart from the British parts the Peninsular was driven into stagnation and decay. With the decline of the Ottoman Empire British forces moved north and east to occupy Cyprus 1878, Egypt 1882, and southern Persia 1907. When oil spurted out of the Persian ground on 26 May 1908 Britain had in place a regional monopoly and network of political domination over the local feudal ruling classes that ensured an efficient imperialist exploitation of this most valuable new resource.

The US challenge to Britain

The 'lucky strike' was made by the Anglo-Persian Oil Company (later, 1951, BP) using Burmah Oil funds. Anglo-Persian paid £20,000 in cash to the Grand Vizier in Tehran for a concession on an area almost twice the size of Texas. With the defeat of Turkey in World War I, Britain and France started carving up her possessions. The 1916 Sykes-Picot Agreement gave southern Mesopotamia (Iraq) to Britain, the north to France. In 1914 an Armenian businessman, Calouste Gulbenkian, used money from Anglo-Persian (BP), Royal Dutch-Shell and the Deutsche Bank to form the Turkish Petroleum Company (later the Iraq Petroleum Company). The agreement between the parties went into abeyance during the war and in 1919 the German share went to France instead. Despite US resentment the British government argued that the USA had not declared war on Turkey and should be excluded from the oil deal. After the 1922–23 Lausanne Conference Mesopotamia became the British Mandate of Iraq. The British military commander of Baghdad refused to let US oil scouts explore the territory. Consistent US economic and diplomatic pressure finally forced the British to accept US corporate participation in the Turkish/Iraq Petroleum Company. In 1928 Exxon (Esso) and four other major US oil companies gained a 23.7 per cent stake in the company. Thus the US entered into Middle East oil. Iraq was discovered to have some of the largest oil reserves in the world.

In 1931 Standard Oil of California (Chevron) struck oil in Bahrain. Two years later they bought oil concessions in Saudi Arabia for £50,000. Oil production began in 1939. King Ibn Saud rewarded the US firm by extending the concession to cover an area equal to one sixth of the USA.

At the end of World War Two US economic power gave it the means to supplant British imperialism as the dominant force in the Middle East. In 1947 when Britain announced it would have to end its aid to Greece and Turkey the US stepped in with dollars and military personnel. India

49

gained its independence in 1947, Britain could no longer afford the costs of maintaining military forces in the Middle East sufficient to repel all challengers, the Arab rulers were growing richer and intent on wielding a greater measure of state power for themselves and Arab nationalism was on the rise. Indicative was the January 1948 Portsmouth Treaty which replaced the old British military mission in Iraq with a proposed Anglo-Iraqi Defence Board. In practice the Treaty meant that in the event of a threat to BP's interests Britain would send forces into Iraq, the RAF would have access to bases in Iraq should it wish to use them and Britain would train and arm the Iraqi government's forces. The Labour Foreign Secretary Ernest Bevin said the Treaty was 'the beginning of a new series of treaties, regularising and expressing the friendship between this country and the Arab world'. Naturally, it provoked huge riots in Iraq and the British placeman, head of government General Nuri el-Said, was forced to resign. He returned to power the following year. Nevertheless, while British imperialism was intent on holding onto its position in the Middle East it was increasingly less able to do so. The denouement came with Suez in 1956; however it was indicated in Iran in the years preceeding it.

In May 1951 the new Prime Minister Dr Mossadeq, leader of the liberal bourgeois nationalist National Front, announced the nationalisation of the Anglo-Iranian Oil Company. British Labour Prime Minister Atlee asked the Chiefs of Staff to draft a plan to occupy the main AIOC refinery at Abadan. The US opposed the plan and it was shelved. The AIOC organised a world-wide boycott of Iranian oil which was backed by a Royal Navy blockade of the Gulf.

Abadan's refinery was the largest in the world, supplying oil to the US forces in the eastern hemisphere. Forty per cent of total production of aviation fuel outside the socialist countries came from the Abadan refinery. Iran accounted for over a third of Middle East oil supplies. The loss of output that resulted from Britain's conflict over the nationalisation damaged the US military campaign in Korea. British military intelligence officers approached the CIA to devise jointly a plot to overthrow Mossadeq.

Between 1942 and 1948 the Iranian armed forces were under the command of US Brigadier General Norman Schwarzkopf (father of 'Stormin' Norman). Schwarzkopf returned to Iran and made contact with officers friendly to the USA. Several hundred US agents were activated in Tehran. Mossadeq was overthrown in a coup on 19 August 1953. The Shah was restored to the Peacock Throne behind which stood the US rather than the British embassy.

British imperialism had been too weak to act effectively alone and the dispute over nationalisation was a nuisance to the USA. After the coup the US oil transnationals joined BP in control of Iranian oil.

During 1955 British-recruited and led forces clashed with Saudi-backed forces at Buraini Oasis on the borders of Oman and what is now the United Arab Emirates. The Saudi forces were US-equipped and fighting in the interests of the US–owned Aramco company. Accusations flew back and forth between the contending powers about bribing sheiks (the British termed them 'annual subsidies'). Foreign Secretary Harold Macmillan said the oasis was 'vital to our interests'. The Saudi forces were expelled with two SAS squadrons and BP not Aramco gained two-thirds of Abu Dhabi's oil.

In October the following year British forces, with French and Israeli support, attacked Egypt, which had nationalised the Suez Canal. The British government intended to remove Gamal Abdul Nasser's government and seize back the Canal. US imperialism, alarmed at the revolt provoked by the British action that swept across the Arab nations and intent on enforcing its regional dominance to secure a steady flow of oil, acted swiftly. The US Federal Reserve Bank sold sterling and in one day a sixth of Britain's gold and dollar reserves vanished as the Bank of England tried to defend the pound. The US forced a humiliating end to the invasion: within three months British troops had departed and Prime Minister Anthony Eden resigned. Although the British ruling class surrendered its dominant role to US imperialism it allied with it against the threat of Arab nationalism and communism to British-owned oil supplies.

United States global strategy

In 1950 oil accounted for 27 per cent of world energy demands while in 1973 it had reached 48 per cent. Who controls oil controls much of the world. Between 1937 and 1967 the volumes of West European oil imports multiplied thirty fold, Japanese twenty fold and those of the USA fourteen fold. In 1939 Britain controlled 60 per cent of Middle East oil, the USA just 13 per cent. By 1960 Britain had 30 per cent while the USA had 65 per cent.

In the course of World War Two the US government decided to get its hands on all the means of lifting, refining and distributing oil as an instrument of foreign policy. After 1945 the winning of sources of 'strategic materials' corresponded more than ever before to the military-strategic aims of the USA as the dominant power in NATO.

The Gulf states provide Western Europe with about 40 per cent of its oil needs, Japan 75 per cent and the highest US dependence was around 20 per cent, reached in the 1970s; it is often nearer just 10 per cent. Substantial as US domestic oil reserves are, US consumption of oil 1945-75 grew at approximately twice the rate of US domestic production. To reduce its own dependence on Middle East supplies and thereby increase its manoeuvrability in the region and power over its capitalist allies, the US ruling class diversified its oil supplies to Venezuela, Ecuador, Mexico, Trinidad and Tobago, Nigeria and Indonesia. In particular the Korean War accelerated US control over Canadian oil output: by 1953 the US owned 73 per cent of Canada's known oil reserves. When the Suez Crisis cut Middle East supplies to Western Europe by two-thirds, the US transnationals were able to maintain 90 per cent of normal purchases by their NATO allies by increasing output elsewhere around the world.

Middle East oil proved not only strategically important to the US ruling class but extremely profitable. Low labour costs, plentiful supplies and the terms of local concessions meant that every dollar invested in the Middle East in the 1950s generated three and a half times as much oil as each dollar invested in the Caribbean Basin. The rates of profit of US investment in the Third World reveal the following: in 1966 all industrial investment yielded an average of 17.1 per cent, manufacture 9.4 per cent, oil 25.7 per cent; in 1979 all industries 29.5 per cent, manufacture 13.5 per cent, oil 103.9 per cent. Similar figures obtain for most of the 1970s when the OPEC cartel was supposedly creating an 'energy crisis'; the reality was the super-profits of the US and British transnational corporations' cartels.

US Central Command

As the Vietnamese drove on to victory, a revolutionary wave covered 14 countries in the period 1974–80. Included among the victories which the US saw as specifically threatening its hold on oil were Nicaragua, Grenada, Mozambique, Angola, Zimbabwe, Ethiopia, Afghanistan and Iran. Of these only Angola and Iran were oil producers but US imperialism saw its domination of the sea lanes threatened.

In 1977 President Carter announced the formation of a Rapid Deployment Force, to be prepared for instant response to events in the Caribbean Basin and Middle East. A string of forward bases (naval and air) was established in Turkey, Israel, Somalia, Oman, Kenya, Saudi Arabia, Egypt and Diego Garcia. By 1981 US military strength in the Indian Ocean and Gulf exceeded the defence forces of all the region taken together. Plus, nuclear weapons were moved onto Diego Garcia. From January 1983 a permanent US Central Command was established to protect 'vital US interests', consisting of over 350,000 men. Those interests are deemed as covering 19 countries from Morocco to Pakistan. The US ruling class had in place a force intended to maintain its rule over oil and dominance over the Middle East, thereby to sustain its role as the world's major imperial power.

1.8 THE DESTRUCTION OF IRAQI COMMUNISM
EDDIE ABRAHAMS
FRFI 100 · APRIL/MAY 1991

Modern Iraq is the product of a long history of British intervention in and manipulation of the borders of Middle East states. This history – and the frequently overlooked tragedy: the destruction of the Iraqi communist and workers movement at the hands of the Baath Party – is recorded well in *Iraq Since 1958 – From Revolution to Dictatorship* by Marion Farouk-Sluglett and Peter Sluglett (IB Tauris, 1990, 346pp, £9.95)

The carve up of the Middle East and the birth of Iraq

In 1920 General Edward Spears wrote that:

> '... the French and the British ... satisfied each others' appetites after the First World War, by serving up strips of Arab land to each other.'

Until World War One, the Arab world fell within the domain of a decaying Ottoman empire. This oil rich area became a battleground as Germany, Britain and France fought to replace Ottoman rule. In their struggle, the French and British won Arab support with promises of democracy and independence. But in secret they concocted the 1916 Sykes-Picot agreement which gave Lebanon and Syria to the French whilst the British got Palestine and Iraq. With Germany's defeat and the collapse of the Ottoman empire, the victorious allies were free to carve up the region.

Between 1915 and 1921 British troops 'liberated' Baghdad and Basra provinces from Ottoman rule and completed their new territorial unit by attaching to these Arab provinces the oil rich Kurdish province of Mosul. Their hopes of imposing direct rule after the fashion of the 'Indian Raj' were dashed by nationalist opposition. The British therefore altered tactics and prepared to rule indirectly. They created a dependent ruling class from among the most backward sheiks, landlords and tribal leaders.

These elements were bribed with enormous tracts of land which had hitherto been state property. They were provided with a state, a civil service, an army and, of course, a team of British 'advisers' who had powers of veto. In 1921 the British authorities engineered the election of King Faisal to lead this ostensibly Iraqi government. Anglo-Iraqi treaties ensured the safety and security of British interests both before and after formal independence in 1932. Thus was born modern Iraq.

Between 1932 and the revolution of 1958, Iraq's British-imposed ruling class ruled the roost, making massive fortunes from collaboration with British capital. They did so however amidst the increasing impoverishment of the Iraqi peasantry, a growing class polarisation and the birth of an Iraqi working class.

By 1958 1 per cent of landowners owned 55 per cent of all land held in private hands. At the other end, 64 per cent held just 3.6 per cent of all cultivated land and 600,000 rural heads of households were completely landless. Hundreds of thousands of dispossessed peasants flooded into slums circling the main cities in search of food and work. Thus grew in the construction industry, small factories and most significantly in the oil industry, a small but militant working class. And by its side a larger, impoverished petit-bourgeoisie of shopkeepers, artisans, teachers, civil servants and professionals.

The Iraqi Communist Party

Formed in 1934, the Iraqi Communist Party (ICP) drew its support from these classes and became a significant force by the early 1940s. It built its influence by uniting the social struggle for better wages, conditions and housing with the national struggle against British control. It targeted for strike action numerous British-owned economic interests and oil in particular. Thus it succeeded in harnessing the ambition and anger of the urban poor – working class and petit-bourgeois. Equally significantly the ICP developed a widespread following in Kurdistan with its policy of autonomy based on self-determination. It was the first Iraqi political party to develop a progressive position on the Kurdish struggle and ICP members edited the first Kurdish political paper.

In the late 1940s, the Party came into its own during a massive nationalist upheaval against the infamous Anglo-Iraqi Treaty. The so-called Portsmouth Agreement was being renegotiated during 1947 and 1949. When the terms of the treaty, prolonging British control for a further 20 years, were announced Iraq exploded into the *al-Wathba*, the leap, the great national uprising. The ICP was a 'fundamental force' in a series of massive strikes and demonstrations which led to bloody street battles. Government soldiers massacred 300–400 protesters. Hundreds of communists were arrested and in 1949 two leading Party members were hanged in public. Their bodies were left dangling for several hours 'so that the common people going to work would receive a warning'.

The 1958 Revolution and the defeat of communism

For ten years these class contradictions intensified and then exploded into a massive political and social upheaval. On 14 July 1958, the Supreme Committee of Free Officers led by Generals Abd al-Salam Arif and Abd al-Karim Qasim overthrew the British-installed monarchy. The coup unleashed enormous pent-up social energy which almost overnight created mass organisations, trade unions, political parties and popular militias. Rapidly General Qasim became the acknowledged leader of a popular revolution.

The revolution succeeded because it was able to unite two distinct anti-imperialist forces. On the one hand the working class and oppressed whose social and economic conditions spurred them on to a social as well as national revolution. On the other hand a whole strata of the new urban bourgeoisie and petit-bourgeoisie whose nationalism pitted them against the monarchy and the British but who remained hostile to socialism.

With its militant record, its links with the working class and its underground organisation, the ICP effectively took command of most trade unions and mass organisations. It set up its own militia to defend the revolution. It also took the leadership of the Students' Union, the Youth Federation, the Women's League and the Engineers', Lawyers' and Teachers' Unions. The masses flocked to it. In January 1959 the Party was forced to announce that it could not accept any more new members as its administrative machinery could not cope. The Party and the masses controlled the streets of Baghdad and with demonstrations of up to 500,000 began pressing for fundamental social and economic change and in particular for land reform.

The spectre of communism began to haunt the imperialists. CIA boss Allen Dulles stated that the situation in Iraq was 'the most dangerous in the world'. The threat of a genuine social revolution led to a split in the alliance which carried through the revolution. At a governmental level this expressed itself in the rift between Abd al-Karim Qasim who relied on communist support and Abd al-Salam Arif who unfurled the banner of Pan-Arabism and anti-communist nationalism.

Central to the programme of Pan-Arabism was the call for the political union of all Arab states. However the populist and radical rhetoric was but a cover for a systematic struggle against Arab communism. Nasser, the outstanding exponent of Pan-Arab nationalism, had by the end of 1958 launched an all out attack against Arab communist parties, and the Syrian and Iraqi parties in particular. Arif and his supporters, in calling for union with Egypt, hoped to deploy Egypt's anti-communist laws against the Iraqi Communist Party and thus strengthen the hand of the anti-communists.

But these measures promised no immediate return. The communists still controlled the streets. Something more decisive and forceful was required to stem the advance of the working class. At hand and ready to wield the cudgel for the Iraqi and imperialist bourgeoisie was the Baath Party and the less significant Nasserite and other nationalist organisations.

The Baath Party in Iraq was formed in 1951 and developed support from the anti-communist elements of the Army. It was tiny compared to the ICP, never enjoying the latter's support and popularity. It did not need any popularity, its main function being to provide the counter-revolution with a base in the army and with gangs of thugs and killers.

From late 1958 the Baath Party, with the help of the police, organised systematic murder and terror against communists. In October 1959, a gang of Baath Party assassins carried out an unsuccessful attempt on General Qasim's life. The leader of the gang was Saddam Hussein who subsequently rose to the top of the Party. By 1961 the ICP reported that 286 Party members and supporters had been murdered and thousands of families forced to leave their homes. By such means the Baathists slowly pushed the communists off the streets.

These actions however failed to eliminate the ICP or destroy the working class movement which remained a force to be reckoned with.

The Baath Party therefore plotted and prepared for its total and thorough destruction. In 1963, in alliance with other nationalist army officers, it organised a successful military coup. Its single-minded purpose was to finish off the Iraqi communist movement. To quote from Sluglett and Sluglett:

> 'The months between February and November 1963 saw some of the most terrible scenes of violence hitherto experienced in the post-war Middle East. Acts of wanton savagery and brutality were perpetrated by the Baath and their associates . . . [as they] set about the physical elimination of their rivals.'

Party members were shot in the streets, or herded into concentration camps, tortured to death or executed after mock trials. For nine months during which the Baath remained in power the killing and the torture continued. In this struggle the Baath received lists of communist names from the CIA. These massacres marked the effective demise of the largest and most popular communist movement in the Arab world: a movement which could have acted as a vanguard for socialism in the entire region.

PART TWO

Palestine and Zionist Colonialism

2.1 ZIONISM: THE SECOND APARTHEID
EDDIE ABRAHAMS
FRFI 69 · JUNE/JULY 1987 – UPDATED JULY 1993

The current stage of the Palestinian national liberation struggle began in 1967. Then, in the so-called Six Day War, the Israeli military machine defeated Egyptian, Syrian and Jordanian forces and occupied large areas of Arab land. The West Bank was seized from Jordan, the Gaza Strip and Sinai Peninsula from Egypt and the Golan Heights from Syria.

Since then, the Palestinian and Arab people have been subjected to a catalogue of Zionist land-grabbing, repression, racism, murder, war and massacre. But this period also witnessed the emergence of the PLO as a major force challenging not just Zionism, but imperialism and Arab reaction. In response, all the imperialist powers, with the USA in the lead, utilised their financial, political, diplomatic and ideological assets to sustain Zionism and help it contain the Palestinian anti-imperialist struggle. To this end they were accomplices in the extension and consolidation of a new apartheid in Israel and the Occupied Territories.

Extending the second apartheid

'The Jews took Israel from the Arabs after the Arabs had lived there for a thousand years. In that I agree with them. Israel like South Africa is an Apartheid State.'

> (Hendrik Verwoerd, South African Prime Minister 1962)

' . . . there are two societies and the norms of the democratic society stop at the ethnic divide. Arabs just don't count. The occupation has become an excuse for inequality; democracy applies only to the master race.'

> (Meron Benvenisti, an Israeli working for the
> West Bank Data Base Project, 1987)

Imperialist and social democratic apologists for Zionism depict the Six Day War as a brilliant victory by a small, defenceless democracy against a 150 million-strong mass of Arab reaction, anti-Semitism and backwardness. This was a consciously cultivated deception to conceal Israel's fundamentally colonialist character.

Zionism is an expansionist colonising force whose first principle is land robbery entailing the violent removal of the Palestinian people from their land. Between 1967 and 1991 over 50 per cent of the Gaza Strip was confiscated by Zionists. 65 per cent of land in the West Bank is now controlled by 100,000 armed Zionist settlers. Meanwhile one million Palestinians have access to only 35 per cent of the land, a percentage which is constantly shrinking. The process of confiscation has accelerated rapidly since the end of the Gulf War as part of an Israeli government plan which, by the year 2005, aims to limit Palestinian land in the West Bank to a 'cluster of cities, interspersed with some villages'.

Besides land confiscation, the Zionist colonisers use other means to systematically destroy the basis for an independent Palestinian agriculture and economy. On land which requires intensive water irrigation, Palestinians have been permitted to drill only two new wells since 1967 while settlers have drilled more than 20, many of them deep enough to divert water from Palestinian wells. Today, 100,000 settlers consume 80 per cent of the West Bank's water. Palestinian farmers pay enormous taxes on their crops which are often confiscated while subsidised Israeli produce floods the West Bank and Gaza markets.

Israeli authorities have the power to control virtually every aspect of Palestinian economic life. For Palestinians to do anything in the West Bank they need to have a permit: to buy land, to open a business, to import raw materials, and even to obtain a telephone. These permits are issued at the discretion of the military authorities and are used by the state to obstruct the development of any local industry in the West Bank.

Forced off their land and thrown into poverty, Palestinians became a reservoir of cheap labour for Israeli industry. Until recently over 150,000 were migrant labourers in Israel. Rising at 3am they travel to Israeli slave markets in the hope of finding a day's work. Not allowed to live in Israel they have to travel back to the West Bank or Gaza Strip each day. They pay the same taxes on wages which are one-third to one-half of the average Israeli wage, but are not entitled to any state benefits. Concentrated in low-wage industries, they are sacked at will and cannot join the Israeli trade unions. As in apartheid South Africa, they are treated like animals by the 'master race'. A Palestinian worker explains, 'The biggest word in the boss's mouth is "donkey". There is no respect.'

The first achievement of 'Israeli democracy' was thus to transform the Occupied Territories into a South African-style bantustan. The land that Palestinians had worked for generations has become a site for over 112 military/agricultural settlements. Besides affording the Zionist settler-colonialists enormous material and social privileges, these settlements are strategic military strongpoints in Zionism's long term design to destroy the Palestinian nation. Zionism will not voluntarily relinquish these territories. Yitzak Shamir, Israeli Prime Minister, in 1991 only confirmed in words what the Israelis have been confirming in practice every day since 1967: 'We will never give up one inch of our sovereign territory.'

Violence as a method of rule

Such colonial conquests can be defended and secured only by means of the most comprehensive violence and brutality. To this end the Zionists retain and regularly use the British Mandate Defence (Emergency) Regulations inherited from the previous British colonial administration. These allow for administrative detention – up to six months (extended during the Intifada to 12 months) imprisonment without trial, house arrest and deportation. Since 1967 over 1,300 people – leading activists, trade unionists and nationalist militants – have been deported.

Military regulations allow the authorities to arrest and detain anyone for up to 18 days without appearing in court. On the West Bank the majority of all convictions are based on forced confessions extracted during these 18 days when detainees are denied access to friends and lawyers. Between 1967 and the commencement of the Intifada in 1988 over 250,000 Palestinians had passed through Zionist prisons. In April 1987 3,000 Palestinian political prisoners went on hunger strike to protest against gross overcrowding, lack of air and natural light, health hazards due to asbestos lining on cell windows, use of tear gas in cells and pressure on prisoners to become collaborators.

12- to 17-year-olds are regularly subjected to 'beating sessions' as punishment and then doused with tear gas. The most notorious prison, An Ansar – the camp of slow death – has been a target for protesters who regularly organise hunger strikes and other protests. Prisons under Zionism are concentration camps. Since the Intifada began there have been 17,000 people in prison at any one time, with up to 40,000 passing through the system each year.

From 1967 to 1979 all trade unions in the Gaza Strip were banned. They were then legalised . . . but not permitted to recruit new members or hold elections to committees! In 1987 19 union leaders were subjected to administrative detention. Union offices are regularly raided, materials stolen and premises sealed. In 1986 the military authorities sealed the Construction and General Institutions Workers Union in Ya'abad for one year. The union however continued to function without offices. Working class militants have braved arrest and closure of their offices to organise elections. And during the Intifada, working class militants have played a critical role in the formation of numerous popular committees which have become the bastion for the uprising.

In the course of the Intifada, the Israelis have reduced the age of criminal responsibility to 12 and issued a decree applying collective punishment to families of children who throw stones! Among the most vicious of collective punishments is the destruction of the family homes of those arrested for resisting Zionist rule. Between 1967 and 1987, 16,000 family dwellings were demolished. Such repression has increased during the Intifada where in less than three years more than 5,000 people have lost their homes. The destruction of homes is accompanied by numerous forms of economic repression including the uprooting of over 52,000 olive and fruit trees which provide for the livelihood of tens of thousands of people.

Apartheid in Israel

Attention focused on the Occupied Territories can easily lead to ignoring the systematic oppression of the 700,000 Palestinians living in Israel itself where they constitute 17 per cent of the population. Unlike the 1.7m in the Occupied Territories, they are supposedly Israeli citizens sharing equal rights with their Jewish compatriots. But here too the principles of apartheid reign.

Since the establishment of the Zionist state, 80 per cent of Arab land in Israel has been confiscated and the process continues today – especially in the north. 92 per cent of the land of the state of Israel is reserved for Jews only. Palestinians cannot buy, lease or rent in these areas. In Israel today, there are only two Arab towns with sewage systems. Not a single Jewish town lacks one. Nazareth, one of the main Palestinian towns, has an operating budget 25 per cent of an equivalent Jewish town, while many local council budgets in Arab towns are only 8-10 per cent of their Jewish equivalents. In 1989 the Zionist government spent $80,000 to settle one Zionist family on the West Bank. The entire annual budget of Um al-Fahm, with a 25,000 population, is $100,000.

Among Palestinians, infant mortality is double that of the Jewish population, while three times more Palestinian children die of unknown causes than Jewish children. In Jerusalem, the Palestinian sector has only four mother and child clinics, while the Jewish sector has 28. Even according to Zionist newspapers, Palestinians in Israel live in 'sub-human conditions, and in buildings more like stables or archaeological

65

sites at best'. In Jerusalem since 1967 over 30,000 new homes have been built for the Jewish population and only 450 for the Palestinians.

Israel – the military wing of US imperialism

The racist Israeli state, this regime of colonial oppression is, and until its destruction will continue to be, sustained entirely by imperialist capital. Since its foundation in 1948 it has received more than $38bn in economic and military aid. From 1983 onwards it has received an average of $3–4bn a year! Zionism has built for imperialism one of the most powerful military machines in the imperialist world and given most of its Jewish citizens an imperialist standard of living. Thus it has created a powerful counter-revolutionary social/military force. Israel is US imperialism's 'strategic asset' not only in the Middle East but internationally.

Besides its wars against the Palestinian and Arab peoples (Suez – 1956; Six Day War – 1967; Yom Kippur War – 1973; Lebanon – 1982), the Zionist state has actively collaborated with and aided such regimes in South Africa, Chile, Taiwan, El Salvador, Guatemala, Sri Lanka and Honduras to name but a few. Whenever the US has difficulties in supplying fascist regimes with guns and bombs, Israel fills the breach.

It is for reasons of such services that the imperialist powers consistently refuse to take any action against Israel's gross violations of international and UN law. Margaret Thatcher, when applying sanctions against Argentina during Britain's war to retain colonial control of the Malvinas islands, declared in the case of Israel that sanctions were 'unworkable'. The 'new' Labour Party fashioned by Kinnock followed the 'old' in unfurling the banner of Zionism. In 1984 he declared that as long as he remained Labour leader 'the Israeli Labour Party can rely on support from me and my party.' He went on to 'contest those whose history is one of refusal to acknowledge and understand the permanence of the state of Israel'. Like the Conservative Party, the Labour Party puts itself in opposition to the Palestinian people.

Resistance

'The odds appear hopeless, but young West Bank Palestinians continue to defy Israel.'

(Newsweek)

'There is definitely a change of attitude among the new generation. They are not intimidated by the army, they are willing to lose their lives in confrontations.'

(Meron Benvenisti)

Despite the terror, repression and poverty of the first 20 years of the occupation of the West Bank and Gaza, the popular movement remained undaunted. In a poll conducted at the end of 1986, 77 per cent of respondents expressed support for a democratic Palestine covering the whole of Palestine and replacing Israel. 60.7 per cent considered the armed struggle as the most effective way forward in contrast to 7.3 per cent who chose 'diplomatic initiatives.' As in South Africa, though not on the same scale, mass confrontations with the occupying army and armed actions by the PLO and individual groups were regular daily occurrences for the first 20 years of the occupation. By the 21st year of occupation this resistance exploded into the Intifada.

2.2 THE INTIFADA
EDDIE ABRAHAMS
FRFI 75/76 · FEBRUARY/MARCH 1988

The mass uprising which swept across Palestine in December 1987 and January 1988 has raised the Palestinian national liberation struggle to a new and higher stage. After suffering repeated setbacks in the diaspora – Jordan 1971, Lebanon 1982 and elsewhere in the Arab world – the Palestinian resistance has re-emerged within Palestine itself on a firmer footing than ever before to present Zionism, imperialism and Arab reaction with its most intractable challenge yet. Their worst fears have come to haunt them.

The uprising – the Intifada – is a rebellion of the entire community, led by the most oppressed – the poor, the refugees, the workers and peasants, within the heart of Zionist colonialism itself. The backbone of the rising are the 'shababs' – the impoverished and unemployed youth. It is they who lead the street battles, build the barricades, enforce the strikes and deal with collaborators. Commenting on the class character of the Intifada the *Observer* noted:

'... most of the blood being spilt does not belong to the merchant class. It flows from the rough boys whose families never got out of the refugee camps. They are the real dispossessed.'

'The Intifada is where the real war is' declared an Israeli paratroop captain in Gaza. A sustained, mass popular resistance has come onto the stage which challenges Zionism directly and uncompromisingly. 65-year-old year old Ali Abbas expressed the sentiment of this movement:

'We will die or we will succeed. We have no choice.'

Zionism's hopes of subjugating and permanently 'pacifying' the Palestinian population under its rule have been smashed. The uprising further represents a blow to those reactionary Arab regimes who, eager to gain US favour, dropped the Palestinian question from the top of the Arab summit's political agenda.

Uprising and resistance

'What is happening now is a revolution of all Palestinians – being led by the very young.'

(West Bank Palestinian)

Since 9 December 1987 thousands of Palestinian youth have daily fought Israeli soldiers with rocks and petrol bombs. In almost every town and refugee camp – in Nablus, in Jenin and Jerusalem, in Gaza City and Jabaliya, in Khan Younis and el Bureij – blazing barricades marked the battle lines. In Jerusalem protesters burnt down Israeli banks and fire-bombed the US consulate. Stunned by the popular onslaught a Zionist soldier confessed that he would rather 'choose to do two months in Lebanon instead of three weeks in Gaza.'

While daily street fighting continued in the West Bank and Gaza, the resistance spread to Israel itself. On 21 December 1987, Israel's 750,000 Palestinians staged an unprecedented and total general strike. Less than a month later on 11 and 12 January 1988 the West Bank and Gaza were also gripped by a solid industrial and commercial strike.

Israeli repression, far from deterring the movement, spurred the entire population to greater resistance and organisation. Hitherto inactive villages and areas joined the struggle, as did women, the old, whole families, shopkeepers, merchants and traders. From a spontaneous movement, the Intifada has become a highly organised political battle with the PLO at its core.

Within weeks of the uprising, a Unified National Committee for the Uprising (UNCU) was formed incorporating all the main PLO trends. Despite the capture of printing presses, the UNCU still issues tens of thousands of leaflets directing the battle and warning against the imperialist plots presented to Palestinians as 'peace plans'.

Committees have been formed for food distribution where curfews are being imposed, to defend those arrested and to organise demonstrations, protests and funerals. Leaflets on the art of street fighting are supplemented by radio broadcasts on how to make petrol bombs, set up trip wires and use rocks. Industrial and commercial strikes are organised with instructions to open shops a few hours a day for the people to obtain basic necessities.

In dozens of towns and villages notorious collaborators have disappeared. On 24 February 1988 an armed collaborator in Qabatiya opened fire on a demonstration at his home killing a four year old boy. The people hanged him beneath a PLO flag.

Zionist repression and barbarism

'Consciously or unconsciously they [the youth] are engaged in a first serious and mass attempt to take control away from the Israeli police. They will lose this battle . . . But this is not the last gasp of a dying movement. It is the opening battle in a new movement.'

(*Christian Science Monitor* 1988)

In a futile effort to destroy this movement, the Israeli government deployed its entire repressive arsenal. The number of colonial troops in the West Bank and Gaza was increased five-fold. By January 1988 at least 76 people had been killed by gunshot or tear-gas and 500 maimed. Over 2,000 alleged organisers and 'inciters' had been arrested and detained in freezing makeshift prison camps. Brought to court blind-folded and handcuffed, hundreds have been processed before tribunals which sentenced one youth to eight months for throwing a stone at a car. In the same period 30 activists were gaoled for six months without trial under British Mandate Laws and four were deported to Lebanon.

By February 1988 more than 116 had been killed and thousands maimed by live ammunition, tear gas, rubber bullets and brutal beat-ings. On 5 February, four youths in the village of Salim, near Nablus, were buried alive by an Israeli patrol. On 26 February two Palestinian youths had their bones smashed by Israeli troops wielding rocks. The British Foreign Office expressed 'shock and horror', claiming that such actions were 'incompatible with the professional standards of the Israeli defence force'. That the opposite is the case was admitted by an Israeli army report:

> 'We must emphasise that the exception is now the norm. Officers or commanders in the field are giving orders to break property and to break hands and feet, to beat people not only during demon-strations as ordered but at all times and not only to subdue.'

The repression is directed against the entire Palestinian population. Kitty Warnock from War on Want reported Israeli troops snatching patients from Shifa Hospital and returning them eight hours later, one with a broken leg, another with a broken arm and others with broken ribs. In the same hospital Israeli troops smashed into the intensive care unit and dragged out a patient jeering 'now you really will have a heart condition'. Pregnant women have suffered miscarriages after their homes were tear-gassed. On 15 January 1988, firing tear-gas, Israeli police stormed two of the Muslim world's holiest sites, the Al Aqsa and Dome of the Rock mosques.

The level of Zionist barbarism is genocidal. A liberal American medical team, Physicians for Human Rights, citing 3,000 casualties described this 'democratic' and 'civilised' Israel as being responsible for:

> 'an uncontrolled epidemic of violence . . . on a scale and degree of severity that may not be clear to the public.'

Dr Jack Geiger of the same body said:

> 'The numbers, rate and scope of beatings and the trauma we have seen cannot be considered aberrations or deviations.'

Dr Leon Shapiro testified that:

> 'If this were a war, many of the actions whose results we have seen would be declared atrocities.'

Virtually every city, town, village and refugee camp has been subjected to punitive curfews with hundreds arrested. Food supplies have been trampled and destroyed to show 'that the curfew will not be broken'. To prevent youths from organising all educational establishments have been closed indefinitely. And to exhaust and starve the population, money from the diaspora is being prevented from reaching the Occupied Territories.

Despite the Nazi-like ferocity of repression, the will to resist has not been broken. A West Bank leaflet was defiant:

> 'May the earth burn beneath the feet of the occupiers and let the whole world know that the volcano ignited by the Palestinian people will not be extinguished until we have accomplished an independent Palestine with Jerusalem as its capital.'

Imperialism and Zionist repression

The Intifada has seriously weakened the political standing of the collaborationist bourgeoisie in Palestine and the Arab world as a whole. It inspired mass demonstrations in pro-imperialist Egypt and Jordan which were only contained by riot police, tear gas and mass detentions. In Lebanon the uprising forced Syria to lift its three year siege on

Palestinian refugee camps. Savage Israeli repression will only accelerate the development of a regional mass anti-imperialist movement and threaten instability in the oil rich Gulf. A US State Department official noted that Zionist repression 'would make heroes of the most radical elements within the Palestinian community.' David Mellor, whose clash with the Zionist authorities was much publicised, stated in Parliament that the effect of unbridled repression 'is to brutalise the situation in a way that builds up more problems.'

But such critical advice costs little. The substantive issue of US money and arms to Israel was not affected one iota by Zionist savagery. A week after voting against the impending deportation of four Palestinians, the US abstained on a UN vote condemning the actual deportations! In the same week, President Reagan signed a $2bn debt relief provision for Israel and agreed to finance 80 per cent of a $130m Zionist military aircraft project. Despite US unease, Secretary of State George Shultz affirmed that:

> 'The US regards its friendship and the strength of its relationship with Israel as a key and unbreakable relationship.'

On arriving in Israel just as two more Palestinians were murdered Shultz stated:

> 'The friendship and ties between Israel and the United States have never been so strong. On behalf of President Reagan I assure you of America's unwavering committment to Israel's security and prosperity.'

Small wonder the Zionists respond to international criticism with the calculated scorn of a client that knows its worth to imperialism. The US will continue to financially and militarily underwrite the Israeli state in return for its counter-revolutionary services in the Middle East and elsewhere.

Imperialist 'criticism' of Israel is no more than 'brotherly' advice to moderate repression lest it lead to an even mightier revolutionary conflagration which would threaten to destroy imperialism's control of the region. Thus, parallel with Israeli repression, the US Secretary of

State proposed a 'new' 'peace plan'. Shultz suggested the Palestinians accept a form of 'autonomy' for the Occupied Territories, to be agreed by the end of 1988 in preparation for a final 'settlement' 12 months later. The popular movement ensured that no Arab regime or Palestinian collaborator accepted this sell-out plan.

Former Palestinian Mayor of Ramalla, Karim Khalaf, dismissed it as 'power to collect garbage and exterminate mosquitoes.' The PLO rejected the proposal stating:

> 'There is no word about self-determination or about the PLO as the sole legitimate representative of the Palestinian people. There is no word about the aim of the proposed talks – whether there is going to be an independent Palestinian state or not.'

The uprising has become a warning that the future of Palestine and the region will not be determined in imperialist or Zionist drawing rooms or by collaborators ready to surrender Palestinian self-determination for a 'political settlement' which leaves the Zionist entity intact.

International solidarity

With the Intifada, the Palestinian masses have opened up a critical battlefront against imperialism. The objective difficulties they face are enormous. Zionism's overwhelming military might and the sophistication of its repressive apparatus are daunting. Imperialism, as in apartheid South Africa, will continue backing the Israeli state given its decisive role in maintaining regional imperial interests.

In addition, the Palestinian people are fighting virtually alone. The reactionary Arab regimes have done nothing to aid the uprising. On the contrary they have repressed all manifestations of solidarity. In the imperialist countries, the opportunist labour movements have watched indifferently as the Zionists unleashed their terrible repression.

The lessons of the past period will be learned by the revolutionary wing of the PLO leadership as it prepares to embark on a prolonged peoples' war based in Palestine itself. Such a war will naturally be fought by forging links with the revolutionary Arab masses of the region. But the communist and democratic movement in the imperialist countries also has an important role.

Zionism depends entirely on support from the major capitalist powers. These countries also provide a lucrative market for Israeli exports, many of which are produced by cheap Palestinian labour. A serious solidarity movement in Britain and other imperialist countries can begin by a campaign to boycott all trade with Israel.

Isolate the racist, Zionist state!
Self-determination for the Palestinian People!

2.3 THE STRUGGLE FOR PEOPLE'S POWER
EDDIE ABRAHAMS
FRFI 76/83 · APRIL 1988/JANUARY 1989

Comparing Zionist atrocities in the Occupied Territories to the Nazi holocaust, the March 1988 issue of *Civilita Cattolica*, journal of the Italian Jesuits, said:

> 'Faced with such a spectacle one cannot but think of more horrendous crimes, of those same crimes the Jewish people endured in the worst periods of persecution when they seemed destined to disappear, destined for the final solution.'

This was no rhetoric. The scale of repression in Palestine is staggering indeed. From the beginning of the uprising on 9 December 1987 to April 1988 over 130 Palestinians were killed, an average of one a day. In proportion to the British population, the dead would number 5,200. Over 3,500 were arrested and detained in make-shift prison camps. The British equivalent would be 140,000 interned, many indefinitely and without trial.

Promising yet more repression, fascist Prime Minister Yitzhak Shamir, speaking from a Zionist military fort on the West Bank, warned the risen Palestinian people:

'Anybody who wants to damage this fortress and other fortresses we are establishing will have his head smashed against the boulders and walls.'

With racist invective capable of warming Hitler in his grave, Shamir went on:

'We say to them from the heights of this mountain land from the perspective of thousands of years of history that they are like grasshoppers compared to us.'

The struggle for power

It is the emergence of revolutionary people's power and the prospect of dual power in the Occupied Territories that is driving the Zionists to unprecedented levels of repression.

The uprising has moved swiftly to challenge the very foundations of Zionist power and rule in the West Bank and Gaza. The carefully constructed civil and municipal administration, staffed by Palestinian collaborators, is collapsing. Guided by UNCU and enforced by the shababs, the equivalent of the young South African 'comrades', the uprising, while destroying the old apparatus of power, is slowly and consciously building an alternative people's administration.

For example, on 6 March 1988, 40 Arab employees of the Israeli income and property tax division in Gaza resigned en masse. On Tuesday 8 March, a second Palestinian collaborator was executed in the Aqabat Jabber refugee camp. Then on 15 March, 500 of the 1,000 Palestinian policemen serving in the Occupied Territories handed in their uniforms.

In its latest leaflets, the underground PLO leadership has instructed all Palestinians employed in the Zionist 'civil' administration to resign. Leaflet No 12 warns that:

'Those who remain in office are liable for retaliation, both in person and against their properties. To those we say that the masses will crush them.'

In its battle to destroy the basis of Zionist rule, the leadership of the uprising is also organising a tax boycott, as well as a boycott of Israeli goods and banks.

In place of the collapsing Zionist administration, the network of people's committees continues to expand. These now exist in every town, neighbourhood, village and refugee camp. They organise food distribution, medical aid and defence. They deal with collaborators and scabs and keep a watch on Israeli troop movements. They deal with prisoners' welfare, with orphans, education and social organisation. Working under the direction of UNCU these popular committees represent the first forms of dual power, the beginnings of an alternative Palestinian state apparatus.

Zionism cannot, however, coexist with organisations of people's power. So it moved rapidly to suppress them. By August, the Israeli authorities had banned all popular committees. Henceforth association with or membership of a committee carries a ten year prison term. Simultaneously, 250 alleged leaders of these committees have been arrested and 25 of them deported. By the end of August, the Palestinian Federation of Charitable Associations was closed down and the offices of seven professional associations were also sealed.

To disrupt the incredibly efficient and ingenious underground organisation, Palestinians are being stopped from travelling to and from the West Bank and Gaza Strip. Telephone links between the Occupied Territories and the outside world have also been curbed. The mass arrests have as their target anyone considered a supporter of the PLO and in particular its left wing – the Popular Front for the Liberation of Palestine (PFLP) and the Democratic Front for the Liberation of Palestine (DFLP).

In an attempt to drive a wedge between the masses and the cadre organising the Intifada, the Zionists are resorting to 'collective punishment' on a massive scale hoping to terrorise the community. On 'security grounds' supplies of petrol, kerosene and diesel essential for cooking and heating have been halted. Money from the diaspora to sustain the poorest families has been blocked. Palestinians will only be given permits for import and export business if they prove they have paid their taxes. Where collaborators have been attacked or killed, fruit and vegetable markets have been closed down and villagers prevented from exporting their produce.

In the run-up to the annual Land Day celebrations on 30 March, the West Bank and Gaza were declared 'closed military zones' with Gaza under a total curfew and widespread restrictions in the West Bank. The Palestine Press Service was banned for three days and the Israeli Communist Party's Arab language daily newspaper was banned for a week. These measures nevertheless failed to prevent mass demonstrations throughout Palestine.

In resisting Zionist repression, the leadership of the Intifada has been conscious of the treacherous role of the major imperialist powers. In its latest leaflet, it urged a general strike and mass demonstrations and protests to confront the US Secretary of State on his planned return to the region in April 1988. His mission remains the same as ever – to work out, in conjunction with Israel and Arab reaction, a 'formula' to halt the uprising and the development of revolutionary people's power.

The revolution under pressure

In order to destroy the revolutionary character of the Intifada, imperialism, in tandem with the Arab bourgeoisie, has put unprecedented pressure on the PLO to recognise Israel, guarantee Zionism's permanent existence and abandon 'terrorism' – ie the revolutionary and the armed struggle.

Just as the Intifada was entering its second year, the Palestine National Council (PNC – the Palestinian Parliament) in November 1988, following a bitter debate, voted to accept UN resolution 242. This resolution, previously universally condemned, recognises Israel and guarantees its security, but refers to the Palestinian question merely as a refugee problem. The vote, with 253 in favour, 56 against and 10 abstentions, was a major victory for the right wing of the PLO led by Al Fatah.

The left-wing, headed by the PFLP fought against acceptance. Its General Secretary George Habash declared that:

'After the Intifada, Israel should be making concessions not us.'

Nevertheless Yassir Arafat, Al Fatah leader and Chairman of the PLO, reiterated the PLO's new line at a UN General Assembly and at a press conference in Switzerland on 14 December 1988 in which he said:

'I repeat, for the record, that we totally and absolutely renounce all forms of terrorism, including individual, group and state terrorism.'

The Palestinian movement is caught in a terrible dilemma. The uprising remains isolated from the Arab masses in the surrounding countries and has no support from the working class in the imperialist countries. There is therefore enormous pressure on a section of the PLO, the bourgeois section, to achieve some form of state on the West Bank and Gaza through the intervention of imperialism. Hence the new 'moderate', and 'realistic' position. Yassir Arafat hopes by these means to persuade imperialism to force Israel to the negotiating table and to accept a two-state solution.

The US and British governments, by making no more than gestures towards the PLO and by appearing ready to negotiate with it, are attempting to keep their options open in the event that Zionism fails to quell the uprising of the masses. Zionism, however, cannot forever fend off the rising tide of the Intifada. The imperialists, particularly the British, have long experience in dealing with the bourgeois forces within national liberation movements. By their recent 'sympathy' for the Palestinians and redoubled talks of 'negotiations' and 'political solutions' they are trying to secure the political forces necessary for a neo-colonial, bantustan-like Palestinian 'independence' should this eventually prove necessary.

If ever the imperialists, to defend their own interests, have to force Israel to the negotiating table for a 'two-state' solution, they want the Arab and Palestinian bourgeoisie to act as guarantors not just for counter-revolutionary Zionism, but for imperialist capital in the region as a whole. But even as imperialism urges Israel to 'negotiate' it steadfastly refuses to halt savage Zionist repression in Palestine. Such repression of popular revolutionary forces, is a necessary parallel to imperialism's 'political solutions'.

2.4 THE INTIFADA UNDER SIEGE
EDDIE ABRAHAMS
FRFI 90 · AUGUST/SEPTEMBER 1990

The Palestinian Intifada, now two and a half years old, is passing through an extraordinarily difficult stage. Events in May and June 1990 were forceful reminders of the harsh conditions confronting the Palestinian national liberation movement. Isolated internationally and regionally it is being forced to fight alone against a relentlessly barbaric Zionist state which continues to enjoy consistent imperialist support.

In an attempt to disguise their limitless ambitions for profit and plunder, the imperialists claimed that developments in 1989, and the collapse of the socialist countries in particular, ushered in an era of 'democracy'. 1989 was the year that 'peace broke out' and 'democracy' proved victorious. In Palestine such claims are unmasked. Zionism, an obscene product of imperialism, is a bloody refutation of all imperialism's claims to be 'democratic' and 'civilised'.

On Sunday 20 May, Ami Popper put on his brother's Israeli army uniform, took his army-issue M16 rifle and went to the Gan HaVradim road junction outside Rishon leTzion. Gan HaVradim is the 'slave market' where Israelis hire Palestinians who commute there from Gaza every morning in the hope of finding a day's work. Popper opened fire on them killing seven and wounding ten.

He was immediately labelled a lunatic. Fascist Prime Minister Yitzhak Shamir considered it politic to publicly condemn the murders. But only as a 'shocking act of lunacy'. A Palestinian worker commented: 'They always say it is a madman when something like this happens.' Subsequent events proved that Popper's crime, far from being a 'lunatic act', was entirely consistent with Zionism's response to Palestinian resistance in general and the Intifada in particular.

Survivors saw dozens of Israeli cars pass by. Not a single one stopped to help. Hours later one driver did stop, to survey the bloodstains. He cheerfully demanded 'Why only seven?' An Israeli soldier commented: 'Seven killed. Good. I've been stoned so many times I don't give a fuck. We should shoot a whole lot more and this crap would stop.' These people represent the average Zionist for whom Palestinians are valued less than dogs. They express the mentality of colonial settlers who live in constant fear of the Palestinian people's struggle to reclaim the land which was stolen from them.

Throughout the Occupied Territories and in Israel itself, Palestinians mounted massive and angry protests. Shamir, claiming that they had 'exceeded the bounds of the permissible', sanctioned the murder of 11 more Palestinians and the wounding of at least 400 before the week was finished. This was no act of 'lunacy'. It was calculated colonialist butchery in an attempt to terrorise Palestinians into submission.

Those who claim that Popper was a 'lunatic' wilfully cover up the fact that the Israeli state survives and can only survive by resorting to the worst reactionary violence. The entire edifice of the Zionist state is built on the expropriation, oppression and plunder of the Palestinian people and their land. In the face of a mass democratic movement fighting for self-determination, such a state can survive only by means of fascist technique. Israel's response to the Intifada is evidence enough.

Indeed by the second anniversary of the Intifada, 823 Palestinians ranging from two to 83 years old had been killed by Israeli bullets, tear gas and beatings whilst estimated serious injuries were put at 80,000. Besides the official terror, the Israeli army is now employing shoot-to-kill tactics. In December 1989 an Israeli death squad, disguised as Palestinians, entered a Nablus barbers shop and shot dead four members of the Palestinian Black Panthers (a unit of militant youth responsible for executing collaborators). All were unarmed. None was given the chance to surrender. At the same time a decree was introduced applying collective punishment to families of children who throw stones and the formation of armed Zionist militias was authorised in the Occupied Territories.

Imperialism and Arab reaction bolster Zionism

Following the 20 May events, Yassir Arafat, at a UN General Assembly, demanded that a UN team be sent to the Occupied Territories. The US vetoed the proposal. On 21 June, in a further act of solidarity with Zionism, the US broke off political contact with the PLO. President Bush and his Secretary of State Baker found their pretext in the 30 May 1989 Palestine Liberation Front's seaborne military operation against Israel. The PLO, they insisted, had failed to condemn forcefully enough this 'Palestinian terrorist action' in which no Israeli was killed or injured and in which Israeli soldiers killed four and captured seven Palestinian guerrillas!

Imperialism will not take serious action against Zionism and is incapable of acting in a democratic manner. Even after the collapse of the socialist bloc, Israel remains its major 'strategic asset' in the Middle East. It is the most stable and reliable counter-revolutionary force in a region where mass poverty and oppression are always on the verge of exploding into anti-imperialist uprising.

The 'final solution'

As the Intifada approaches its third year, the Palestinian people are preparing to confront a massive new danger. From over the horizon they can already see the spectre of the 'final solution' – the expulsion of all Palestinians from the West Bank and their replacement by a new flood of Zionist immigrants. This is no fantasy.

In 1990 alone, over 200,000 Soviet Jews will settle in Palestine, all demanding homes and land. Responsibility for their settlement will be in the hands of the new Housing Minister Ariel Sharon. Sharon is a ruthless murderer who would uproot millions to defend Zionism. He is known as the Butcher of Lebanon for organising the 1982 invasion of Lebanon and the murder of 20,000 Lebanese and Palestinians. It was he who gave the go ahead for the unspeakable massacre of 3,000 unarmed Palestinians at Sabra and Shatila after Israel conquered Beirut in 1982.

Commenting on the new Jewish immigration, the PFLP magazine

Democratic Palestine notes that 'Israel has received a new reserve force for the occupation army' and is 'getting a new injection of professionals and other skilled workers who will be useful in further development of industry.' The PFLP goes on to note that the new immigration 'increases the danger that the Zionists may opt for "transfer" as a "final solution" '.

The future of the Intifada

Political developments over the past year, and the collapse of the socialist bloc in particular, have sharpened the international and regional isolation of the *revolutionary* Intifada. The lack of forward political development following the heady days of the 1988 Declaration of the Palestinian State has induced a degree of passivity and strengthened the hand of bourgeois forces within the Intifada. And no doubt the weariness resulting from two and a half years of Zionist repression has forced the less revolutionary, less consistent sectors into retreat.

However, despite all these factors and the unrelenting repression, the Intifada survives. The popular will to fight, the determination to resist Zionist colonisation, the willingness to die for freedom remains unbending. The Intifada survives because the material conditions that gave rise to it survive. When the Intifada first exploded in Palestine *Hadashot*, a Zionist newspaper, commented that the Occupied Territories:

'have become more and more like Soweto . . . densely populated, poor, with shameful living conditions and full of hatred.'

The Intifada is a revolt against unbearable conditions of poverty, oppression and enslavement. And now with talk of 'transfer' assuming ominous dimensions, it is literally becoming a matter of life and death for the Palestinian nation.

2.5 IMPERIALISM PLANS TO BURY THE REVOLUTION
EDDIE ABRAHAMS
FRFI 104 · DECEMBER 1991/JANUARY 1992

The dominant image that accompanied the Middle East conference, of an obdurate Israel 'being dragged screaming' to negotiate peace with the Palestinians, was a massive exercise in deceit. The conference, which opened on Wednesday 30 October 1992, was not designed to secure a just settlement of the Palestinian question.

Having crushed Iraq, the imperialists and Zionists, with the willing aid of the Arab ruling classes, are turning to silence their greatest and most effective foe in the Middle East – the Palestinian revolution. In concert they plan to annihilate the force which became a vanguard inspiring hundreds of millions to fight against imperialism and the poverty, squalor and oppression it imposes on them. Riding the tide of international reaction, imperialism is designing a new colonial stability for the region disguised as a negotiated settlement of the Arab-Israeli conflict.

The conference charade

At the heart of this conflict is the right of the Palestinian people to form an independent state in Palestine. This right is rejected, even in principle, by the USA and Israel. How can one talk of a serious conference when Palestinian self-determination does not even feature on the agenda?

All that is on offer is a 'transitional period' of 'autonomy' . . . lasting some three to five years . . . following which the promise of a final settlement. An old scheme, dismissed in 1988 by the then Palestinian mayor of Ramalla as 'power to collect garbage and exterminate mosquitoes'! Nevertheless, today , with the Intifada beleaguered and isolated, imperialism hopes that offering the Palestinian bourgeoisie the sop of 'autonomy' will be enough to silence the challenge of the Intifada.

As the so-called peace conference began, the Israeli authorities accelerated, to unprecedented levels, their colonisation of Palestinian land. Every plea for a halt to settlement building, even as an earnest to honest intentions, was rejected. There is no commitment to halt land confiscation – amounting to the annihilation of the very foundations of the Palestinian nation – during the 'transitional' period.

How can one talk of serious negotiations when the PLO, the sole legitimate representative of the Palestinian people, was not permitted to attend the conference? How can one talk of justice or equality when even the composition of the joint Jordanian–Palestinian delegation was subjected to a US and Israeli veto?

The real aim of the conference was to initiate bilateral negotiations between Israel and individual Arab states. This is then to lead to Arab recognition of Israel but without an Israeli recognition of Palestinian self determination and without Israel's withdrawal from the Occupied Territories.

Despite media impressions, Israel is not opposed to such a 'peace' treaty. It signed one with Egypt in 1975 – the infamous Camp David Agreement. Israel is opposed to a peace which leads to Palestinian self-determination. Such a peace would obstruct its long-standing ambition to incorporate all of Palestine into a 'Greater Israel'.

Zionism and the question of Palestine

Zionism cannot and will never recognise Palestinian self-determination. Despite the myths, it did not even accept the 1948 UN plan which divided Palestine into a Jewish and a Palestinian state. Israel's first Prime Minister, Ben Gurion, then stated:

> '. . . after the formation of a large army in the wake of the establishment of the state, we will abolish partition and expand to the whole of Palestine.'

The history of Zionism is the bloody story of this colonial expansion. Today, more than ever in the past, the Israeli ruling class is being driven towards its 'Greater Israel'. The collapse of the socialist bloc and the demise of Arab nationalism has generated significant debate in imperialist circles about Israel's continuing strategic value. These considerations, together with the massive US economic crisis, open up the prospect of an end to limitless US financial aid – Zionism's nightmare.

In response the Israeli government is desperately building a relatively independent economic and military foundation for the state. But this is almost impossible within Israel's current borders. Indeed, the economic unviability of a divided Palestine was recognised by the UN in 1948 when it urged close economic unity between the proposed Israeli and Palestinian states. Zionism is therefore colonising the Occupied Territories and its critical water and agricultural resources.

Zionism is colonialism and racism

Neither before, during or since the conference has the US Administration done anything to halt Israel's racist, colonial and illegal expansion. The 1949 Geneva Convention states that:

'The occupying power shall not deport or transfer parts of its own civilian population into the territories it occupies.'

Yet shortly before going to Madrid, Yitzhak Shamir, Israel's Prime Minister, who in 1988 said that Palestinians 'are like grasshoppers compared to us', reiterated:

'All the territories that we have available for construction will be populated by Jews up to the horizon's edge.'

In just over a year, between January 1990 and July 1991, Israel confiscated 7.3 per cent more of Palestinian land. This brings over 70 per cent of the West Bank and 50 per cent of the Gaza strip under the Zionist jackboot. The 239,000 settlers, who account for only 13 per cent of the population, also consume 80 per cent of water in the Occupied Territories. According to the Israeli Central Bank the government's proposed 1992 budget of $39bn includes $2bn for settlements and related infrastructure: roads, electricity, water, security zones and army encampments.

A leaked government document outlines plans to build 100 more settlements by the year 2005. These will circle the three main Palestinian towns – Ramalla, Nablus and Hebron – with 100,000 more Zionists and reduce the Palestinian area of the West Bank to a 'cluster of cities, interspersed with villages'. This genocidal strategy merely continues that developed during Zionism's first expansionist war in 1948. Then Ben Gurion explained:

> 'The strategic objective was to destroy the urban communities, which were the most organised and politically conscious. This was ... done by ... the conquest and destruction of the rural areas surrounding most of the towns ... Deprived of transportation, food and raw materials, the urban communities underwent a process of disintegration, chaos and hunger which forced them to surrender.'

As if to underline Zionism's bantustan policy, the infrastructure for the settlements by-passes Palestinian villages and towns. Palestinians are not allowed to rent, buy or live in, the settlements. These are reserved for Jews only who are subject to Israeli law, can vote and enjoy democratic rights. The majority of Palestinians on the other hand live under military rule and have no rights.

Israel is a racist, settler–colonial expansionist state. It has an infamous Law of Return giving Jews of any nationality, from anywhere in the world, the right to settle in any part of Palestine, but which denies Palestinian refugees driven out since 1948 the right to return to their homes. The Zionist Law of Citizenship and the Israeli High Court have confirmed that there is no such thing as Israeli nationality. Only 'Jewish nationality' conveys full citizens' rights in Israel. None of this is, of course, negotiable at the conference. And the US is even endorsing Israel's campaign to reverse the 1975 UN Resolution 3379 condemning Zionism as 'a form of racism'.

The clash between Zionism and the United States

While US imperialism endorses fundamental Zionist strategy it cannot give unqualified support to its every tactic or policy. The two states' economic and political interests do not necessarily coincide. The assets.

of major US oil multinationals are based in the Arab world. Arab petro-dollars play a significant role in sustaining the world capitalist economy. Additionally, the European and Japanese ruling classes are challenging the US in the Middle East via an alliance with the Arab ruling class.

Thus, whilst remaining firmly pro-Zionist, the US is bound to take account of Arab bourgeois interests. Especially so since the Gulf War and the 'return' it owes Arab states for their support in the anti-Iraq crusade. Adjusting US policy to suit today's changing US needs will necessarily entail disputes with Israel. Thus the 'arm twisting' and 'hostilities' in the run-up to the conference. Thus the dispute over Israel's request for $10bn worth of credit guarantees – a dispute over timing not substance. A massive handout to Israel just before the conference would have tarnished the US's 'impartial' posture.

But at the end of the day the US and Israeli position coincided: no PLO representation, no Palestinian independence, no end to settlement building. One day before the conference US Defence Secretary Dick Cheney expressed the US's current stand:

'Rest assured that the United States will continue to support Israel's qualitative military edge over all possible enemies. And we remain committed to ensuring Israel's security in the years ahead.'

The Arab ruling class and the Palestinian revolution

The Arab bourgeoisie participated in the conference, because, as the PFLP puts it:

'...the Arab regimes as a bloc have officially relinquished the concept of liberation... the Zionist entity is [now] dealt with as a natural state in the region, rather than a colonial settler society. Thus, the Arab states' conflict with Israel is no longer about to whom Palestine belongs, but about which borders Israel might accept.'

The Arab ruling class has also taken its own independent steps against the Palestinian revolution. The Syrian government's 'uncompromising', 'anti-Zionist' stand at the conference had nothing to do with Palestinian self-determination. It was part of their own battle to win back the Golan Heights. The Syrian government's attitude to Palestine is evident in Lebanon. There it is trying to break the highly organised Palestinian community which has been a bedrock of the Palestinian revolution.

The Syrian-imposed Lebanese government is planning to deport 120,000-200,000 Palestinians on the grounds that they are 'illegal immigrants'. It has forbidden the reconstruction of Palestinian refugee camps destroyed after 15 years of Israeli and Syrian sponsored attacks. Syrian and Lebanese troops circle these camps to prevent any construction materials being moved in. Palestinians are rapidly becoming second class citizens. They now need identity cards and work permits to get employment. They are being forced into the worst and lowest paying jobs. They pay 18 per cent of their earnings into a social fund but cannot claim from it. The UNRWA is cutting down camp feeding centres, limiting free school supplies and reducing medical care. Confronted with such conditions a Palestinian mother cries out:

> 'Our future here is zero. This is not a life, this is a garbage pit with rats.'

The Palestinian revolution and the Palestinian bourgeoisie

Under enormous pressure from imperialism and from the Arab and Palestinian bourgeoisie, the PLO after much debate also agreed to endorse the conference. Only a left-wing minority, led by the PFLP, opposed this.

Within the PLO, the bourgeois trend is in control, its position strengthened from severe repression and exhaustion suffered by the Intifada and from the collapse of the socialist bloc. With support from the Arab world at its lowest ever level and with no hint of serious imperialist pressure on Israel, the Palestinian bourgeoisie is desperate for any solution, however limited – even autonomy. Its overriding aim is to defend from Zionist colonisation what small privileges it still enjoys and to secure its substantial economic positions in the Arab world by avoiding a clash with the Arab bourgeoisie. A prominent Nablus businessmen graphically expressed their position on the conference:

> 'No military option is open. The Arab card is lost. The Soviet card is lost. The socialist card is lost. The only card in our hand is the conference card. We have to get on this train even if we don't yet know where it is going.'

The Palestinian masses – the workers, the peasants and the poor – have nothing to gain from this train. Their organisations in the PLO are continuing the battle for a revolutionary anti-imperialist struggle against Zionism. Central to this is reviving and strengthening the mass movement – the Intifada. How the political struggles within the movement will develop, especially with the rise of Muslim fundamentalism, remains to be seen.

The outlook appears grim, the struggle awesome. While sections of the Palestinian bourgeoisie have the political and economic resources to survive or escape the Zionist onslaught, the masses have no alternative but to fight. They cannot leave. They are unwelcome in the Arab world. So inevitably, a new generation of fighters must emerge to continue the Intifada. With the rich experience and lessons of popular power and organisation they can take up the banner of the revolution and self-determination.

2.6 THE COLONISATION OF PALESTINE
EDDIE ABRAHAMS
FRFI 113 · JUNE/JULY 1993

In January 1993 Israeli soldiers shot three-year-old Palestinian Nuriman Iliyaan nine times at close range with plastic-coated metal bullets. In another incident, 40-year-old Aiysha Suleiman, a bystander in a minor clash, was shot 12 times. On 11 February Israeli soldiers using anti-tank missiles destroyed 19 homes suspected of harbouring 'wanted men'. In March Walid Honsheia was told that the home he was building on family land was to be destroyed because it fell outside Israeli imposed planning boundaries.

In the context of the wars in ex-Yugoslavia and the Caucuses, it appears grotesque to condemn Israel for genocide and ethnic cleansing. But anything less damning distorts the truth. In August 1992, Yitzhak Rabin's Labour Party victory was universally welcomed as a harbinger of compromise and peace. But Rabin's government is proving even more brutal than the Likud Administration. It is slaughtering Palestinian civilians, targeting children in particular, in a vicious offensive to suppress an increasingly armed Intifada.

Between August 1992 and January 1993, 76 people were shot dead by Israeli troops compared to 63 in the previous six months. During the same period, the number of children killed rose from six to 17. Of the 23 Palestinians murdered in January, 13 were under 16. Of the 496 treated for live ammunition wounds, 150 were under 15. Between January and March this year 58 Palestinians were murdered, 20 of them children. In the same six months, 100 homes were destroyed by anti-tank missiles, grenades and rockets leaving hundreds homeless.

These crimes are committed with the active collusion of the US and EC governments and concealed by the silence of the imperialist media. There have been no angry editorials, no calls for sanctions, no demands for action to force Israel to abide by UN resolutions. Quite the contrary. Following the illegal deportation of 415 Palestinians in December 1992 the PLO withdrew from the Madrid 'peace-process'. In the name of safeguarding the 'peace process' it was subjected to enormous pressure until it rejoined in April. Meanwhile US Secretary of State Warren Christopher ensured that the UN did not take any action against Israel's continued failure to comply with Resoluton 799 demanding the repatriation of all deportees. He further guaranteed the $3bn annual grant necessary for Israel's survival.

Israel and the new colonialism

Imperialist support for Israel's barbarism has sound foundations. Since the end of the Cold War the USA has been reorganising its strategic relationship with Israel. A leaked Pentagon document argues that the US now intends:

'to retain the pre-eminent responsibility for addressing selectively those wrongs which threaten not only our interests but those of our allies and friends, or which could seriously unsettle international relations.'

To this end the US is expected to:

'maintain the mechanisms for deterring potential competitors from ever aspiring to a larger regional or global role.'

This mechanism in the Middle East is Israel. It will help the US retain control of the region's oil resources in its fight to fend off EC and Japanese competitors. Israel will become a strategic US base in the Eastern Mediterranean to fight fundamentalism and regional 'terrorism.' An Israeli official predicts that Israel could become the US's 'biggest carrier in the Mediterranean.'

Israel's Haifa port is already accommodating larger US naval vessels. The US has allocated funds for its expansion. US weaponry to equip a mechanised battalion is being sited in Israel. All US F-15 fighter planes are now serviced by Israeli Aircraft Industries and US ships are serviced in Haifa by Israel Shipyards. This is additional to existing shared intelligence and military research.

According to the *Washington Post*, Israeli strategists:

'will present Israel to Washington as a figurative home port in a sea of regional crisis'.

But to play this role, Israel has first to eliminate the 'Palestinian problem.' It remains a source of severe instability and upsets US relations with Arab states. Israel is therefore setting about a planned, methodical colonialist destruction of the Palestinian nation itself.

The 'peace-process'

This is clear from Israel's apartheid-style 'peace talk' proposals on Palestinian self-government. All land occupied by Zionist settlers, all roads, military zones and public land, including the Jordan Valley and the West Bank Highlands, will come under complete Israeli jurisdiction. This amounts to over 70 per cent of the Occupied Territories.

Palestinian autonomy over the remaining portions of land will be the autonomy of a bantustan. Israel will retain control of internal security and foreign relations. It will in addition control the infrastructure and water supplies, all land which is not privately owned and will have power to determine who shall or shall not reside in the Occupied Territories. These proposals merely transfer to Palestinians an existing colonial administration over which Israel will retain ultimate power through parallel structures of 'residual authority'.

The 'peace-process' remains a critical component of Zionism's strategy. By incorporating the Arab states into a settlement with Zionism, it isolates the Palestinian national liberation struggle. By seeking to incorporate the Palestinian bourgeoisie into an effectively colonial settlement, the Israeli state is then left free to turn against the Palestinian masses – the working class, the peasantry, the poor – who have nothing to gain from the process, not even an independent Palestine.

The effect of this strategy on sections of the Palestinian bourgeoisie is already clear. In the face of fierce mass opposition, Faisal Husseini, a prominent east Jerusalem Palestinian, explained, according to *Middle East International*, that Palestinians had to rejoin the peace process because 'it was impossible for [them] to go against everyone – the Arabs, Europeans and Americans.' Sari Nusseibeh, another prominent right-winger, argued that the talks were more important than the issue of the deportees.

The colonisation of Palestine

For the sake of the 'peace-process' Rabin promised to stop new settlement building. But he did authorise completion of 11,000 housing units constituting the largest ever building programme in the Occupied Territories. Filling them will add 60,000 settlers to the 110,000 already there. A commentator noted:

'With 144 Settlements, many tiny, and scattered all over the West Bank, there is no need to build new ones.'

In contrast to Likud's uncontrolled and unnecessarily provocative settlement building campaign, Rabin plans to rationalise their expansion and development. Their strategic distribution and the network of roads and military zones linking them secures Zionist control of the largest part of the Territories and restricts Palestinians to four enclaves in the West Bank, and two in the Gaza, all isolated from each other and totally dependent on Israel.

Israel has also imposed new planning boundaries in nearly 300 Palestinian villages. No Palestinian building, even on their own land, is to be permitted outside these boundaries. These limits are in marked contrast to the large boundaries looped around Zionist settlements. Sarah Helm in *The Independent* notes that:

'With the pool of land available for confiscation drying up, Israel is now focussing on curbing the growth of the Palestinian population on land that remains theirs.'

The colonisation of Palestinian land extends into Israel proper. Under the 'Seven Stars' plan the Palestinian populated northern Triangle will be overwhelmed by Israeli population centres, industrial parks and infrastructure. Today the area has 130,000 Palestinians and 40,000 Israelis. By 2005 it is intended that there be 393,000 Israelis and only 142,000 Palestinians.

By such means Zionism plans to utterly fragment Palestinian demographic continuity and thus forever destroy the foundation for any Palestinian state – either a democratic secular state across the the whole of Palestine or even the two-state solution advocated by the PLO's bourgeois trends.

Occupied Territories sealed off

Every step of Israeli policy is infused with this colonial calculation. On March 30 1993, the Rabin government sealed off the Occupied Territories and stopped all Palestinian workers entering Israel. This measure aimed to stem the rising number of Palestinian armed attacks inside Israel. At a stroke 120,000 workers and their 700,000 dependents were deprived of their livelihoods. With the closure now in its second month, starvation is a real possibility as one-third of all income in the Occupied Territories is earned by working in Israel. East Jerusalem, officially annexed to Israel but critical to Palestinian economic and social life, has also been sealed off causing incredible hardship.

Despite idiotic press speculation, the closure is not intended to terminate the flow of Palestinian migrant labour to Israel. Nor does it mark Israel's attempt to separate off the Occupied Territories from Israel. On the contrary, it will tighten and better control the movement of Palestinian labour and trade. It will therefore merely reaffirm the colonial status of the West Bank and Gaza.

Israeli employers will not do without cheap Palestinian labour, paid 20-50 per cent of an Israeli wage. Already the government has been forced to issue 23,000 permits for agricultural and other workers. When the closure ends, economists believe that a further 70,000 permits will have to be issued.

The Occupied Territories are too profitable to be separated from Israel. For example, the Qatif Block of settlements in the Gaza Strip produces 40 per cent of Israeli tomatoes destined for export and a substantial portion of cut flowers. Israeli textile and footwear factories use thousands of small workshops in Gaza, producing to precise Israeli instructions and using Israeli raw materials or unfinished products. Zionist employers contract out work to home workers working 12 hours per day for $3.50.

Revolutionary resistance

Zionism has no intention of relinquishing Palestine and is assured of imperialist support in furthering its expansionist ambitions. But the majority of Palestinian people are not willing to bow their neck to their executioner. Despite the 'peace-process', the Intifada continues, and is indeed entering a new stage. The formation of Freedom, Independence and Return Committees, initiated by the left wing of the PLO, has galvanised popular opposition to the 'peace-process'. The revival of mass action is also combined with growing armed guerrilla operations.

In 1990 there were 168 Palestinian shootings; by 1992 the figure was 508. In the first three months of 1993 the rate of shootings had doubled. In 1991 22 Israeli civilians and soldiers had been killed. In 1992 the figure was 39. Expressing Zionist concern the Israeli Environment Minister, justifying the shooting of children, said:

' . . . [the]character of the struggle in the Territories had changed, such that in several places there is outright war.'

While many attacks are carried out by unaffiliated individuals, the Israeli government is seriously concerned by the development of guerrilla war organised by both the PLO and the Muslim fundamentalists. Israeli military correspondent Ze'ev Schiff writes that:

'For the first time guerrilla warfare – even if only in its beginning stages – is being conducted in the [Occupied] Territories.'

Schiff notes that guerrilla units have good intelligence, counterfeit documents, disguises and mobility, though they do not come under one operational command.

The number of guerrillas – identified by Zionists as 'wanted men' – grew from 60 at the beginning of 1992 to 104 at the end even though 180 had been arrested, killed or had fled to Egypt. Commenting on the close connection between the mass movement and this emerging guerrilla war, Israeli journalist Dani Rubinstein notes that unlike in the past:

'today the implementation of collective punishment is no longer sufficient to pressure the residents of the Territories into distancing themselves from the wanted men (ie guerrillas) from their midst or turning them in.'

The destiny of Palestine has yet to be decided. Whatever the corrupt and reactionary nature of the 'peace-process', those in Palestine who will gain nothing from a compromise with Zionism and imperialism are fighting on. It rests on democratic and socialist forces in Britain, the EC and the US to halt all external support for Israel, external support without which it would be unable to continue its war of genocide against the Palestinian people.

2.7 COMMUNISM, FUNDAMENTALISM AND THE QUESTION OF PALESTINE
EDDIE ABRAHAMS
FRFI 111 · FEBRUARY/MARCH 1993

The December 1992 killing by Hamas of Israeli border-guard Nissim Toledo and the subsequent deportation to Lebanon of over 400 alleged Hamas and Islamic Jihad supporters has brought to the fore the role of Muslim fundamentalism in the Palestinian revolution. The deportations, illegal under international law, reveal the anti-democratic and uncivilised character of the Israeli state. None of those expelled have been charged with any crime related to the killing of the border guard, let alone found guilty of one in a court of law. None had the opportunity for an effective appeal. They were summarily dumped, in mid-winter, into arid mountains with no more than a blanket and some clothes.

As the 400 plus deportees freeze on the Lebanese mountain sides, the United Nations is again shamelessly exposing itself for what it is – the public relations office for US imperialism. With UN diplomatic blessing the US bombs Iraq in the name of UN Resolutions and international democracy. Israel meanwhile, a reliable ally of the US and UN, neither faces nor expects any retaliation for its repeated defiance of numerous UN Resolutions including Security Council Resolution 799 demanding a return of the deportees.

These illegal deportations – among an arsenal of repressive measures Israel inherited from the British mandate including collective punishment, detention without trial, destruction of homes and orchards – are more than just retribution for the death of Nissim Toledo. They are part of stepped-up repression against an Intifada resurgent since the November 1992 hunger strike by Palestinian political prisoners. More particularly they were designed to disable Hamas which is emerging as a major force in the West Bank and Gaza Strip.

Fundamentalism – reactionary, pro-capitalist populism

The rise of Hamas – an acronym for the Islamic Resistance Movement – has paralleled the wave of Islamic fundamentalism sweeping the Arab world. In Algeria, the Islamic Salvation Front commands massive support among the poor and is waging a terror campaign in its drive for power. Egypt's largest opposition group is the Muslim Brotherhood. It has the support and the means to seriously destabilise Mubarak's pro-US government. The Jordanian branch of the Brotherhood extends its influence into every sector of the state, while fundamentalist forces gather influence in Tunisia, in Iraq, in Lebanon and elsewhere. In Palestine they claim to command anything between 25 per cent and 40 per cent of popular support, reaching 60-70 per cent in certain areas of the Gaza Strip.

With the collapse of the USSR, the Great Powers are targeting Islamic fundamentalism as the 'evil enemy' undermining world order, the market economy and democracy. Such propaganda combined with fundamentalism's radical, anti-western and anti-Israeli rhetoric can generate illusions that it has progressive, democratic, anti-imperialist features. Hamas's record and role shows this is not the case. Islamic fundamentalism – like its Christian and Jewish variants – is an anti-democratic, reactionary and pro-capitalist political trend. It cannot represent the interests of the working class, the poor, the unemployed, the peasantry or the impoverished petit-bourgeoisie.

In the West petit-bourgeois and bourgeois anti-working class, chauvinist, xenophobic and sectarian movements assume the form of populist reactionary nationalism and racism. In Israel they have long assumed the form of Zionism. Islamic fundamentalism is the form they take in the Arab world. Today it represents the most dangerous obstacle to the development of a new movement capable of representing and enforcing the interests of the poor and exploited.

While each fundamentalist movement differs according to the character of the economy and class relations in each particular country, they by and large all share an essentially similar ideological and political standpoint. Committed to the defence of private property and capitalism, Islamic fundamentalism harbours a particular and savage hatred of communism and Marxism. It has acted as the ruling class's terror squad in the struggle against communism in the Middle East. Fundamentalism is characterised by an unremitting hostility to equality, democracy and rationalism. It opposes the right of the working class to organise independently of Islamic institutions. It is also uncompromisingly opposed to the emancipation of women from domestic slavery and is intent on driving them out of all spheres of public life.

Fundamentalism represents a ruling class alliance of less privileged sections of the bourgeoisie and petit-bourgeoisie. It is the political movement of those sections of the ruling and privileged classes who were by-passed and marginalised during the period of post-colonial economic development. This stratum did not share fully in the post-colonial feast that the nationalist ruling class enjoyed as it squandered national wealth and degenerated into corruption and crime. Today, with an international economic crisis devastating the Third world and further discrediting the nationalist bourgeoisie, the fundamentalists see their opportunity to redress past grievances.

Despite fundamentalism's reactionary pro-capitalist character imperialism is determined to control its expansion and if possible defeat it. Today's fundamentalist forces, whilst prepared to co-exist with imperialism, are demanding a better deal for themselves. Imperialism will not readily countenance this. It prefers its traditional allies among the existing dominant sections of the ruling class whose demands are more 'moderate'. Furthermore, fundamentalist forces, resting upon mass support which is fired by hatred for imperialism, are inherently unstable and therefore ill-fitted to act as imperialist servants.

The distinctive and most dangerous feature of fundamentalism is this capacity to command support among the desperately poor and impoverished rural and urban population which sees no future for itself or its children. Experiencing the bitter results of opportunism among Arab communist parties, the poor and sections of the working class abandoned communism for fundamentalism. Most communist parties, essentially Menshevik organisations, were incapable of conducting an uncompromising class struggle against the rich and privileged ruling class. In the name of 'national unity' they all too often abandoned the needs of the poor and moderated the class struggle in favour of an alliance with a corrupt and pro-imperialist national bourgeoisie.

Without manipulating and exploiting popular discontent the fundamentalist leadership would not have the social power to mount a challenge to the long-established ruling class. Thus it promises to make the poor rich without, however, making the rich poor and without abolishing private property. On the basis of Islamic mores it promises to restore the social stability, cohesion and security which has been destroyed by capitalist development. The growth and evolution of Hamas reveals precisely the general conditions which have enabled fundamentalism to so displace communism and socialism as the ideology of the poor and exploited.

Hamas divides and weakens the Intifada

Hamas, the main fundamentalist force in Palestine, was formed in 1987 by the Palestinian branch of the Muslim Brotherhood. The Brotherhood initially opposed the Intifada but was rapidly forced to change tack. Refusal to join an uprising of the overwhelming majority of the Palestinian people risked losing the fundamentalists all the popular support they had built through welfare, educational and religious work. But given the popular, revolutionary and anti-imperialist character of the movement, the Brotherhood decided to retain its distance and intervened one step removed by forming Hamas.

Hamas entered the political arena, but only to undermine the democratic and anti-imperialist struggle. The revolutionary wing of the Palestinian movement has always fought to destroy the racist and sectarian Zionist state and replace it with a democratic and secular

Palestine. In such a state Arabs and Israelis, Muslims, Jews and Christians would have equal rights irrespective of race or religion. Hamas is opposed to this and aims to establish an Islamic state in which even many Palestinians who are Christians would be second class citizens.

Within the Intifada Hamas divided and weakened the popular movement. It not only opposed the PLO but refused to unite with it or collaborate with UNCU. It refused to participate in the popular committees which in the Intifada's early stages developed into the beginnings of organised popular power. Hostile to the independent organisation of the poor and working class it opposed the left-wing's call for a civil disobedience campaign to incapacitate the Zionist administration on the West Bank. In a direct challenge to the unity of the Palestinian resistance it organised strikes on days and times that the UNCU decreed as no-strike periods. Its anti-Christian sectarianism led to the founding of a Christian Resistance Movement (Hamam) in Ramallah.

Most significantly it violently opposed women's participation in the Intifada. *Democratic Palestine* comments:

> 'Hamas supporters launched a large-scale campaign against Palestinian women and their participation in the Intifada . . . This deprived the Intifada of about 50% of its activists.'

The PFLP's overall assessment of Hamas' role is sobering for those who mistake it for a genuine component of the Palestinian revolution:

> 'In the final analysis, Hamas has, whether consciously or not, contributed to the Israeli occupation's effort to undermine the Intifada. And here Palestinian leftists and other progressive nationalists are partially to blame, for they somehow closed their eyes to what was happening in the name of national unity, whereas they should have stood up to Hamas.'

Hamas – an anti-communist terror squad

The left's and progressive nationalists' toleration of Hamas was a terrible mistake. The Muslim Brotherhood and Hamas reserve their vilest venom for the left. A Hamas slogan makes the organisations purpose clear: 'Communism is a cancer inside the nation's body and we will cut it out.' For such reasons these movements have for decades been nurtured and financed by the ruling class in its struggle against communism, Marxism and popular democracy in the Middle East. In Egypt and in Syria, the fundamentalists were used to oppose strong working class and communist organisations. In the Palestinian arena both Zionism and Arab reaction, while attacking the Palestinian and Arab left, financed and facilitated the growth of fundamentalism. Ze'ev Schiff and Ehud Ya'ari, in their book *Intifada – Israel's Third Front*, comment:

' . . . the Civil Administration has contributed considerably to the development of the Muslim groups . . . Many Israeli staff officers believed that the rise of fundamentalism . . . could be exploited to weaken the power of the PLO . . .

'For the better part of a decade, the Israelis had allowed fundamentalist Muslims to move into positions of power in the religious establishment.'

Haim Baram, writing in *Middle East International* (8 January 1993), notes:

'The Israelis pumped millions of dollars into the Muslim coffers as part of their grand design to circumvent the PLO at any conceivable price.'

But the Muslim Brotherhood's major financier was the pro-US Saudi regime, notorious for its bankrolling of the fascist Mojahedin in Afghanistan, its support for the US war against Iraq and its support for counter-revolutionary forces in the Arab world. While it abstained from participation in the national struggle, with Saudi funding the Muslim Brotherhood built a vast network of support through Islamic endowments, welfare organisations, societies, universities and mosques it controlled.

With Saudi money and Zionist licence the Brotherhood launched a veritable civil war against the democratic and particularly Marxist and left-wing forces in Palestine. A few examples demonstrate this. In

January 1980 they attacked and severely damaged the Palestinian Red Crescent offices in Gaza claiming it was dominated by communists. In 1982 they did so again, attacking twice. In 1981 Dr Mohammad Hassan Sawalhah was thrown out of a third floor window of Al Naja University because he was a left-winger. In 1983 fundamentalists launched attacks on leftists and nationalists in the Universities of Bir Zeit and Gaza. In 1984 they dispersed a demonstration in Al Bireh refugee camp claiming it was supported by the 'atheist left'. In the Gaza Strip PFLP and Palestine Communist Party members have been subjected to acid and razor attacks. Violence against PLO supporters continued and in June 1992 fundamentalists tried to drive PLO supporters off the streets in Gaza.

Class character and social and economic base of fundamentalism

How have such reactionary forces won the loyalty of large sections of the poor and oppressed – not only in Palestine but in large parts of the Arab world? An answer is offered by *Democratic Palestine*. The rise of fundamentalism is:

> 'a reaction to the failure of the Arab regimes to achieve the goals and aspirations of the Arab peoples, most importantly national liberation and social progress . . . It is equally a reaction to the inability of the secular opposition . . . to constitute a real alternative in terms of achieving these goals.'

In the Arab world, as in other parts of the Third World, imperialist-dominated capitalist development has generated a terrible social polarisation. A tiny post-colonial ruling class, allied to imperialism and steeped in corruption and crime, lives a life of unbelievable luxury. In sharp contrast are the devastated lives and shattered hopes of the poor and exploited: the working class, the unemployed, under-employed, the city dwellers forced off the land and now living in hopeless urban squalor and a huge and impoverished petit-bourgeoisie. The central issue of the class struggle has revolved around the question of who was to organise the poor and impoverished. Would it be the ruling class in alliance with the fundamentalists or the powerful communist forces based within the small working classes?

For decades the Arab ruling class spared no violence to defeat communist and working class organisations whose membership was banned, imprisoned, executed and massacred. Parallel to repression, Gulf oil money funded the fundamentalists to organise among the poor and oppressed and undermine the appeal of socialism, democracy and secularism. In the absence of state welfare provision, fundamentalist organisations posed as alternative welfare providers. But at a price: provision of some cheap services in return for supporting fundamentalism, passivity in the class struggle and abandonment of communism. This assault, facilitated by the widespread opportunism within the communist parties, succeeded in severely weakening the left in the Arab world.

Within the Palestinian context Zionism and the Arab ruling class waged a similar struggle to debilitate the left and revolutionary nationalist currents. In September 1970, King Hussein's army suppressed a mass insurrection and drove the PLO out of Jordan. In 1976 Assad's Syrian regime used its army to save the Lebanese fascist falange from defeat at the hands of a joint democratic and leftist Lebanese/Palestinian alliance. The same forces were used to stifle a resurgent alliance in 1984. These repeated assaults severely weakened the position of the left and revolutionary nationalist forces.

As a result the dominant bourgeois faction of the PLO increasingly tied its fortunes to the Arab ruling class and abandoned the revolutionary struggle. In return it hoped that imperialism would reward it by pressurising Zionism into a compromise settlement. The dominant PLO leadership, representing a substantial Palestinian bourgeoisie – both inside and outside Palestine, underwent a process of degeneration, developing an anti-democratic, bureaucratic stratum. Its privileged existence decisively separated it off from lives and experience of the majority of the Palestinian poor and exploited. The current 'peace process', which, has produced nothing for the Palestinians, has accelerated popular disillusionment with the PLO. Such developments have provided fertile ground for the fundamentalists, enabling them to pose as defenders of the poor and oppressed. Their rhetoric of total opposition to Zionism and to any negotiations with the Israelis is winning them growing support from a population which has no faith in the bourgeois course of appeasing Zionism and imperialism chosen by the PLO leadership.

The collapse of the socialist bloc and the retreat of the anti-imperialist movement internationally has also enormously benefited the fundamentalists. The Palestinian people, abandoned first by the Arab bourgeoisie and imperialism, now find themselves internationally more isolated than ever from the world working class and peasantry. Their economic and material conditions continue to deteriorate as a result of the international recession, the consequences of the Gulf War and the crippling effect of Zionist colonisation. Such circumstances strengthen the appeal of Islamic populism, apparently more radical and promising than a Soviet socialist experiment that failed.

However, Hamas's vociferous denunciation of the PLO and its radical rhetoric are designed only to lull the people whilst it negotiates a better position for itself at the table of the privileged. Whilst its street slogans denounce 'autonomy', its respected leaders such as Dr Mahmoud al-Zahar state that 'The Islamic movement is ready to enter into negotiations concerning autonomy for the Palestinians'. While condemning the PLO, Hamas is demanding 45 per cent representation in its institutions as a condition for joining it. The recent crisis over the deportation of Hamas supporters has in fact driven the PLO leadership and the Muslim Brotherhood leadership even closer.

The immediate future suggests no rapid defeat of fundamentalist forces by communist or progressive movements. But as the class struggle unfolds, life itself will prove that fundamentalism is incapable of resolving any of the problems facing the Palestinian and Arab people. The mass movement will then pass its own ruthless judgment and sentence upon a movement which has caused so much damage to the cause of national and social liberation. They will return more vigorously to defending and developing their own independent organisations. To do this they will turn to those forces within the Arab, Palestinian and international movement who are guided by science, by rationalism, by democracy – in other words by scientific socialism, by communism, by the heritage of Marxism and Leninism. The collapse of the socialist bloc may have been a body blow to such forces, but they exist and are continuing their struggle for socialism and progress.

2.8 ISRAEL/PLO AGREEMENT: THE GREAT BETRAYAL
EDDIE ABRAHAMS
FRFI 115 · OCTOBER/NOVEMBER 1993

The Declaration of Principles (Declaration) signed by the Israeli government and the PLO on 13 September 1993 is a contemptuous and humiliating insult to all who have died and all who continue to fight for national and social liberation in Palestine. The agreement proposes to establish a Palestinian Interim Self-Governing Authority (PISGA) across the whole of the Occupied Territories beginning with the poverty-stricken and strategically insignificant Gaza Strip and the 100 square kilometres around Jericho city. A 'final settlement' is then scheduled within five years of the formation of the Self-Governing Authority. This 'peace'-plan is neither new nor radical (see 2.5 – Imperialism plans to bury the revolution).

Less than one year after the start of the Madrid Peace Process in October 1992, the leadership of the PLO has abandoned all the national and democratic ideals of the Palestinian revolution. In exchange for what amounts to a neo-colonial, apartheid bantustan-style 'autonomy', Arafat promises to try and terminate not just the Intifada but the armed struggle and the Palestinian revolution itself. While Palestinian workers and peasants continue to suffer aggravated poverty and are gunned down in their own streets, Arafat has committed the PLO to:

> 'encourage and call upon the Palestinian people in the West Bank and Gaza Strip to take part in steps leading to the normalisation of life . . . '

> (Letter to Norwegian Foreign Minister,
> *Financial Times* 10 September 1993)

In another letter to Israeli Prime Minister Yitzhak Rabin, equating the revolutionary armed struggle of the oppressed with violence and terrorism, Arafat stated:

'... the PLO renounces the use of terrorism and other acts of violence and will assume responsibility over all PLO elements and personnel in order to assure their compliance, prevent violations and discipline violators.' (*ibid*)

It is hardly surprising that the PLO has now split, with the left-wing PFLP and the DFLP resigning from the PLO executive along with a number of other opposition groups. George Habash has urged the Palestinian movement to hurl Arafat into the 'dustbin of history'. These forces are attempting to forge an alliance to organise and mobilise popular opposition to the deal.

This 'peace'-plan does nothing to advance even the most elementary requirements of the vast majority of Palestinians for popular power, self-determination and independent economic development. The response of the underground leadership of the Intifada in the West Bank and Gaza Strip makes the issues abundantly clear:

'The agreement reached between a branch of the PLO and the Zionist enemy does not meet the minimum demands that were raised by our masses when the uprising started. No Israeli withdrawal has been achieved, no recognition of Palestinian national rights, no establishment of a Palestinian state and no freeze and removal of the settlements.'

(*International Herald Tribune* 21 September 1993)

The signing of the Declaration marks the final end to the PLO's role as a vanguard anti-Zionist, anti-imperialist movement in the Middle East. It represents a victory for Zionism, imperialism and the Arab bourgeoisie. The Palestinian bourgeoisie have abandoned the struggle for a secular and democratic state across the whole of Palestine, a struggle which could set the stage for real national and social emancipation for all the workers and peasants of the region – Arab or Jewish. They are making their final peace with Zionism and imperialism and are being willingly incorporated into a reactionary alliance against the working class, the peasantry and the poor.

The 'peace'-plan for a bantustan

The neo-colonial, anti-working class character of the PLO/Israel agreement is hard to dispute. The PISGA, once it is established, will have no power whatsoever over Zionist settlements, which include the richest and most fertile areas of the Occupied Territories. It will have no jurisdiction over any Israeli citizens in any part of the Occupied Territories. It will have no authority over refugees or foreign affairs or relations with neighbouring countries. And it will have no control over Arab east Jerusalem. The Israeli police and army will have free use of all roads within the PISGA.

The PISGA itself will be a glorified local council with 'power' over health, welfare, education and tourism. It will also be required to form a Palestinian police force to keep law and order. This plan is but a modification of Israeli proposals advanced earlier this year. It does not halt land confiscations or settlement expansions which effectively destroy any basis for an independent Palestinian state (see 2.6 – The colonisation of Palestine).

26 years of Israeli occupation have already destroyed the economy of the West Bank and Gaza, subordinating it totally to the needs of the Zionist settlers and Israeli capital. The combined Gross Domestic Product of the West Bank and Gaza is five per cent of that of Israel. Gross National Product per head in the West Bank is just $2,000 while in the Gaza it is $1,200. The Israeli figure is $10,800. In this context it is downright treachery to speak of an independent Palestinian state even in the Occupied Territories as a whole, let alone in just Gaza and Jericho. In the Gaza Strip at least 260,000 of the area's 780,000 people live in squalid refugee camps. Male unemployment now stands at 62 per cent and poverty is becoming desperate. An UNRWA official, Alex Pollock, notes that nearly all the area's infrastructure is 'either missing or in a deplorable state'.

This makes talk of the PISGA being merely a preparatory stage towards an independent Palestine, in a 'final settlement' five years hence, nothing but a deception. By then no Palestinian entity will exist! The Israeli government has repeatedly made clear, along with the US, its total opposition to any independent Palestinian state. Even as the 'peace'-deal was being signed in Washington, Israel issued a statement via its Paris embassy reiterating its 'opposition to the creation of an independent Palestinian state'.

The Declaration says nothing about the 'right of return' for Palestinian refugees expelled from their homeland from 1948 onwards. It leaves intact the entire Zionist colonial-settler state and military machine, ready to be used against resurgent revolutionary movements or other forces hostile to imperialism. Since the agreement President Clinton has assured Israel that there will be no cut in the billions of dollars the US gives in aid and military assistance.

The Accord unites imperialist capital and the PLO against the people

The leaders of the USA, EC and Japan welcomed the Declaration as a decisive step to end the Palestinian revolution which, over the decades, has presented the greatest threat to imperialist control over the region and its oil riches. They all understand however, that the devastated economy of the Occupied Territories cannot sustain a stable PISGA. Poverty and desperation will breed opposition and threaten a revival of the revolutionary challenge. It is necessary therefore to take precautions.

First they will try to bribe and silence this opposition. In the words of Alex Pollock:

> '. . . a well-funded programme could immediately provide jobs, alleviate [not eliminate] suffering and defeat political opposition.'
> (*Financial Times* 10 September 1993)

An EC diplomat put the same message in a different way:

> 'Steps will have to be taken to support the population there otherwise the politics of despair will take over very quickly.'
> (*The Guardian* 1 September 1993)

To this end imperialism is preparing a financial package with promises from the EC, the US, Japan and a number of Scandinavian countries. Meanwhile Arafat is touring the oil-rich Middle East governments begging for money to help buy support for the plan.

Lest this bribery does not work, the *Financial Times* reminds us that the Declaration:

> 'commits the new Palestinian police force to co-operate with Israeli security forces in combating Hamas and other radicals in the territories which remain committed to the armed struggle.'
>
> (*Financial Times* 15 September 1993)

Abdullah Hourani, an independent member of the PLO Executive who has now resigned, quite correctly said:

> 'This agreement transforms the Palestinian autonomy authority into a repression apparatus against our people in favour of Israel.'
>
> (*Financial Times* 13 September 1993)

Large sections of Palestinians, even those among the ranks of Arafat's Al Fatah, see through the fraud of the Declaration. 180 Al Fatah guerrillas in Jordan issued a statement refusing to join the proposed Palestinian police force:

> 'We are ready to serve in a nationalist police force in an independent Palestinian state, but not to be tools to suppress our people's resistance against the Israeli occupation.'   (*ibid*)

Who gains, who loses?

The only beneficiaries of the Declaration are the imperialists, the Zionists and the Arab/Palestinian bourgeoisie. The end of the Palestinian revolution will mean greater security for imperialist oil profits in the region. For the Zionists it opens the possibility of a much more systematic and peaceful colonisation of Palestine.

These accords will enable Israel to rapidly sign agreements with surrounding Arab regimes and end the regional blockade against it.

Israel then expects to emerge as a dominant economic force in the area; already Israeli economists are talking of 'major opportunities in terms of export markets and imports of natural resources' and are expecting a 22 per cent increase in exports.

As for the Arab and Palestinian bourgeoisie – with the termination of the Palestinian revolution and with financial help from imperialist and Arab capital it hopes to carve itself a little niche as a subordinate partner of Zionism and Arab reaction. Preparing to enter the imperialist fold, the Palestinian bourgeoisie is eager to reassure imperialism that the PLO will abandon all ambitions for an economically independent and socially just Palestine. Hisham Awartani, a bourgeois Palestinian economics professor, is urging the PLO to:

'recast itself to face the challenge: first it must resist socialist voices calling for a state-controlled economy and nationalist voices demanding economic isolation from Israel.'

(*Financial Times* 10 September 1993)

Awartani is forthright about the need of the PLO to remove itself from the influence of 'trade unions, labour groups and old-time socialists.' The PLO must, in other words, oppose these groups' demands for social and economic justice – demands which represent the interests of the vast majority of Palestinians.

The PLO, the Palestinian bourgeoisie and the Revolution

The fundamental issue that today confronts socialists and anti-imperialists is to explain why and how the PLO, once a powerful symbol of anti-imperialist struggle, has surrendered with such a whimper. Why has it signed a 'peace'-accord which, in the words of Ali Jiddah, a PFLP supporter who spent 17 years in a Zionist prison (*interviewed in* FRFI *101 June/July 1991*), is 'a total subjection of the Palestinians to Israeli and American conditions'?

Current developments are the culmination of a long process spanning some two-and-a-half decades during which the right-wing, bourgeois and petit-bourgeois trends within the PLO, represented primarily by Al

Fatah, have sought to seize control of the organisation and curtail and stifle the truly popular, anti-imperialist, anti-capitalist struggle of the Palestinian masses.

In the 26 years of Zionist occupation and economic subjugation of the West Bank and Gaza Strip, the Palestinian bourgeoisie and wealthier sections of the petit-bourgeoisie have become internally integrated into the Zionist economy. Externally they are dependent on the flow of aid from the oil-rich, pro-imperialist Gulf states. Within the Arab diaspora, the wealthy Palestinian bourgeoisie has always tied its fortunes to the bourgeoisie of the Arab world rather than the popular democratic struggle of the masses. As a result, the Palestinian right-wing's commitment to the national liberation struggle has always been qualified by its own narrow class interests, interests opposed therefore to a consistent and uncompromising struggle against Zionism, imperialism and capitalism.

The Palestinian bourgeoisie sees the national struggle as no more than a stepping-stone to greater profits, unfettered by Zionist rule. It opposed Israel's occupation of the West Bank and Gaza not because it devastated the lives of the masses, but because the occupation curtailed its own economic advancement. For the Palestinian bourgeoisie, the mass popular revolution was a bargaining counter to be used in its selfish dealings with imperialism and Zionism. Like the bourgeois trends in all other liberation movements, the right-wing of the PLO could not express or fight for the needs of the majority. On the contrary, it has always opposed the popular, socialist and revolutionary nationalist trends within the PLO.

At the peak of the PLO's anti-imperialist role, these left-wing and revolutionary nationalist trends were serious contenders to take over the leadership of the struggle. Imperialism therefore, in alliance with Zionism and the Arab bourgeoisie, spared no violence to destroy them. In particular, from 1988 onwards the imperialists and Arab regimes ensured the total isolation of the Intifada. This facilitated the Zionist repression which worked to drain and exhaust a mass popular movement which was moving to establish popular power and dual power. Repeated assaults severely weakened the position of the left and revolutionary nationalist forces. This allowed the bourgeois forces to consolidate their position within the PLO, which underwent a process of degeneration. Gulf oil money helped to nurture a privileged anti-democratic, bureaucratic stratum whose comfortable existence decisively cut it off from the lives and experiences of the majority of the Palestinian poor and exploited. The Gulf War marked a crucial turning point for these forces. The Arab ruling classes' willing alliance with the US in its war to crush Iraq marked its submission to imperialism and the final humiliation and disintegration of the Arab nationalist movement. This isolated the Palestinian bourgeoisie, especially when the PLO, due to mass Palestinian anti-imperialist sentiment, was forced to support Iraq during the War. With an end to Gulf oil funding and with support from the Arab world at its lowest level, the PLO faced a major political and financial crisis. Meanwhile, on the West Bank and Gaza accelerated Zionist colonisation was threatening the remaining Palestinian bourgeois privileges. Under these conditions, the PLO's bourgeois leadership threw in the towel and prepared to sue for peace on any conditions. They got the Madrid Conference and now the Declaration of Principles.

The national bourgeoisie and the democratic revolution

The Palestinian bourgeoisie reflects, in a concentrated form, the character of the Arab bourgeoisie, and indeed the bourgeoisie of most oppressed nations in these post-Soviet, new colonial times. Today they have abandoned all programmes for genuine independent national development and are prostrating themselves before their imperialist masters.

During the great anti-colonial and anti-imperialist struggles of the post-war period the strength and economic performance of the USSR stood as an example, even to the vacillating bourgeois and petit-bourgeois trends, of independent economic development. The existence of the Soviet Union was a fetter on imperialism and offered the anti-colonial and anti-imperialist movements a greater degree of freedom to manoeuvre in their struggles. Liberation movements were able to hope and to fight for political and economic independence from imperialism as a first stage in improving the material conditions of the masses.

In this context left-wing forces within liberation movements wielded significant power. In relation to the Middle East US Secretary of State Warren Christopher admitted as much, asserting that the Soviet Union, whilst it existed:

'emboldened radicals, intimidated moderates and left Israel, save for the friendship of the United States, in a lonely state of siege.'
(*International Herald Tribune* 21 September 1993)

However, the collapse of the Soviet Union and the socialist bloc has enabled imperialism to decisively reassert unrivalled international economic, political and military power against all Third World opposition. In consequence, the dependent bourgeoisie, weakened by its own corruption and subordination to imperialist capital shamelessly submits to imperial dictates in exchange for a few perks, whilst the conditions of the masses touch levels of unprecedented poverty and suffering.

James Connolly, a great Marxist and fighter for Irish national liberation murdered by the British in 1916, aptly noted that in the national struggle the working class cannot rely on 'the leadership of a class whose social character is derived from oppression.' All 'bourgeois movements end in compromise' and the 'bourgeois revolutionist of today becomes the conservative of tomorrow.' In the epoch of imperialism therefore, only 'the working class remains as the incorruptible inheritors of the fight for freedom.'

The future of the Palestinian revolution

For over five months the West Bank and Gaza Strip have been sealed-off from Israel and from Jerusalem. Hundreds of thousands of Palestinians and their families, who rely on slave labour in Israel for their meagre living, are now desperately hungry. Imperialism, Zionism, Arab reaction and the PLO hope that the promise of international aid to release the masses from their desperate position will reconcile them to the neo-colonial autonomy plan and marginalise the opposition.

This task will not be easy. There have been numerous strikes and demonstrations against the deal. The left within the Palestinian movement, having withdrawn from the PLO, is organising against the sell-out. But confronted with the radical rhetoric of the fundamentalist forces, the left's fortunes will depend on how clearly and persuasively it can demonstrate that in this epoch the struggle for national liberation cannot be separated from the struggle for social liberation, that for success the struggle against Zionism and imperialism must be united with the struggle against capitalism.

The influence of Muslim fundamentalism among the poor and dispossessed of Palestine will seriously hinder this task. Despite its radical rhetoric opposing the agreement Hamas, the major fundamentalist organisation, is already engaged in secret negotiations with Al Fatah. It is not so much opposed to the deal as to the apportioning of the spoils. In any event, fundamentalism's opposition to the PLO has never had any revolutionary or democratic content.

The Palestinian revolution confronts difficult days ahead. The least we can do in Britain is to continue exposing the reactionary role of imperialism and Zionism in sustaining an order in the Middle East, the end result of which is abject poverty, war and death for the majority, whilst enormous riches are siphoned-off to feed the greed of a tiny rich minority in the imperialist heartlands.

2.9 BRITISH LABOUR AND ZIONISM
STEVE PALMER
FRFI 29 · MAY 1983

The genocidal butchery perpetrated by the Zionists in Lebanon in 1982 may seem far away. Yet the responsibility for establishing the Zionist state of Israel lies right here, in Britain.

The 1917 Balfour Declaration of the British government supported the 'establishment in Palestine of a national home for the Jewish people'. Though the Balfour Declaration had been issued by the Tories, it was rapidly endorsed by the Labour Party and the TUC in their 'War Aims Memorandum', adopted in December 1917:

'Palestine should be set free from the harsh and oppressive government of the Turk, in order that this country may form a Free State,
under international guarantee, to which such of the Jewish people
as desire to do so may return, and may work out their salvation free
from interference by those of alien race or religion.'

The Declaration had several imperialist aims. One was an attempt to
counteract the struggle of the Bolsheviks to overthrow the Russian
government and take Russia out of the imperialist war then raging. A
later Colonial Office memorandum, written for Winston Churchill in
1922, explained:

'The earliest document is a letter dated 24th April 1917 in which a
certain Mr Hamilton suggested that a Zionist mission should be
sent to Russia for propaganda purposes. It is clear that at that stage
His Majesty's Government were mainly concerned with the question of how Russia [then in the first stages of revolution] was to be
kept in the ranks of the Allies. At the end of April the Foreign
Office were consulting the British Ambassador at Petrograd as to
the possible effect in Russia of a declaration by the Entente of sympathy for Jewish national aspirations. The idea was that such a
declaration might counteract Jewish pacifist propaganda in
Russia.'

The British imperialists were contemptuous of the indigenous Palestinian population – and said so quite openly to one another. Balfour
explained in a Memorandum to Curzon that:

' . . . in Palestine we do not propose even to go through the form of
consulting the wishes of the present inhabitants of the country . . .
Zionism, be it right or wrong, good or bad, is rooted in age-long
traditions, in present needs, in future hopes, of far profounder
import than the desires and prejudices of the 700,000 Arabs who
now inhabit that ancient land.'

The Declaration had been made without reference to the Palestinian
people, who overwhelmingly opposed it. It was therefore inevitable

that a Zionist state in Israel would be a racist state, and an outpost of imperialism in the Middle East.

It was the racist British Labour Party which was to be the midwife to the birth of the Zionist state. This was the logical outcome of the strong Zionist ties and sympathies of the Labour Party, allied to its unswerving support for British imperialism. In 1920, Poale Zion, the British section of the International Organization of Socialist Zionists, had affiliated to the Labour Party, and from the early twenties, the Zionist current in the party grew rapidly.

The central problem which taxed the Zionists, following the Balfour Declaration, was the need to build up the Jewish Zionist colony in Palestine, the Yishuv: in 1918, Jews in Palestine – the supposed homeland – formed less than ten per cent of the Palestinian population. Without massive Zionist immigration into the country, the plan for a Zionist state would have collapsed. By 1929 the Jewish population had nearly trebled to 156,000. The Zionists owned four per cent of the land, but 14 per cent of the cultivable area. The Zionists, vigorously supported by their racist trade union Histradut, strictly enforced a policy of exclusively Jewish employment, both on the land and in industry.

The MacDonald letter

In August 1929, weeks after a new Labour government had taken office, hundreds were killed and many more injured in violent riots in Jerusalem. A government inquiry showed that the root cause of the hostility between Palestinian Arabs and Jewish settlers was the expulsion of peasants from land acquired by the Zionists, and recommended curtailing further Zionist immigration. Labour Colonial Secretary, Lord Passfield (formerly Sidney Webb), issued a White Paper recommending caution over unrestricted immigration to Palestine.

The Zionists unleashed a storm of fury. The Labour Prime Minister, Ramsey MacDonald, took control of Palestine out of Passfield's hands and passed it over to a Cabinet committee which, jointly with the Zionist Jewish Agency, drafted a letter which MacDonald read to Parliament on 13 February 1931. The letter, addressed to Chaim Weizmann, the Zionist leader who was to become Israel's first President, overturned the White Paper:

'the obligation to facilitate Jewish immigration and to encourage close settlement by Jews on the land, remains a positive obligation of the Mandate, and it can be fulfilled without prejudice to the rights and position of other sections of the population of Palestine.'

It was a testament of Labour support for Zionism and, as Weizmann remarked, the reversal in policy had a decisive effect on the establishment of the state:

'it was under MacDonald's letter to me that the change came about in the Government's attitude, and in the attitude of the Palestine administration, which enabled us to make the magnificent gains of the ensuing years. It was under MacDonald's letter that Jewish immigration into Palestine was permitted to reach figures... undreamed of in 1930.'

MacDonald also expressed the Labour government's support for the Zionists' policy of apartheid in employment, which was directed against the Palestinian Arabs:

'it is necessary also to have regard to the declared policy of the Jewish Agency to the effect that in "all the works or undertakings carried out or furthered by the Agency it shall be deemed to be a matter of principle that Jewish labour shall be employed." His Majesty's Government do not in any way challenge the right of the Agency to formulate or approve and endorse such a policy.'

Labour's complete contempt for the Palestinian Arabs was further confirmed by another incident recounted by Weizmann:

'The first indication I had of the seriousness of MacDonald's intentions was when he consulted me with regard to the appointment of a new High Commissioner to replace Sir John Chancellor.'

There is no record that the Labour Party consulted the Palestinian Arabs, expelled from the land acquired by Zionists, over who they would prefer as High Commissioner.

Throughout the 1930s, Arab resistance in Palestine to Zionist encroachment increased until it broke out into open rebellion against the British state in 1936. The rebellion began in April with the launching of a general strike which lasted six months. The British responded by dynamiting houses, criminalising Palestinian freedom fighters, and killing 1,000. Even as the general strike was still in progress, the British TUC, meeting in Plymouth, showed its racist support for Zionism and contempt for the Palestinians:

> 'the Congress earnestly hopes that the British Government . . . will take all the necessary means to bring the present disorders to an end.'

The government followed this advice. The rebellion was crushed after three years by 20,000 British troops who left more than 5,000 Arabs dead and 14,000 wounded.

A Zionist militia had been formed, armed and trained by the British, called the 'British Settlement Police'. It was similar in composition and purpose to the 'B Specials' or UDR in British-occupied Ireland, and by 1939 it numbered 21,500 Zionists – one in 20 of the Jewish population. The British also formed joint terror squads with the Zionists, similar to the SAS, known as the 'Special Night Squads'. Led by a British officer named Orde Wingate, these provided training for future members of the Zionist terror gang known as the Irgun. The Zionist deputy head of these squads was Moshe Dayan, later to become notorious in the 1967 'Six Day War'. Dayan later remarked that:

> 'In some sense every leader of the Israeli Army even today is a disciple of Wingate. He gave us our technique, he was the inspiration of our tactics, he was our dynamite.'

After the rebellion was crushed, remaining opposition was further undermined by the policy spelt out in the Tories' 1939 White Paper. This recommended sharply restricted Jewish immigration, regulation of land sales, and rejected a Jewish state, holding out promises of Palestinian self-government in the future. At its May conference, the Labour Party condemned these immigration restrictions at a time when European Jews were being brutally massacred by fascism, but it became clear that this criticism was simply ammunition to further Zionist designs:

> 'This Conference reaffirms the traditional support given by the British Labour Movement to the re-establishment of a National Home for the Jewish people in Palestine. It recognises that considerable benefits have accrued to the Arab masses as a result of Jewish immigration and settlement. This Conference is convinced that under the policy of the Balfour Declaration and the Mandate, the possibility exists for continued and increasing peaceful co-operation between the Jewish and Arab peoples in Palestine.'

1944: 'The Static Arab'

In December 1944, the annual Labour Party Conference passed its strongest pro-Zionist motion to date:

> 'there is surely neither hope nor meaning in a "Jewish National Home", unless we are prepared to let Jews, if they wish, enter this tiny land in such numbers as to become a majority. There was a strong case for this before the war. There is an irrestible case, now, after the unspeakable atrocities of the cold and calculated German Nazi plan to kill all Jews in Europe. Here too, in Palestine there surely is a case, on human grounds and to promote a stable settlement, for transfer of population. Let the Arabs be encouraged to move out as the Jews move in. Let them be compensated handsomely for their land and let their settlement elsewhere be carefully organised and generously financed. The Arabs have many wide territories of their own; they must not claim to exclude the Jews from this small area of Palestine, less than the size of Wales. Indeed we should examine also the possibility of extending the present Palestinian boundaries, by agreement with Egypt, Syria or Transjordan.'

The racism behind this motion was made clear by its drafter, Hugh Dalton, later Labour Chancellor:

> 'in Palestine we should lean, much more than hitherto towards the dynamic Jew, less towards the static Arab.'

This shameless racism proved embarrassing even for the Zionists. Commented Weizmann:

'I remember that my Labour Zionist friends were, like myself, greatly concerned about this proposal. We had never contemplated the removal of the Arabs, and the British Labourites, in their pro-Zionist enthusiasm, went far beyond our intentions.'

The 1945 Labour government

After the war, another Labour government was returned to power. Its policy towards Palestine was dictated by the Labour Party's concern to safeguard Britain's overall imperial interests. The war had weakened British imperialism. Britain had negotiated a massive dollar loan from the US imperialists. Since sterling could not be freely exchanged for currencies, scarce US dollars had to be conserved to pay off the US imperialists. Since oil from the Middle East did not have to be purchased with dollars, the control and security of these resources was therefore of vital importance to British imperialism. Bevin, the Foreign Secretary, expressed Labour's problem very clearly:

'His Majesty's Government must maintain a continuing interest in the area, if only because our economic and financial interests in the Middle East are of great importance to us and to other countries as well. I would like this fact faced squarely. If these interests were lost to us, the effect on the life of this country would be a considerable reduction in the standard of living. Other parts of the world would suffer too. The British interests in the Middle East contribute substantially not only to the prosperity of the people there, but also to the wage packets of the workers of this country. Nor can we forget our old and valued friendships with the peoples of the area.'

To defend its empire, the Labour government, as Bevin hints, attempted to draw conservative elements of the Arab states into support for its designs. From this perspective, the establishment of a Zionist state in Palestine was, at this time, a threat to imperialist interests. Richard Crossman, strongly pro-Zionist, claims that this was because Bevin identified Zionism with communism:

'I tried to convince him that it was just *because* the leaders of the Yishuv were of Russian origin that nearly all of them were fanatically opposed to Russian Communism. Moreover, apart from a minority of fellow travellers, I added, the leadership of the Histradut ... felt that the one Labour movement in the world whose ideals they shared was the British. But nothing could shake his *idée fixe* that the British position in the Middle East was threatened by a Jewish-Communist conspiracy ... '

More plausibly, Mayhew, then Bevin's Under-Secretary, argues that Bevin was opposed to a Zionist state because it would stimulate radical nationalism in the Arab states which might be directed against imperialist interests:

'its success would condemn the Middle East to decades of hatred and violence, and above all – this was the immediate concern – that by turning the Arabs against Britain and the Western countries, it would open a highroad for Stalin into the Middle East.'

Bevin's fears of communist influence in the Middle East were not fanciful: the Labour government was already waging war against the Greek people led by communists, and in Azerbaijan and Kurdistan autonomous republics with Soviet backing had been established after the war.

But the Zionists began a war of terror against the British in Palestine; in the Labour Party, tension on the question mounted. Within the Cabinet there was deep sympathy for the Zionists. At one point Richard Crossman visited John Strachey, a member of the Cabinet Defence Committee, and asked his advice about an act of sabotage planned by his Zionist friends:

'The next day in the Smoking Room at the House of Commons, Strachey gave his approval to Crossman. The Haganah went ahead and blew up all the bridges over the Jordan.'

It is impossible to imagine a British Cabinet approving a similar IRA operation!

Michael Foot

The political atmosphere inside the Labour Party can be gauged from a pamphlet which Michael 'Peacemonger' Foot wrote together with Crossman entitled *A Palestine Munich*. Dismissing the danger to the future Zionist state from the surrounding Arab states, the pamphlet remarks:

'there is nothing which any of these states can do in the nature of formal warfare either individually or collectively, that could not be countered by an airborne brigade or even an airforce demonstration.'

The pamphlet explained the conflict in racist terms:

'tribal, dynastic and religious antagonisms take more fanatical forms in the Oriental than in the Western world . . .

. . . the liberal era has never dawned on these countries. Such political mass movements as exist have a closer resemblance to the mass movements of the European Middle Ages than to those in the era of enlightment.'

Although it might be expedient to preserve friendship with the states of the Arab League, this would backfire and threaten British imperialism:

'Once we had defeated the Jews for them, the Arabs would demand immediate withdrawal of our troops from Palestine, and stage a revolt if this were not conceded. Then the last base for the defence of Suez would have gone.'

Far better to back the Zionist settlers and to partition the state:

'the government of the Judean State would be eager to negotiate a treaty of alliance with Great Britain . . . such a treaty would leave in British hands the port of Haifa and such airfields and installations as we require . . . Britain would be in a far stronger position than she is at present.'

In the event, it was the Zionist terror campaign and not the danger of nationalism or communism which threatened imperialist stability. With the encouragement of US imperialism, the Labour government announced that it would withdraw British troops from Palestine by 15 May 1948. The Labour Party breathed a sigh of relief, and Weizmann remarked, 'Now, thank God, we can live on friendly terms.' Labour had created Zionist Israel, and paved the way for genocide against the Palestinian people.

The terror squads were now turned on the Palestinian people. On 9 April 1948 the Irgun, led by Menachem Begin, conducted the massacre of Deir Yassin, when the Zionists butchered 254 Arab men, women and children in cold blood. This was only a particularly gruesome example from a wave of genocidal terror which drove 900,000 of the 1,300,000 Arab population out of Palestine, and left the Zionists holding 77 per cent of the land.

Suez 1956

With their state established, the Zionists began to threaten the countries bordering their statelet, carrying out repeated attacks on them. When the Egyptian leader Nasser requested arms from the United States to defend his country, he was told he could have them provided that he joined the US puppet states in the anti-Soviet Baghdad Pact. Nasser refused and negotiated for arms with Czechoslovakia. The US imperialists then withdrew finance from the Aswan Dam project, vital to irrigating the Egyptian land. On 26 July 1956, Nasser announced the nationalisation of the Suez canal; instead of its revenues going to enrich imperialists, they would be used to finance the Aswan Dam.

The British and French imperialists were up in arms. And so was the 'socialist' Labour Party which condemned the nationalisation as 'high-handed and totally unjustifiable'. A week later, Labour leader Gaitskell likened Nasser to Hitler and Mussolini, and called on the government to supply the Zionists with British arms. Labour also made it clear that it did not rule out the use of force.

Despite weeks of imperialist wheeling and dealing, it became clear that Britain and France did not have the support of the USA to use force, while the socialist countries and oppressed nations were siding with Egypt. Labour became increasingly worried that the use of force might endanger imperialism's wider interests. This opposition was entirely limited to criticising the government's tactics, and had nothing to do with anti-imperialism.

On 12 September, Gaitskell told the Commons that:

> 'If the government do this, they will leave behind in the Middle East such a legacy of distrust and bitterness towards the West that the whole area will be thrust almost forcibly under Communist control. This is the greatest danger of all.'

The British and French secretly arranged for puppet Israel to invade Egypt at the end of October, so that they could intervene 'to keep the two sides apart' – in fact to attack the Egyptians. When the news of the British invasion broke, the Labour Party did not attack the violation of Egyptian freedom nor did it utter even a whisper against the slaughter of the Egyptian people. Instead it condemned the government for losing an opportunity to attack the socialist countries, threatened with counter-revolution in Hungary.

The British and French imperialists backed down after the US showed its opposition for its own imperialist reasons – and after the Soviet Union threatened Britain and France with rocket attack.

The Six Day War

In the 1960s the Zionists staged a series of provocations against the Arab states. These reached a point where they could no longer be ignored, and Egypt, when it responded, was drawn into the carefully-laid Zionist plans to occupy the Sinai and other territories. Nasser closed the Straits of Tiran on 22 May 1967. The British Labour Cabinet met the following day. According to Wilson, the Cabinet decided that:

> 'Though several ministers were committed friends of Israel and of Israeli leaders, we were all agreed to urge the utmost restraint, at a very difficult time, on her.'

In fact, the Labourites had decided to give the Zionists full imperialist backing. The same day, Abba Eban flew to London:

'From the airport in London, I drove with Ambassador Remez to Downing Street . . .

Wilson's reply was forthright. The Cabinet had met that morning and had reached a consensus *that the policy of blockade must not be allowed to triumph; Britain would join with others in an effort to open the Straits.*'

Some 'restraint'! When George Thompson, Minister of State at the Foreign Office, was dispatched to Washington, he was accompanied by a senior member of the naval staff in order to co-ordinate British plans to open the straits with the Pentagon.

Labour's plans to send a British-American naval force to sail through the Straits of Tiran had been delayed by the reluctance of the French imperialists to join in the adventure, and w·ns pre-empted by the Zionists' own attack on the Arab countries. Although the force never attempted to open the blockade, Labour had exhibited its usual enthusiasm for imperialist schemes. And this particular scheme had, without doubt, encouraged the Israelis to begin the Six Day War.

The Yom Kippur War

In his book *The Chariot of Israel*, Harold Wilson explains the Labour Opposition's reaction to the war of October 1973, waged by the Arab states against Israel, and which threatened to liberate the Occupied Territories from Zionist rule:

'It was Labour who provided all the activity. As soon as news of the invasion became known I telephoned the Israeli Ambassador . . . I was in contact with him each day to hear of developments. The first thing he told me was that Mr Heath's Government had placed an embargo on the shipment of spares and ammunition to Israel needed for the Centurion tanks Britain had supplied when Labour had been in power. As soon as the Prime Minister, Edward Heath, returned to London, I went to No.10 to press him to change Government policy on spares and ammunition. When he refused, James Callaghan and I took up the issues publicly.'

With such obliging support from the Zionist errand-boys of the Labour Party, it is a wonder that the Israelis bothered keeping their own ambassador in London. Wilson goes on to quote the Israeli Foreign Minister, Abba Eban:

'The decision of Edward Heath and his government in London came as a specially harsh blow ... the British example affected other European countries ... It was only when Harold Wilson's Labour Government came to power that the scar in our relations began to heal.'

Conclusion

This brief survey of recent Palestinian history shows Britain's responsibility for conceiving and nurturing the Zionist monster. It also exposes the key role consistently played by the Labour Party in this process throughout the entire period – at times even outdistancing the Zionists themselves. A golden testimony to services rendered by Labour comes from the late Zionist Prime Minister, Golda Meir:

'one of the greatest factors in helping us to overcome our initial difficulties was the fact that from the very first, since 1917, we constantly received encouragement from the British labour movement.'

The fact is that today's Labour Party is true to its history. It is thoroughly pro-Zionist and pro-imperialist. Some 120 MPs are members of the Labour Friends of Israel. Among the Zionists are many of the so-called 'left', including Tony Benn and Eric Heffer. Another Labour MP is Greville Janner, who returned from a visit to Zionist-occupied Lebanon, remarking that 'the soldiers' restraint has been remarkable'. Opportunists like this form the core of the Labour Party and determine its political standpoint. The wretchedly pro-imperialist Labour Party did not call for a single demonstration during last summer's Zionist butchery in Lebanon. Surely that says it all?

A battalion of PKK guerillas

PART THREE

Kurdistan – The struggle for national liberation

3.1 IMPERIALISM AND THE COLONISATION OF KURDISTAN
TREVOR RAYNE ·

For over 2,500 years Kurdish land has seen some of the most illustrious empires in history come and go, and still the Kurds are fighting for their identity and their nation. The Persian Empire, the Assyrians, the Greek Macedonians of Alexander the Great, the Romans and Byzantines came and went. As classical history gave way to feudalism so the land was occupied by the Ottomans and the Shahs of Iran. However, throughout their history the Kurds can seldom if ever have confronted such brutality and barbarism as that inflicted upon them by their modern oppressors.

The struggle for the liberation of Kurdistan poses a critical threat to imperialism. Located at the heart of the Middle East, Kurdistan covers a territory over twice the size of Britain with about 30 million people. It cuts a swathe through one of the most strategic and mineral-rich regions in the world with oil, natural gas and iron ore resources, all of which have been developed, and coal, phosphates, copper, silver and gold which are largely underdeveloped, and with reported uranium deposits.

Kurdistan is strategically vital; geo-strategically and historically it straddles the old silk routes from Europe to China and India, and from Russia to Arabia, Egypt and Africa. It contains the headwaters of the

Tigris and Euphrates: these rivers are vital in the region, both for agriculture and hydro-electric power. More specifically today the suppression of Kurdistan is vital for the survival of the Turkish, Syrian, Iraqi and Iranian states and through them imperialism's domination of the entire Middle East and its 66.3 per cent of the world's known oil reserves. For the imperialist powers, relying as they do on cheap oil, the struggle for a free Kurdistan is a challenge to the 'New World Order' and imperialism's continued domination of the raw materials and labour resources of the Third World. This is why, when British Foreign Secretary Douglas Hurd visited Ankara shortly after Turkish troops perpetrated the Newroz 1992 (21 March, Kurdish New Year) massacres, he chose to sympathise with the state murderers and describe the Kurdistan Workers Party (PKK) as 'terrorists'.

The importance of Kurdistan for imperialism can be seen in the tortured history of the country, which has been bartered, divided and enslaved. As the Ottoman Empire went into decline towards the end of the 19th century Britain, France and Germany cast their predatory gaze on the potential spoils. With the discovery of oil in the region, first in the Caucasus, later in Persia and then in the Kurdish Mosul and Kirkuk regions, the rivalry, the promises and the treachery accelerated into the conflagration of World War One.

Mosul and Kirkuk contain two-thirds of Iraq's oil reserves. They are in the Kurdish region. Between 1915 and 1925 the British, variously in the guises of Lawrence of Arabia, Royal Dutch Shell and the Foreign Office, offered Mosul first to the Grand Shereef of Mecca, then to the French, then to the Kurds at the 1920 Treaty of Sevres, and finally to the Standard Oil Company of the Rockfellers. These offers were made to induce allegiance to British imperialism against the Turks and Germans. This land was being handed out to people even though British troops were nowhere near it and it certainly was not British to give away.

In the end when British troops had managed to occupy and subdue a Kurdish revolt the British under Lloyd George awarded it to themselves and to the Anglo-Persian Oil Company (later, 1954, to become the British Petroleum Company), a move which was internationally blessed by the League of Nations and the Treaty of Lausanne in 1923.

Initially, the British government considered forming a Kurdish 'buffer state . . . interposed between Iraq and Turkey' (Winston Churchill) to shield its oil possessions from a perceived Turkish nationalist/Bolshevik alliance. By the end of 1921 the Turkish nationalists were seen as potential allies against Bolshevism.

Despite Kurdish protests, Kurdistan and even the name Kurd were not even mentioned in the Treaty of Lausanne which laid the basis for a reconciliation between imperialism and Turkish nationalism, as personified by Kemal Ataturk. By the end of the 1920s Turkey played the role of 'buffer' against the Soviet Union. So for the benefit of British capital Kurdish lands were partitioned between Iran, Iraq, Turkey and Syria – consequently Kurds rebelled and have done so periodically ever since.

The precedent was set for the subsequent seven decades of brutal repression by Winston Churchill, then Secretary of State for Oil and War, who ordered the RAF to use gas bombs on Kurdish villages. Having practised on the Red Army – at least 500 bombs were dropped on the Red Army in Archangel in September 1919 – Churchill turned his attention from the 'Bolshevik baboons' to the 'uncivilised tribes' of Kurdistan. Such was the first ever aerial bombardment of civilians in 1922 and the commencement of a military strategy, carried out in the Gulf even to this day, of control by air supremacy – replacing the need to deploy ground troops in dangerous territory with mass slaughter from the skies. 'Bomber' Harris, who was to command the 1,000 bomber flights that burned down Cologne, Hamburg, Berlin and Dresden in World War Two, learnt the effectiveness of aerial war on bombing missions against Kurdish villages.

Divide and rule

The partition of Kurdistan has resulted in the cultural, economic and political suppression of the Kurdish people. In Iran in 1975 Kurdish per capita income was one-ninth that of Iran as a whole. Over 70 per cent of the Kurdish population were illiterate. In 1966 50 per cent of Kurdish families, which averaged five to six people, lived in single room accommodation. Kurds working in cities did a 54 hour working week. Again for 1975, 40 per cent of Kurdish girls and 25 per cent of boys aged seven to 15 years did not attend school. While east Kurdistan (Iran) was one of the most underdeveloped parts of Iran it was the most developed part of all Kurdistan!

In Turkey today, the average per capita income in all Turkey is about $1,500, but in north west Kurdistan it is $350 per person. That is a standard equivalent to Bangladesh.

In Iraq just 7-12 per cent of the budget for development went to Kurdish areas which contain 30 per cent of the total population. This is when these Kurdish areas have consistently contributed over 70 per cent of Iraq's oil income. These figures of poverty and degradation are from one of the most mineral rich places in the world.

While the Treaty of Lausanne denied the existence of the Kurds as a people, the requirement of Turkish and Persian capitalism for markets and labour denied Kurds even the right to Kurdish language and culture. The newly emergent bourgeoisies felt their territorial, economic and political power threatened by the Kurdish identity: borders would be ineffectual, and thereby open to incursions by rival powers and neighbours; peasant labour would be rendered unavailable while tied to feudal landholdings and clan systems; and rival poles of power among Kurds would draw dissident elements of the bourgeoisie and working classes and communists to them. All of which, in fact, happened.

However, the same level of underdevelopment of production that generated and sustained Kurdish feudal lineage, ties and identities tended also to undermine the struggle for Kurdish nationhood and unity. Clan chieftains sought to channel Kurdish demands for rights and political power into narrow local aspirations and the defence of non-democratic feudally-based power: that is, the power of landownership, ties of allegiance and religious tribute. Such leaders have been prepared to ally with one after the other of the regional powers in order to secure their limited ambitions. Above all this has expressed itself as autonomy within the existing territorial divisions of the colonising nations – that is, the feudal and semi-bourgeois Kurdish leaders have sought to get the best terms they can in an alliance with the colonial ruling classes that leaves the more powerful colonial states intact – and the Kurdish people divided and their masses oppressed. That was the lesson of the Kurdish leader Massoud Barzani's alliance with Iraq's General Qasim in 1958 against the Iraqi communists and Kurdish groups. It was repeated in 1970 when Barzani signed an agreement with the Baathists guaranteeing Kurdish autonomy within Iraq; and it was repeated again in 1975 when Barzani's alliance with the Shah of Iran was ended on the say-so of the Shah and the CIA. In each case the sectarian ambition of a section of the Kurdish people has led to the weakening and defeat of the whole. And when the Kurdish struggle has gathered enough momentum to destabilise its regional clients to the point of destruction, imperialism has intervened directly.

The RAF bombed Kurds in Iraq throughout the 1920s. They bombed Barzani's forces when they rebelled in Iraq in the early 1940s, trying to take advantage of World War Two. In 1946, in the Mahabad Republic in Iran, the USA twice threatened the use of nuclear weapons against the Soviet Union if it intervened to protect the Kurdish and Azerbaijani Republics. This allowed the Shah's forces to destroy them. From 1963-4 in Iraq British weapons supplies for war against a Kurdish rebellion were increased. This was done by both Tory and Labour governments. From 1957 onwards Savak, the Shah's secret police, was given a free hand in Kurdish areas. It was trained by the SAS, four of whom were killed in Iran by Fedayeen guerrillas in 1972. The SAS were deployed against the Kurds by Labour and Conservative governments. In 1991 US and British troops and helicopters intervened to protect Turkey from the unity of the Kurds – supported by Labour and Tory alike. US and British planes have provided intelligence to the Turkish Army on Kurdish guerilla movements.

Kurdistan: the key to the Middle East

The Kurdish struggle has proven itself to be a key component of the struggle by workers and oppressed peoples in the region. In Iraq Kurdish people were strongly represented in the Iraqi CP before the

General Qasim coup against the British-installed monarchy. The Kurdish struggle has provided the main opposition to the Baathists in Iraq for 25 years. In Iran the Kurdish Fedayeen were in the vanguard of the forces that overthrew the Shah, and ever since have sustained the guerrilla war, with their Fedayeen and Komala, against the Islamic Republic. In Turkey it is the Kurdish national liberation war led by the PKK and ERNK which has revived opposition to the regime following the effective suppression of the left in the 1980 military coup.

The Kurdish struggle is the key to progress and democracy in Iran, Iraq, Syria and Turkey. Kurdistan is the vanguard of the workers and oppressed peoples of the Middle East. Crucially today there is a revolutionary vanguard organisation based in north west Kurdistan – Turkey – with a mass following that raises Kurdish ambitions above narrow local demands for autonomy to the national level and combines this with a programme of popular democratic demands which mobilise the poor peasantry, the Kurdish working class and the mass of the Kurdish people. This is the PKK, and it threatens to be the ingredient that turns a revolutionary situation throughout Kurdistan into an actual revolution – the conductor that directs the popular struggle against feudal and sectarian restraints, against imperialism itself. This is what the British and US governments fear.

The declaration of the foundation of the PKK was made in 1978. During the 1970s Abdullah Ocalan and a group of young comrades studied Kurdish history and society. They returned from universities in Ankara and Istanbul to begin political work among the Kurds. From its beginning the PKK set itself against 'feudal exploitation, tribalism, religious sectarianism and the slave-like dependency of women'. It would struggle for the 'independence, democracy and unity of Kurdistan.' The PKK would seek unity of the Kurdish and Turkish peoples on the basis of the right of the Kurds to independent organisation and political power.

The 12 September 1980 military coup unleashed terror across Turkey and north west Kurdistan. Significantly each of the three coups in 1960, 1971 and 1980 have claimed to be putting down 'separatist movements', meaning Kurdish nationalists, and 'communists'. The 1980s terror targeted the PKK and the Turkish left. Thousands of Kurds and Turks were tortured, many killed. Leading PKK members were killed in detention, women were raped. Ocalan and other PKK elements withdrew to the Lebanon and began theoretical, political and military preparations for the Kurdish peoples' reply. On 15 August 1984 the armed struggle was launched.

Turkey's armed forces have used a forced depopulation programme; entire villages have been destroyed, towns shelled and bombed, fields and trees have been incinerated and livestock shot. The Turkish airforce has used napalm and chemical weapons. In 1991 the Turkish government brought out a new Anti-Terror Law. This explicitly protects torturers and suppresses reporting of the Turkish military's war effort. In the two years since it was passed 15 journalists have been murdered by Turkish troops and Special Forces in Kurdish areas.

Turkey's policy towards the Kurds is as racist and fascist as apartheid is in South Africa. It is the Turkish state which practices terror with the blessings of the US and British governments. It is the Turkish state which should be branded an international pariah.

3.2 KURDISTAN: AN OPPRESSED NATION
SPEECH BY HATIP DICLE FRFI 102 · AUGUST/SEPTEMBER 1991

Before I explain the human rights violations that are occurring in Kurdistan I would like to pay my respects to the Kurdish people who have fallen in the struggle against tyranny and persecution and a struggle to defend their dignity and national rights. Those people were martyred in the national liberation struggle but they contributed to the fight for humanity against the dehumanising campaigns being waged against our people. Their struggle is recognised in the UN Universal Declaration of Human Rights where it is written that in order to defend your national rights, your basic human rights, all legitimate paths are valid.

The question of Kurdistan is one of the most pressing issues in the world today. All defenders of human rights and defenders of peace should realise that as long as the people are denied their independence and freedom there will be no lasting peace in the Middle East. Britain has the greatest responsiblity for the division of my country; we do not blame the British people for this but we do expect international solidarity from democratic organisations and people in Britain.

58 years of emergency rule

For 58 of their 70 years in the Turkish Republic the people of northern Kurdistan have been under martial law and states of emergency. Today in Turkey the existence of Kurdish people as a national entity is still not recognised. We have no rights for education in our mother tongue. Our children are not allowed to learn their mother tongue and have to learn a foreign language. Our people are face to face with an unprecedented assimilation campaign. We are not allowed to publish books in our own language. We have no right to produce any written works in our own language. Kurdish people are prevented from hearing their own tongue spoken on the radio or television. The penalty for speaking Kurdish at a political meeting or any kind of meeting in a public place according to the new Anti-Terror Law starts at 15 years.

The Turkish government's campaign over the last three months, saying it has lifted the ban on Kurdish, that it is bringing in democracy, is all deception. Only fifteen days ago in Diyarbakir all the Kurdish cassettes that were on sale in the shops were confiscated in an operation. I have not heard of anything like this anywhere else in the world: Kurdish parents are not allowed to give their children the names they would wish to give, they cannot give Kurdish names. If they try to register their child at the local administrative office they are taken to court and prosecuted!

Our folk music is taken by Turkey, translated into Turkish and presented to the world as Turkish culture. They even win awards at international events.

This plunder is not only of our culture but also of our political rights. We are not allowed to establish a party with our own names 'Kurd' and 'Kurdistan'. This has been taken away from us. Our economic wealth has also been plundered. In northern Kurdistan all our economic wealth is being plundered. 95 per cent of the oil that comes within the borders of Turkey is in the Kurdistan area. All the phosphate, chrome and copper resources in Turkey are situated in Kurdistan. 85 per cent of the electricity in Turkey is generated from the hydro-electric plants on the dams of the rivers in Kurdistan.

Despite all this wealth that exists our people live in dire poverty. The average per capita income in Turkey is $1,500, but according to our research the average per capita income in northern Kurdistan is $350. In Izmit, an industrial city in the west of Turkey, the average income is $3,500 a year but in Hakkari in the south-eastern corner of Turkey, in Kurdistan, the average income is $150 a year. In the west of Turkey the standard of living is similar to that of some European countries while the standard of living in Kurdistan is similar to that of Bangladesh. This indicates the level of plunder that has gone on over the last 70 years.

Every delegation that visits Diyarbakir asks the same question: 'What do the Kurds want?' We say that we want the rights enshrined in the international treaties signed by all the countries of the world at the UN. Firstly, we want our national identity to be recognised. We want the bans and persecutions of our language and culture to be lifted. We want to be able to exercise our political rights, to act with our own name – in other words we want democracy in order to have the freedom to organise politically. We want the freedom to decide how our natural wealth is disposed of. We want to determine our own destiny.

Human rights trampled by Turkish military

To begin my description of the human rights situation in northern Kurdistan I will go back to the 1980 military coup. Then the whole of northern Kurdistan was turned into a torture chamber and the whole country was trampled under military boots. All our intellectuals were thrown into prison. There was an horrendous level of torture in the prisons: some people set fire to themselves to defend their human dignity. The period of detention at that time was 90 days and in this period people were subjected to torture. Many people were forced to flee the country and become political refugees in Europe. I am not exaggerating when I say that there is not one house in Kurdistan that did not have a relative or someone they knew who was tortured, shot, killed or thrown into prison. Villagers were forced to gather in village squares and then tortured. Their houses were raided on the pretext of looking for weapons. Men were stripped off in front of their wives and string was attached to their sexual organs and then they were led around the village squares. Relatives of political activists were arrested and tortured just for being relatives. The torture at that time was so intense as to be beyond comparison with anywhere else. But the repression and the torture could not break the spirit of resistance and in 1984, on 15 August, in reply to the repression the guerrilla struggle began.

At the beginning of the guerrilla struggle led by the PKK all the people became a target for the Turkish authorities. The state introduced a Village Guard or Village Protector state militia system wherein villagers were sometimes forced by economic hardship to fight for the government against the guerrillas. Sometimes whole tribes were forced into these militias.

When the Turkish authorities realised that they would be unable to prevent the rise of the revolutionary movement they then brought out, in April 1990, decrees with the force of law which provided powers even Hitler and Mussolini did not have. Today, the state of affairs is such that whatever the regional governor says is law. He has the authority to close down newspapers and the printing shop if any newspaper were to tell the truth about what is happening in Kurdistan. He has the power to exile people from Kurdistan – anyone he considers undesirable. There is absolutely no independence of the judiciary. All authority is in the hands of this one man, the Regional Governor. All the repressive measures have been rendered unworkable by the guerrilla struggle and the support they receive from the people.

In August 1990 the Turkish government officially announced to the Council of Europe that it was suspending human rights in Kurdistan. At the time the attentions of the whole world were on Kuwait which had been occupied by Iraq. Between August and November 1990 up to 300 villages were forcibly vacated in the Botan area. This is an area where the guerrilla struggle is at its most intense. According to our research these 300 villages were forcibly vacated because the villagers had refused to become village guards and their houses and orchards were burnt to prevent them returning. These people were made refugees in their own country. When we visited the Sirnak area we saw the people living in tents on the edge of the town. All the woods on the Herkol, Cudi and Gabbar mountains were burnt. Villagers said that as well as their orchards their bee-hives had been burnt. Some people who had refused to leave their homes had their belongings burnt inside their houses. Our research shows some 50,000 people affected by these measures. The aim of this policy is to depopulate Botan. Of these 50,000 those that were better-off moved to Turkish cities to the west. The poorer villagers were forced to live in shanty towns on the outskirts of Kurdish towns. Some lived in barns.

An interesting development took place with the people sheltering near Sirnak. They managed to get some money together, bought mules and went to open-cast mines abandoned by the state and scraped a living selling coal dust. However, the state did not tolerate their presence around Sirnak and the Turkish army took its machine guns and killed 300 mules. These mules were all the people had. 3,000 villagers marched into Sirnak in protest at the barbarous act. The state replied with its troops and special forces who fired on the people killing five and leaving seven more with bullet wounds. These people, who had seen their villages burnt around their ears, driven from their homes and then had their only means of livelihood destroyed, were fired at.

On 19 November in Europe there was a conference on the world reduction in arms. At Turkey's request 34 countries agreed to exclude Turkey from new arms reduction proposals. We condemn those European countries that were signatories to an agreement that is turning Kurdistan into a veritable arsenal. Since 19 November the weapons no longer required in Europe are being transported to Kurdistan. Between Sirnak and Uludere near the Iraqi border there is a military post every two or three miles.

The burning of villages is not the only method used to depopulate Kurdistan. There is a ban on Kurdish nomads taking their flocks of sheep to high pastures in the summer. This affects about one million people. The Turkish authorities' aim is to force the nomads to sell the sheep cheaply and leave the area. Another method is used: many village guards want to give up their weapons and when they present themselves to the authorities to resign they are told to load their belongings on a tractor and to leave Kurdistan and their homes. That is the only way their weapons will be accepted back.

Systematic and widespread torture

As you can read in Amnesty International reports and in the European Parliament, there is an intensive campaign of torture in Kurdistan today. The period of detention upon arrest is now 30 days. During the first two weeks many people suffer severe torture and in the second two weeks their bruising and marks are given time to heal so as not to be visible. Such is the intensity of the campaign of detentions that, whereas once we were able to keep track of the number of people being detained, now it is impossible. If there is a guerrilla attack near a village then all the villagers – men, women and children – are detained and tortured. We can no longer keep track of all the incidents. The people do not need to be taken away to a military or police headquarters to be interrogated; local schools can be turned into torture chambers. People are given systematic shocks, hung up by their arms, made to walk on broken glass, hosed down with pressurised water; all kinds of torture are used.

Massacres to depopulate Kurdistan

Here are some recent examples of violations of human rights. I have a list covering the last year. If I detailed them all I would be here talking for another three hours, so I will tell you just about some of the most striking examples. This list covers only about ten per cent of all the violations that occurred over the past year.

On 10 June near Sirnak in the village called Gere, or its new Turkish name Gevrimli, 27 women and children were massacred. There was a big campaign on Turkish television stating that the women and children had been massacred by the PKK; this was state propaganda. We organised a delegation of lawyers and journalists to visit the village and talk to the people, but we were prevented from making the visit for 11 days. When we finally got into the village we discovered the following: the villagers who were killed were from families who had refused to become village guards. The villagers said that those who had committed the massacre wore T-shirts and flak jackets. There is a military base just 15 minutes walk from the village. We are absolutely certain that those responsible for the massacre were the Turkish security forces – the Special Forces counter-insurgency teams. This massacre was timed to coincide with a European Security Conference held in Copenhagen. At the time Turkey was being pressurised by human rights organisations, so the Turkish authorities create this scenario – 'Look what the PKK has done. This is why we must have these new laws'.

The same thing happened in a village near Hakkari called Sete. Again nearly 30 people were killed and again the victims were from families that had refused to join the state militias. On 30 June 1990, in the Mardin province, a driver who refused to take troops to a military operation was taken to a military post and shot in the head. You may wonder what happened to the officer that committed this murder; he is still free despite the efforts of the family of the murdered man to have him brought to trial. He was not brought to justice, no enquiry took place into the murder. The officer said that the murdered man was inspecting the officer's revolver when it went off and the man accidentally shot himself. With this explanation the authorities took the matter no further.

On 6 August 1990 in Hakkari Province it was reported on the news that seven PKK 'terrorists', as they call them, had been killed in a clash. We investigated this incident and discovered the seven were poor villagers who made a living by taking things from Turkey to Iraq to sell and then bringing things back. They carried their wares on their backs; it was very simple smuggling but they were taken to a military headquarters and shot out-of-hand. The bodies of these people were not returned to their families for burial. Instead, a ditch was dug and they were tipped in on top of each other, unwashed, in the clothes they had been wearing. Such is the condition of the Turkish state that they no longer respect even the dead.

Until three months ago the bodies of dead guerrillas were not returned to their families. Before 1986 the bodies of guerrillas in the Siirt area were tied to the backs of vehicles, dragged around the streets and then thrown on the municipal dump. In 1988 there was a campaign to have the dump called the Butcher's River dug up – it is estimated there are 100 bodies there – but the campaign was unsuccessful. The dump remains uninvestigated.

Turkey does not conform to the Geneva Convention: it uses napalm and gas and captured guerrillas are thrown from helicopters. A taxi driver disappeared on 11 June 1990. He had previously been arrested for having a Kurdish cassette in his car. Then he disappeared and his car with him. We know about people who disappear in Central America, but perhaps this is the first time someone has vanished together with his vehicle.

On 5 September 1990 a mental patient who had been released in Elazig only the day before was shot only 200 yards from his house and the security forces announced on the evening news that he was a 'terrorist'.

In recent times resistance to repression has grown among the religious priests. In September last year one was taken to a local military post and a different form of torture was used on him: a strict Moslem, he was forced to drink raki, an aniseed alcoholic drink. It was forced down his throat. This Imam had advised the people not to join the militias.

In November 1990 another villager was arrested and detained for a week. After a week his body was returned to his family with a doctor's note saying he had died of a heart attack. The priest who washed his body said the back of his head had been caved in and that blood was still seeping from it. He had been killed under torture in Mardin.

I have a long list of shepherds who have been shot while tending their flocks, of villagers shot and then the authorities claimed it to be an accident, or that they were terrorists.

In March this year before Newroz (the Kurdish New year) there were incidents in Sirnak where the people were killed by the security forces.

Also the refugees who fled from Saddam told us that dozens had been killed at the border by the Turkish army in April.

Some of you may have seen the *Panorama* programme shown two weeks ago where there was a story about three girls who were out on the hills looking for an edible thistle called Kenger. They got lost and the local village guard informed the authorities that the girls had gone into the hills to join the guerrillas. Following this they were taken to a village military post, tortured, kept in cells and shown photographs of three people who it was claimed had encouraged the girls to join the guerrillas. The girls had no knowledge of this but they were forced to put their thumbprints on a confession which incriminated these three people, two of whom had been imprisoned before as PKK suspects. One was a local official of the Popular Labour Party whom the state wanted to incriminate. He was arrested and is still in detention.

The new Anti-Terror Law

In April 1991 the Turkish government brought out the new Anti-Terror Law. It came in the context of a mass mobilisation of the people in Kurdistan. There is now mass opposition to the Turkish government: the people close their shops for days, they go on hunger strike protests and thousands of people go to the funerals when guerrillas are killed. People are going to democratic associations and joining in the activities there. The main aim of the Anti-Terror Law is to suppress this democratic mass movement. The Turkish government announced to the world that it has lifted the ban on Kurdish, that it has removed the notorious articles 141, 142, and 163 – those laws that prevented freedom of thought and speech. They say they have separated such acts from terror offences, but in fact the same offences exist in the new Anti-Terror Laws. Indeed, under this new legislation for saying what I have said today I could be charged with a terror offence, I could be defined as a 'terrorist'.

No newspaper can print the truth of what is happening in Kurdistan for if they did they would be fined 500m Lira (£70,000). Newspapers cannot print the names of the torturers; there are heavy fines for that. The Turkish state is so hypocritical: it was the first state to sign the Anti-Torture Convention, but with the new Anti-Terror Law it is

143

protecting torturers; they will not be charged for their torture. Those people who kill our people in the villages, even if they are charged, their defence costs and solicitors will be paid for by the state.

The torturers must have been encouraged by this new law for, only a month after it came into effect, three brothers in Norsin – a town near Bitlis – were forced to eat dog excrement by the military. Despite all the efforts of the solicitor working for the three brothers, he was unable to get an enquiry into the officer responsible. In fact, a major who had forced villagers to eat human excrement in Yesiyurt near Cizre in 1988 was not punished – on the contrary, he was promoted.

When I got on the plane to come here I opened a newspaper and read that on 25 June our Human Rights Association building in Diyarbakir had been bombed. The Turkish government hopes to frighten us into ending our services to the national liberation struggle but they will be mistaken. We will continue to expose their violations of human rights and send our reports to the world.

3.3 THE TURKISH STATE, THE TURKISH WORKING CLASS AND THE KURDISH REVOLUTION
MURAD AKIN FRFI 105 · FEBRUARY/MARCH 1992

The Turkish working class and Kurdish oppressed masses are facing very conflicting tasks and dangers. Any analysis of the political conditions resulting from the early general election and of the policies of the newly established liberal-social democratic coalition must begin with an examination of the revolutionary dynamic of the labour movement in Turkey and the Kurdish resistance.

1991 proved to be the high point of the growing class resistance in the form of unofficial mass action which began in 1989 – the '1989 Spring'. The miners' strike in Zonguldak, December 1990 – January 1991, was the first nation-wide anti-government challenge to the Motherland Party Government (ANAP) since the 1980 military coup. But after the intervention of local social-democratic politicians and trade union leaders during the final stages of the strike, a collective agreement was signed and imposed on the strikers and the unofficial and widely legitimised mass movement was isolated. This development revealed both a weakness in class solidarity and the inability of the revolutionary movement to influence the course of the strike and combat the influence of the local trade union leaders. Nevertheless, the positive example of the miners' strike spread to other worker's struggles against job losses, for higher wages and better working conditions. The glass workers of Pasabahce in Istanbul followed the example of the workers of Zonguldak, converting workplace protest into a locally-based unofficial mass movement.

The Turkish and Kurdish workers suffer from a relatively new and pragmatic layer of trade unionist leaders, both local and national, who have benefited from post-coup legislation. This legislation allows higher ranks of trade unionists to be highly paid and to control a huge volume of financial sources. It was this trade union aristocracy which pushed the working class into an organisationally premature general strike ('general action' in their terminology) on 3 January 1991 during the last days of the miners' strike. They reduced this action to 'general absenteeism' – the workers merely stayed at home, although the 'general strike' was a concrete demand among the politically advanced workers. This contributed to the liquidation of the Zonguldak resistance and the spreading of a general climate of defeatism in the class movement.

After this, the trade union leadership limited the agenda to economic issues, depoliticised strikes and offered an indecisive opposition to the ANAP government. This was consistent with their call for a coalition government of social-democrats and liberals. Such a government was formed after the elections in November 1991.

'Serhildan Ciyane' – 'to resist is to live'

Kurdish resistance (*Serhildan*) not only demonstrated the mass basis of the struggle led by the PKK but a new stage of struggle in the cities complementing the guerrilla warfare in the rural areas. Today the Turkish cities realise that the Kurdish resistance now incorporates an urban mass movement, although there is still a problem of interaction between the class movement in the cities and the *Serhildan* against the Turkish state and propertied classes.

During the imperialist military assault against Iraq, the PKK adopted a clear anti-imperialist policy risking isolation and repression by pro-imperialist Turkish forces. Nevertheless, this anti-imperialist policy, unique on the Kurdish left, helped the *Serhildan* to gain ground in the largest parts of Kurdistan.

On the other side, the majority of the metropolitan Kurdish left look towards American and European intervention for a 'democratic' mid-way 'autonomy' solution to the Kurdish question. This wing includes Talabani and Barzani of the Kurdistan Patriotic Front in southern Kurdistan.

This policy has been disastrous for the Kurdish people once again. The growth of mass support for the Kurdish national liberation movement allowed some local Kurdish politicians and ex-social democratic party managers to be involved in Kurdish resistance on a more pragmatic, collaborationist basis. These elements tried to exploit the anti-imperialist patriotism of *Serhildan*. They want to narrow the scope of resistance to the interests of the Kurdish national bourgeoisie, using the support of European and Turkish liberals to compromise with the Turkish state. These elements welcomed Özal's 'liberal' intervention in northern Kurdistan. They joined the Social Democratic Populist Party which has no democratic or anti-imperialist standing. This layer of Kurdish politicians and propertied classes also supported the new coalition.

Today these 'realistic' politicians, European-based Kurdish organisations and some sections of the Kurdish intelligentsia are planning to organise a 'Kurdish conference' with the help of pro-imperialist European and American MPs in such a way as to exclude the PKK. Using the 'liberal' policies of the Turkish bourgeoisie, they are aiming, primarily, to channel the grassroots radicalism and anti-imperialist socialist orientation of Kurdish resistance towards the lines approved by the Turkish liberals and new world 'realism'. The 'Kurdish conference' has claimed that: 'Today is not the age of socialism and national liberation movements but democracy and human rights'. This is taking place at a time when Kurdish guerrillas are being buried at mass funerals and the people are being shot by Turkish 'special teams' in the Kulp and Lice districts of Kurdistan. The PKK denounced the call for this 'Kurdish conference' in a press release on 2 January 1992.

There is nothing new in the new government's approach to the national liberation movement. Demirel, the new prime minister of the coalition government, is repeating the brutal-liberal approach of the Turkish state under Turgut Özal in the period prior to the elections. This policy depends on the recognition of Kurdish identity as an ethnic group, a rhetoric of democracy and tolerance, and armed suppression of any sort of resistance by those fighting for Kurdish independence. This policy is sponsored by American and European 'democrats'. It is basically aimed at the creation of a collaborationist layer within the Kurdish liberation movement.

Demirel promised everything during his post-election trips with his partner Inonu (leader of the Social Democratic Populist Party) through Kurdish cities. But he did not forget to stress the unitary state structure, threatening to destroy the armed struggle 'more brutally than ever'. This policy had the support of ex-ANAP prime minister Mesut Yilmaz. The policy to eliminate the PKK by every means is the common denominator in Turkish bourgeois politics. The aim is to win the representatives of the Kurdish propertied classes away from the Kurdish revolutionary democratic movement – a movement which is based on the poor and oppressed working people and peasants of Kurdistan.

The working class begin to remember Demirel in power

Both the True Path Party (Demirel's party) and the Social Democratic Popular Party spent enormous energy in convincing big business and finance capital about their 'realistic' and conciliatory policies by meeting TUSIAD (Turkish Industrialists' and Businessmen's Organisation) during the pre-election period. It is clear who will pay the bill for economic recession and political instability.

The workers and oppressed masses are beginning to understand the conciliatory declarations of the seventh Demirel government. The new government is subject to the same ideological and economic constraints as the preceding bourgeois governments. The new cabinet was absolutely aware of the 'demands' of TUSIAD before forming a government. The new economic advisers support the master plan on privatisation prepared by the US bank Morgan Guaranty Trust. The first consequence will be the dismissal of a further 125,000 workers from Public Economic Enterprises, over and above the 300,000 job losses in 1990-1991.

The miners' strike had countered the hysteria of privatisation. So the privatisation of coal mines, steel plants (Erdemir), TEKEL (Tobacco Monopoly), TEK (Electricity Company) was slowed down. The new Secretary of State responsible for economic restructuring claims he will deal with privatisation in a more 'humane' way by a process of creating 'autonomous' (independent from the state budget) enterprises. But nobody knows how making those enterprises 'autonomous' will be more 'humane' than privatisation.

TUSIAD has now put more pressure on the legislative and governmental bodies to ensure through rationalisation a reduction of the number of unionised workers to under two million – less than 10 per cent of the work force. So dismissals as a means of deunionisation continue with armed suppression against any attempts at resistance under the new government. The glass workers in Tuzla in Istanbul, for example, protesting against dismissals, were suppressed by the 'mobile force' (a special anti-riot police force) at the end of 1991.

The main form of attack today by capital in industrial conflicts is through layoffs. This is because real wages have risen from their low point in 1988 and over the last two years have shown an increase, regaining the 1983 level. However, even current real wage levels in manufacture are 21 per cent less than the 1970's average. The increased labour costs, despite the low level, were a constraint on profits in the exports sector. Last year's job losses represented 15 per cent of unionised workers. However, the trade union leadership, in close collaboration with the new coalition parties, gives credit to the government and offers no sign of resistance.

The new bourgeois government faces a foreign debt of $55bn, unemployment at 21 per cent, and inflation around 60 per cent. On the other hand, the 500 largest industrial companies in Turkey enjoy a real rate of profit of 30.5 per cent. The share of labour costs as a proportion of sales revenues of these companies means that a worker works 24 days for himself, and 230 days for capital in a year. The recent increases in state employees' wages of 25 to 30 per cent were far below the inflation rate.

There is very little that is 'new' in the policies of the coalition government. The deunionisation and dismissals increasingly consist of occasional workers, privately contracted employees etc. The new economic advisers emphasise the need to reorientate resources towards efficient and productive investments, rather than the speculative income-creating investment of the previous government. The Turkish bourgeoisie is now concerned to reduce the weight of the rentier stratum and increase the productive capacity of manufacturing industry as part of its new climate of consensus and democracy.

There is no pressure from the unions on the new government to reduce unemployment. The official level is 3.1 million; however, including agricultural unemployment and the informal sector, the figure could reach 9.5 million.

The old managers of the misnamed DISK (Confederation of Revolutionary Trade Unions), whose activities were banned by the military regime, now promote their new concept of 'contemporary trade unionism'. This concept is based on the total rejection of class unionism, and has been reinterpreted for the new world of 'peace and compromise'.

The reality is not so promising. Disillusionment has already set in among state employees. Plans to cut VAT repayments to workers and employees will significantly reduce real wages. Government plans to sell Public Economic Enterprises to foreign buyers as a mortgage for foreign debt threaten massive redundancies and more expensive services.

The government also believes that by allowing Kurdish liberals to publish their own newspapers and organise a Kurdish Democratic

Party or something similar it will isolate those leading armed resistance against the Turkish state.

A common struggle against the Turkish state

As 1992 begins the Turkish ruling class in alliance with the Kurdish bourgeoisie are taking measures to retain the political initiative. This is dependent on the ability of the Turkish bourgeoisie to retain the collaboration of the trade union leadership for its economic programme and its success in integrating the Kurdish bourgeoisie in a more stable political relationship as part of the overall US/EC political strategy in the Middle East.

This path will meet resistance. The economic crisis will force the working class increasingly into confrontation with the reformist–collaborationist leadership of the trade unions. Kurdish anti-imperialist resistance is still independent, far away from defeat and liquidation. This is the context in which the ideological and political rejuvenation of the revolutionary organisation of Turkish socialists is the precondition for a united anti-capitalist/anti-imperialist resistance against the Turkish state.

3.4 KURDISTAN: REVOLUTION AT A CRITICAL JUNCTURE
TREVOR RAYNE
FRFI 114 · AUGUST/SEPTEMBER 1993

Events during the past year – Syria's closure of PKK bases in Lebanon, the joint Kurdish Democratic Party/Patriotic Union of Kurdistan (KDP/PUK) and Turkish army assaults on the PKK in South Kurdistan (northern Iraq), the PKK's unilateral ceasefire and resumption of hostilities in the face of Turkish state intransigence – have brought the Kurdish revolution to a critical stage.

Financial Times: Abdullah Ocalan has agreed to extend his cease fire. Are you closer to a solution?

Suleyman Demirel: We never hear him, whatever he says. If you start hearing him, then he becomes a party to the problem . . . We should never deal with him. (*Financial Times* 7 May 1993)

On 17 March 1993 PKK General Secretary Abdullah Ocalan, accompanied by Jalal Talabani, leader of the PUK from South Kurdistan, declared a unilateral ceasefire in the Kurdish liberation struggle to run over the 21 March Newroz (New Year). The ceasefire was extended indefinitely on 16 April when Ocalan made the following demands: an end to the annihilation of Kurdish people and Turkey's military operations; a general amnesty; cultural rights such as Kurdish language radio and television stations, newspapers and books; the right to the unfettered use of the Kurdish language and the legalisation of Kurdish political organisations; the right for displaced persons to return to their homes and be compensated for damage to their houses and loss of livestock; abolition of the system of regional governors and the disarming of the village guards. Ocalan warned that if the Turkish Republic continued its operations then the ceasefire would be meaningless and the guerrilla war would have to be resumed. He appealed to the UN and to the European Parliament to send delegates to Kurdistan to observe the ceasefire.

In an immediate response to the original ceasefire declaration Turkey's Interior Minister ruled out negotiations with the PKK. The army-dominated National Security Council recommended continuing with the big Spring military operations. During the Newroz celebrations the Turkish army killed 41 people, 30 of whom were guerrillas observing the ceasefire. By 24 May, 128 Kurds had been killed since the unilateral ceasefire began, six Kurdish villages had been destroyed and some 2,000 Kurdish civilians arrested and detained without trial. Turkish sources claimed that 74 PKK guerrillas had been killed including 13 guerrillas murdered with chemical weapons at Silvan.

On 24 May 41 Turkish troops were killed by PKK guerrillas at Bingol, in what they described as self-defence. By 8 June when Ocalan announced the unilateral ceasefire over, 44 Kurdish villages had been destroyed since 17 March, 3,500 Kurdish civilians had been arrested and several hundred people had been killed by the Turkish state forces. President Demirel had offered the PKK an 'honourable surrender' with limited amnesty provisions if combatants gave up their weapons, a fate which Ocalan described as 'worse than suicide'. Rejecting the appeal from the PKK to find a political solution to the Kurdish problem the Turkish state showed its determination to crush the liberation struggle militarily. The UN and European Parliament barely acknowledged the ceasefire and the Turkish state felt reassured that it could continue its war unperturbed by international 'concern'.

Ocalan announced the ceasefire over at Bar Elias on 8 June. He said that 'thousands, tens of thousands, will suffer . . . this campaign will be the most ferocious of all our campaigns. We are for a union within the federal rule in Turkey. On that basis we are always ready for a political solution. Until this happens the armed struggle will be escalated . . . '. He warned that Turkey's economy and tourist income would be targeted and blamed Turkish state colonialism which 'bears the responsibility because they have not recognised the minimum of our rights. If they do not recognise the minimum of our rights how can we halt the armed struggle?'

South Kurdistan – uncertainty and hedging

At the beginning of October 1992 the new Kurdish Parliament in South Kurdistan voted for the status of an independent federated state. On 4 October the two leading figures in this parliament – Barzani, leader of the KDP, and Talabani – mobilised 15,000 peshmergas to drive the PKK out of their bases on the border with Turkey. By 28 October the commander of Turkey's army General Dogun Gures said that up to 200,000 Turkish troops were in northern Iraq. Together with the KDP and PUK peshmerga they were pitted against the PKK.

Although the PKK claimed to have lost no more than 100 guerrillas the combined assault drove them from their bases and rendered a section of their command and logistics inoperable. The KDP and PUK said that the PKK could have a political presence in South Kurdistan but could not use this as a base from which to attack Turkish state forces.

Barzani and Talabani and the Iraqi Kurdish bourgeoisie and feudal leaderships are dependent on Turkey, the US and NATO to preserve their autonomous enclave. Turkey provides the six monthly renewable mandate for the NATO war planes which patrol the skies of northern

Iraq. With the Baghdad embargo of the Kurdish region the enclave is dependent on the UN and routes through Turkey for supplies and currency. Barzani and Talabani have thus far shown that they are willing to sacrifice the PKK and Kurds in Turkey to retain their own positions. The Turkish state does not want an independent Kurdish state in South Kurdistan, but its priority is defeating the PKK and for that reason it is prepared to use Barzani and Talabani as allies.

In May the UN began withdrawing its armed guards from northern Iraq claiming that it was short of funds. Throughout the spring there were meetings between the diplomatic representatives of Turkey, Syria and Iran. They appear to have been coordinating attacks on the Kurds. Each state fears the impact that the PKK is having and the implications of an independent South Kurdistan. In April Iranian government forces began bombarding and shelling camps of the Kurdistan Democratic Party of Iran along Iran's border with northern Iraq and adjacent to South Kurdistan. Iranian troop incursions into South Kurdistan followed. Turkey and Syria have agreed to find a 'final solution' to their dispute over the River Euphrates and control over its waters by the end of this year. Additionally, with the Soviet Union gone, Syria is showing itself more accommodating to the US over Israel and has been willing to close down PKK bases in the Lebanon to win US favour. Syria wants the Golan Heights back and for that it needs US pressure on Israel.

Any rapprochement between Syria, Turkey, Iran or Iraq is viewed with apprehension by Barzani and Talabani. Precisely at the moment when an independent Kurdish entity begins to emerge they transform from being useful tools for the colonial powers to use in their contentions into a potential challenge to that colonialism and status quo. Barzani and Talabani recognise that Turkey has only a conditional need of them and that fulfilment of this need is critical to retaining US and EC protection for their enclave. If they are able to subdue the PKK not only militarily in northern Iraq, but more importantly politically in its aspirations and methods throughout Kurdistan they will have earned their keep.

Over the past few years Barzani and Talabani have visited Ankara. Part of the Turkish government's strategy has been to use them to found a Kurdish party to rival the PKK in Turkey. The PKK has attempted to bring other Kurdish political trends in Turkey under its political influence. After the 17 March ceasefire declaration, Ocalan for the PKK and Kemal Burkey, leader of the Kurdistan Socialist Party, signed a protocol ending animosity between the two parties. Representatives from other Kurdish political parties were present at the ceasefire declaration. Between 18-20 June representatives of 11 Kurdish political organisations, including the PKK, met and agreed to start preparations for a National Front. These parties include representatives of more bourgeois and petit-bourgeois currents in Kurdish society. Their incorporation into the liberation movement is positive in so far as it diminishes the ability of the Turkish state to create a Kurdish entity to rival the PKK, but potentially negative in that bourgeois and petit-bourgeois influences, may compete with the socialist forces to determine the political line of the liberation movement and the PKK. This would manifest itself over the methods of revolutionary struggle and the objective of independence, with the bourgeoisie and petit-bourgeoisie making concessions to colonialism and imperialism.

Ocalan himself has stated that he does not want 'separatism', but for relations with Turkey to be 'reorganised on a free and equal basis'; 'to be in a state of unity is not contrary to independence'. He does not take the Iraqi Kurdistan development as a model, criticising the endeavour towards federation in Iraq as unrealistic unless put on a basis of democracy and equality with Arab and other people in Iraq. 'What is important here is the Kurdish people being able to guarantee their political and military existence, having the power to do that.' This formulation may appear to be a concession towards autonomy and away from an independent Kurdistan. However, self-determination as a democratic principle is not identical with complete separation. What matters is the role of the working class and peasantry for whom democratic rights and control of the land and means of production would invariably bring them into conflict with the bourgeois colonialist Turkish state. Federalism as Ocalan defines it above necessitates the democratisation of the Turkish state. The dominant elements in the Turkish state, led by the military, assess that the PKK has been strategically and significantly weakened by its expulsion from Lebanon and restriction of its activities in northern Iraq. In this context, an intensified military assault should, they gauge, diminish support for self-determination within Kurdish society as it is rendered unattainable and strengthen the trend towards compromise and ultimately surrender to Turkish state rule.

Hence the significance of Ocalan's 17 March ceasefire declaration in the presence of Talabani, a man whom on previous occasions he described along with Barzani as 'horse-traders . . . who have put our land up for sale'. The expulsion from Lebanon and the attack on its bases in northern Iraq have increased the pressure from bourgeois elements among the Kurds on the PKK leadership. Barzani and Talabani are favoured by imperialism. The PKK is viewed as dangerous with its working class and poor peasant base of support. There were reports that the ceasefire was opposed by sections of the guerrillas in the mountains. The resumption and intensification of the guerrilla war indicates that the pressure of the mass movement has prevailed over the path towards concessions to colonialism and imperialism.

Unlike the PLO, the PKK has no hinterland of bourgeois support to bankroll it and strengthen the position of those who would make concessions to colonialism. The US and EC governments have been pouring weapons into Turkey which will be used to try and destroy the Kurdish struggle. Socialists in Europe must fight against the attempt to isolate the liberation movement and push it onto the path of concessions and subordination to colonialism and imperialism. This means supporting mobilisations such as those of Kurdish communities in 28 cities across Europe on 24 June where they demanded an end to European governments' support for the Turkish state's war effort. That way the attempt to isolate the PKK is fought and the powerful socialist and working class trends within it are strengthened.

PART FOUR

The United Nations and the New Colonialism

4.1 THE UNITED NATIONS: NEW COLONIAL HEADQUARTERS
EDDIE ABRAHAMS/MAXINE WILLIAMS
FRFI 111 · FEBRUARY/MARCH 1993

'The time of absolute and exclusive sovereignty has passed'.
(Boutros Boutros-Ghali, Secretary General of the United Nations)

There is much talk today of a new international order, led by the United Nations, in which the problems of individual nations can be dealt with by international intervention. It would be heart-warming if this was a precursor to seriously tackling problems which are indeed beyond the scope of single states and which are the scourge of humanity – economic crisis, war, poverty, famine and environmental destruction. However, this is not the case. Rhetoric by US and British politicians about 'humanitarian' concerns have resulted in the expenditure of resources not to feed the starving, but to bomb them. And this is being done in the name of the United Nations.

Whilst it is only to be expected that the US and Britain would use the United Nations to mask their Great Power ambitions, it is shocking to see the haste with which sections of the left/liberal 'intelligentsia' have swallowed this. Whilst 250,000 Iraqis lie buried in the sand courtesy of the UN, these intellectuals peddle the illusion that the UN can play a positive international role. One expects the USA to bomb the oppressed; one does not wish to be told by leftists that this ushers in a new dawn of international brotherhood. Thus Martin Shaw tells us in the *New Statesman*:

> 'opposition to western military interventions in the third world . . . is now downright wrong.
>
> 'To uphold national sovereignty and damn intervention is to give a free hand to genocide. The UN and the great western powers are doubtless imperfect tools . . . but only they, in most cases, can stand between the people and those who would destroy them.'
>
> (*New Statesman and Society* 15 January 1993)

Only by exercising great self-control has Shaw avoided calling on the West to shoulder the 'white man's burden'. No doubt he is dusting off his sola topee and khaki shorts at this very moment.

United against the poor

Until the 1989–90 collapse of the socialist bloc, the USSR as a permanent member of the UN Security Council was to some extent able to prevent the UN becoming a rubber-stamp for US imperial policy. This is no longer the case. The US now dominates every aspect of UN policy. What it wants it gets. Hence in 1990 when the US set out to destroy Iraq and prevent the latter challenging US domination of the Gulf, it sought the fig-leaf of UN sanction. Those who have illusions about the UN's neutral and democratic character should recall the methods by which the Gulf War became a UN operation. The US bribed and bullied its way to majority votes:

> 'In crucial votes during the Gulf War, the US repeatedly drummed up support by using its political and economic muscle. At the time of the crisis, India . . . needed billions of dollars from the IMF. Drought-stricken Zimbabwe also needed help from the IMF. Both were acutely conscious that the US enjoyed an effective veto in the IMF . . . As a result both . . . made speeches against UN resolutions and then voted for them.'

'Yemen did vote against the US . . . and its ambassador was told by American diplomat John Kelly . . . that its action "was the most expensive No Vote you ever made." Yemen promptly lost $70m in aid.'

(*The Guardian* 14 January 1993)

So confident has the USA become of UN endorsement that its latest bombings of Iraq in January 1993 did not even have the legal cover of a UN resolution. The US, Britain and France imposed the colonial-style exclusion zones in Iraqi- controlled territory without reference to the Security Council let alone the General Assembly. Emboldened by its success in the Gulf, the US sought and gained UN Security Council approval for invading Somalia – another longstanding strategic ambition. Just as in the Gulf War, its true aims were disguised by phrases about 'humanitarianism'. But the first striking image of the operation in Somalia was of a large white US soldier holding down a handcuffed Somali. That image writ large is the reality behind all the talk of a UN-led new international democratic order. It is a boot in the face of the poor.

Yesterday was bad enough . . .

The UN has never been a neutral, benevolent or democratic international institution. It was formed in June 1945 – along with the International Monetary Fund (1945), the World Bank (1946) and the GATT (1948) – to prevent socialism, restrain the USSR and control emerging independent Third World nations. Even then the US exercised a dominating influence. This reflected its dominant world economic and military position. Among the UN's first operations was a major attack on socialist Korea in 1950 when US President Truman ordered US troops into action against the Korean People's Army. This was approved by the UN and later, US and international forces, operating under 'UN command', waged a war in which four million Koreans were slaughtered.

The United Nations is effectively run by its Security Council whose five permanent members (USA, Britain, France, China and Russia) reflect the balance of world power. In contrast, General Assembly resolutions expressing the standpoint of the majority of UN member states are not legally binding. For example for the past 25 years the UN has, in Resolution 242, demanded Israeli withdrawal from the West Bank and Gaza Strip. Israel and the USA have blithely ignored this, suffering no consequences whatsoever. Under the Reagan and Bush Administration the US used its veto over 25 times to protect Israel, usually with British support.

Tomorrow looks even worse . . .

In the grip of a profound crisis, the main imperialist powers are seeking to overcome this at the expense of the Third World and each other. Each is developing its spheres of influence: the USA in Latin America, Mexico, Canada and the Middle East; Japan in South East Asia; Germany in Eastern Europe and Russia. A new age of colonial conquest and rivalry is being born. Economically challenged by Japan and Germany, the USA today retains its position as sole superpower (with Britain parrot-like on its shoulder) by virtue of its military strength and semi-colonial control of large parts of the world. But both Japan and Germany have military and colonial ambitions of their own. Hence the constitutional changes allowing them to re-arm and engage in overseas military operations. Much to the alarm of Britain and France, they also have eyes on Security Council seats at the former's expense.

Mindful of these potential rivals and seizing the opportunities of its victory in the Cold War, the US is now restructuring the UN to better control it. As John Pilger so rightly puts it:

> 'Boutros Boutros-Ghali was installed by Washington with enthusiastic support from the Foreign Office. He has since set about turning the UN into America's principal colonial office.'
>
> (*New Statesman and Society* 18 September 1992)

The UN charter does not allow the UN to intervene 'in matters which are effectively in the domestic jurisdiction of any state' and prohibits armed intervention other than in self-defence. Whilst noted more in the breach than in the observance, this provides at least a point of appeal for countries under attack. Pilger shows that the US, through Boutros-

Ghali, is using a new concept – 'preventative diplomacy' – to bypass this inconvenience. Preventative diplomacy allows military intervention where 'threats to peace', not necessarily military threats, exist. Anything the US wishes to do can be justified under such terms and no doubt will be. Iraq and Somalia are just the beginning.

The return of Victorian missionaries

Far from a new age of rational international arbitration, we are entering a colonial era where any poor country which defies imperial wishes can be attacked and subdued. Yet the Martin Shaws of this world insist that:

'The West has an historic responsibility to undertake this global leadership . . .

. . . only the West has the economic, political and military resources and the democratic and multi-national institutions to undertake it.'

(Ibid)

This is the racist superiority of the Victorian missionary. The USA, which cannot adequately feed, clothe, house and educate its own population, particularly its black population, has nothing to tell the world about progress. Nor has a Britain which holds down Ireland by brute force. But just as the Victorians had their missionaries to accompany armed intervention with soothing words, so today's colonialists have Martin Shaws to sing lullabies to the intelligentsia.

The imperialists have huge economic, military and political resources. An unequal battle is being waged in which socialists in the imperialist countries must oppose imperialist intervention, fight for the right of nations to self-determination and expose the UN's legalistic cover for a new age of conquest.

4.2 COLONIALISM: BACK WITH A VENGEANCE
EDDIE ABRAHAMS/MAXINE WILLIAMS
FRFI 114 · AUGUST/SEPTEMBER 1993

No phrase has been devalued more quickly than that of 'humanitarian assistance', the banner under which the UN undertook intervention in Somalia. The 70 Somali civilians ripped apart in the UN (ie US) helicopter gunship attack on General Aideed's compound on 12 July are mute witnesses to humanitarianism, New World Order style. This brutal event came only two weeks after US President Clinton unleashed a deadly barrage of Cruise missiles into the centre of Baghdad, killing dozens of civilians, amongst them one of Iraq's leading artists. The less than wafer-thin pretext for this butchery was that an alleged plot to assassinate former President Bush (now that really would have been an act of humanitarianism) had been masterminded by Iraqi intelligence.

A new confidence and belligerence in the tone and actions of the Great Powers is crudely apparent. 'Colonialism is back and not a moment too soon' wrote Paul Johnson in the influential *New York Times*, adding that: 'The civilised world has a mission to go out to these desperate places and govern'. Johnson, a notorious right-winger, was not only articulating the sentiments of US and imperialist triumphalism, but also the views of a section of the left intelligentsia. Writing in the *New Statesman* in January, Martin Shaw said: 'Opposition to Western military intervention in the Third World . . . is now downright wrong.' Not surprisingly he has preserved a discreet silence in the face of recent events in Somalia.

'UN Peacekillers'

Since the UN entered Somalia on 9 December 1992, the Somali people have learned to hate what is essentially a military occupation by the USA. 26,000 UN troops now wage war on the Somali people. The aid agencies, whose blocked relief efforts provided the excuse for the intervention, now complain that their work has been made impossible and is entirely secondary to 'military objectives'. Prime amongst these objectives is the capture of General Aideed on whose head the UN has placed a $25,000 reward 'Dead or Alive'. On 12 June Aideed's headquarters were bombed and when the populace poured into the streets to protest, 20 men, women and children were gunned down as UN troops fired on the unarmed demonstrators. This was the first step in a plan which included house-to-house searches, mass arrests and other ground operations such as the 17 June armed attack on Digfer hospital. By 14 July at least 150 Somali civilians had been killed.

Although sheltering under the UN 'peacekeeping' umbrella, this is effectively a US operation to secure strategic control over Somalia. As another right-wing commentator, Conor Cruise O'Brien, said: 'The subordination of the UN to US domestic policies is not a remote danger. In some areas it is already an established fact.' The UN forces are led by a retired US Admiral, Jonathon Howe. UN officials are rarely even briefed before US troops undertake operations like the bombing of Mogadishu. The pretence that this is a UN operation disappears altogether at the daily press briefings at which the only telephone hotline is one to the Pentagon. The 'peacekeepers' have claimed that women and children are being used as shields by Somali guerrillas (haven't we heard this wherever US imperialism has waged war?) thus explaining why they are murdering women and children.

The likes of Martin Shaw may harbour illusions about the UN and western powers' 'global leadership' for democratic purposes, but the Somali people know otherwise. Their frequent demonstrations echo to the slogans: 'Down with US Imperialism', 'UN Peacekillers' and 'New White Warlords'. They not only understand the character of the intervention but its purpose.

Colonial conquest

Most press commentators, unable to understand US motives in Somalia, have resorted to either 'humanitarianism' or the need for Clinton to boost his image as a 'strong leader'. Why can they not see the explanation which stares them in the face? The US is intent on extending its influence throughout Africa at the expense of the other major imperialist powers. In Somalia it intends to impose a puppet regime or a UN protectorate. Somalia, with a commanding position over sea routes through the Gulf, east and southern Africa and the Indian Ocean, has long been prized by the US which now also has its eyes set on further incursions into the Horn of Africa. US Secretary of State Warren Christopher has stated that 'Now we need to try to apply these lessons of preventive diplomacy to Sudan.' Sudan's profit to imperialism is evident. It controls the headwaters of the Nile and has immense oilfields coveted by Chevron and other US oil companies.

No local opposition will be allowed to stand in the way of these ambitions. The US is today targeting General Aideed because he has not proved to be entirely pliant, just as with Saddam Hussein. Aideed is the most powerful of Somalia's ruling class factions and has resisted total subordination to US designs. He has succeeded in manipulating popular hostility to imperialism to bolster his previously flagging power. The US is therefore intent on destroying him.

Dividing the spoils

Whilst the US is the world's dominant power, other imperialist nations will not sit back and accept its monopoly of colonial acquisition. Italy, the previous colonial power in Somalia, has registered its opposition to US domination of the intervention there and threatened to pull its troops out. Germany, having changed its constitution to allow military operations abroad and seeking a seat on the UN Security Council, is strengthening its contingent in Somalia. The German population is having to be rapidly re-educated to support what the Foreign Minister called 'healthy patriotism' which will mean 'using power, not opting out.' Thus the German state, apparently unable to muster enough policemen to guard immigrant hostels under fascist assault, readily finds the resources for war against black people abroad.

Imperialism cannot be civilised or made humanitarian. A new age of militarism, racist conquest and war is underway. If we do not stand against it now humanity will pay a terrible price. If we do not destroy imperialism, it will destroy us.

4.3 SOMALIA/IRAQ: NEW COLONIALISM IN ACTION
EDDIE ABRAHAMS
FRFI 111 · FEBRUARY/MARCH 1993

The 17 December 1992 US/UN invasion of Somalia and the bombing of Iraq by US, British and French aircraft between 13-18 January 1993 are harbingers of the new post-Cold War colonialism. Until the 1979 Iranian revolution the US dominated the Middle East through its alliances with the ruling classes of Iran under the Shah, Saudi Arabia and Israel. In 1979 Iran's place in the triangle was taken by Egypt. Today this structure of control is increasingly shaky. Imperialism has destroyed the social and economic fabric of the Arab world, driving millions into poverty and destitution. The reigning factions of the local ruling class, degenerated by decades of corruption and parasitism, are totally discredited. As a reaction to this the tide of Muslim fundamentalism sweeping from Iran has reached Sudan, Tunisia, Algeria and is now threatening a beleaguered Egypt.

Zionism does remain a formidable ally in the region. But it is not sufficient to secure US control. Furthermore, Israel is challenged by the Palestinian Intifada which shows no sign of demise. Having destroyed Iraq, once the most powerful Arab military force in the region, the US establishment feels able therefore to experiment with new tactics and strategies of domination. Edward Perkins, US ambassador to the UN, stated that the US invasion of Somalia was:

'. . . an important step in developing a strategy for dealing with the potential disorders and conflicts of the post-Cold War world.'

He added that the world 'is likely to hold other Somalias in store for us.'

The Somali experiment

24,000 US troops, supported by 10,000 more from 21 other countries, are now in effective control of Somalia. They intend to test the possibility of reconstructing Somalia as a protectorate under US/UN tutelage. An official from the previous Bush administration argued that:

'Somalia has no government. It needs some kind of structure . . . You may need a UN protectorate, which the UN would manage and then try and turn back into a state.'

In its current exercise, the US has lessons from the recent past. In 1977 it began financing and arming the now defunct Siad Barre regime as an outpost against the Ethiopian revolution. Over the next decade it supplied the Somali ruling class with over $900m. In return the US took possession of a Soviet-built air and naval base at Berbera which became the staging post for the Rapid Deployment Force capable of striking Khomeini's Iran. An indication of the US's long term designs for Somalia was its embassy, one of its largest and most opulent built at a cost of over $35m.

Today, with the crisis in the Arab world, the US calculates that rebuilding Somalia is economically and politically relatively inexpensive. The US calculates that in a country exhausted and impoverished by war and famine it does not require a vast sum to buy the loyalty of the ruling class and the gratitude of a portion of the population. By 4–5 January, Generals Aideed and Ali Mahdi, who united to overthrow Siad Barre in January 1991, but then waged war for the spoils, were forced to the conference table along with a dozen other factional groupings. These ruling class factions, responsible for much of the war and devastation, are now being groomed by the US. They have since signed a ceasefire agreement and are preparing to set up a joint police force in Mogadishu.

If a dependent and subservient state is formed the US could command a potential bulwark against instability and fundamentalism. From Somali sea and air bases it can project its power across the region right up to Iran, a current target for imperialist aggression. The country's strategic position would enable the US to extend its influence throughout Central and East Africa. This would be a great advantage in the US's contest with other imperialist powers for influence there. The region offers, according to Californian investment banker Daniel Montana:

'immediate prospects for profitable investments. Everything is in place – a legal system, basic transportation and communcations

... this infrastructure will not be ready in most of Eastern Europe and the ex-Soviet Union for 5-10 years.'

The value of US influence in Africa was reflected by former US Assistant Secretary of State for Africa who claimed:

'Even though it is very far away and relatively unknown, news is spreading that you can do business in Africa.'

This is the objective reality behind the hypocritical garbage about helping to save starving Somalis. Tens of thousands of Somalis have been dying since January 1991. But only in September 1992 did the US begin to send in food. To legitimise the invasion as a humanitarian operation, the US and its allies systematically exaggerated the scale of famine and the extent of banditry and anarchy. Famine did destroy up to 200,000 lives. But it did not reach the 500,000 bandied about in the press and was to a great extent concentrated in the south. Most food was not looted. Save the Children Fund for example distributed 4,000 tons of grain without loosing a single bag. Most aid agencies suffered losses of only 2-10 per cent because they collaborated with clan elders in distributing food. The UN suffered most because it refused to do so.

By the time US troops arrived the worst of the famine was over. The most vulnerable of the drought victims – children and the old – were already dead. According to Rakiya Omar, who was sacked as director of Africa Watch for opposing the US invasion, 'the famine is waning' and 'markets in all the main towns are awash with cheap food'.

Famine there still is. But its roots lie not in Somali banditry and anarchy but in colonial domination of the country's economy. With a population of 5-6 million Somalia has water and range land able to service 4 million cattle and 5.5 million camels. It is potentially self-sufficient in livestock and grains. But British and Italian colonial domination – which only ended in 1961 – forced the local population to abandon subsistence agriculture and animal husbandry for cash crops such as bananas and sugar. Cheap 'food aid' also helped destroy local grain production. The result has been deforestation, overgrazing, soil erosion and desertification, abject poverty, famine and death. Somalia has a GNP of $210 per capita, female literacy is 16 per cent and infant mortality 116 per 1,000 live births.

The continued destruction of Iraq

Parallel with the experiment of recolonisation in Somalia, the Great Powers, with unbridled ruthlessness and cynicism, are continuing the work of destroying Iraq. The 13-18 January air and Cruise missile attacks on Iraq were extensions of the January 1991 Gulf War. More precisely they were conducted to enforce the essentially colonial arrangements imperialism has imposed since the Gulf War.

By means of bombs and destruction, the Great Powers demand that the Iraqi government accept the UN's transfer of parts of Iraq's oil-rich border territory to Kuwait and that it also accept a limitation of Iraqi jurisdiction in the imperialist-imposed 'exclusion zones'. The raids were precipitated by Iraq's challenge to these colonial dictates: it had moved Iraqi troops into the UN's southern 'exclusion zone' to take control of Iraqi arms depots, and had attempted to control the movement of UN arms monitors.

These attacks have nothing to do with 'international law', 'humanitarianism' or 'ending Saddam's torture of his own people'. Former US Attorney-General Ramsey Clark, condemning the current bombings as a 'criminal act', went on to say that:

'there are 4,000-5,000 Iraqi children dying each month as a result of the destruction of water and sanitation facilities from the last US bombings.'

Such is the barbarism so evident behind all the democratic rhetoric we hear. Yet in the name of 'humanitarianism' and a 'new internationalism' the Labour Party and a host of one-time anti-imperialists have vociferously endorsed the invasion of Somalia and the destruction of Iraq.

A new invasion is prepared

Beyond the invasion of Somalia and the destruction of Iraq, imperialism is preparing to attack Iran. Robert Fisk, writing in *The Independent*, notes that 'Washington has sounded the alarm that Iran is once more a threat to the Gulf.' Martin Indyk, a Special Assistant to the US President on Middle East Affairs, warned:

> 'Iranian intentions and capabilities [are] a dangerous combination for Western interests . . . If we fail to modify [sic] Iranian behaviour, five years from now Iran will be much more capable of posing a real threat to Israel, to the Arab world and to Western interests in the Middle East.'

Iran is being charged with developing nuclear weapons and building up its fighting forces well beyond 'defensive needs'. It stands accused of orchestrating fundamentalists in Egypt who have conducted armed attacks on tourists. It is accused of subsidising fundamentalists throughout the Arab world and of encouraging Hamas to kill Israelis in return for massive cash donations.

As a preliminary to 'modifying Iranian behaviour' the US is supplying vast quantities of arms to client states. During 1991 and 1992 $28bn worth were sold in the Middle East. In 1992 Saudi Arabia planned to purchase a staggering $17bn worth of arms, while Kuwait is purchasing 236 tanks at $1bn. Meanwhile annual military funding of Israel continues to the tune of $3-4bn. In October 1992, the US Congress passed an act tightening trade restrictions against Iran and in November it called on the G7 to refuse Iranian orders for dual-use technology. Meanwhile countries like Russia, Korea and Argentina are being urged to halt arms sales to Iran.

But in its assault on Iran, the US is confronting Great Power opposition. For their common benefit they permitted the US to tame Iraq and experiment in Somalia. But Germany and Japan in particular do not want to see oil-rich Iran totally subordinated to the US. They are not willing to give the US total control of the Middle East oil upon which they too are dependent. Furthermore, compared to the US they have greater commercial interests in Iran. In 1992 Japan exported $2.5bn to Iran and Germany $5bn. Explaining why Japan refuses to impose a technology embargo on Iran, Japan's Foreign Minister said:

> 'Our ties with Iran go a long way back and are different from US–Iran relations.'

Herein lie the seeds of new inter–imperialist wars. As the Great Powers prepare once more to carve up the world, they will, like a pack of hyenas, viciously fight for their own choice portions. Wars against the Third World will be followed by wars between the hyenas. Millions will be slaughtered on the altar of capitalist industry, trade and profit. This is what the new colonialism holds out for the international working class movement. Truly there is one choice: between socialism or barbarism. For all those who stand for progress, for civilisation, for human dignity and justice it is time to stand up and say: no more!

APPENDIX ONE

IMPERIALISM, OIL AND WEAPONS
TREVOR RAYNE
FRFI 101 · JUNE/JULY 1991

In the 45 years since the end of the Second World War there has been just one single year when official statistics do not record British military personnel killed on active service overseas. British forces have engaged in at least 92 separate overseas military interventions since 1945.

Throughout the 1970s and 1980s only the USA among the major capitalist nations spent more as a proportion of its Gross National Product (GNP) on defence than Britain. The Ministry of Defence is British industry's biggest customer: approximately one in ten of the manufacturing workforce are employed in the weapons industry. Of the top 20 British industrial companies, 11 are involved in arms production or supplies. While during the 1980s Britain became a net importer of manufactured goods, it remained a net exporter of weapons. In 1990 Britain's biggest arms company, British Aerospace, made 65 per cent of its sales abroad; over 50 per cent of these exports went to Third World countries with 41 per cent destined for the Middle East. 38 British firms are known to have sold arms technology to Iraq.

How many of the 20 million-plus people slain in wars and 'counterinsurgency operations' since 1945 were killed by British troops and British-made weapons we shall never know. But we can see in the entire structure of the British economy, in the arming of murderous regimes around the globe and in the near-constant war fought by British forces against oppressed peoples, that Britain is an imperial nation dominated by monopoly capital for which the 'maximum and universal development of militarism' (Lenin) is its life-blood.

In the service of multinational capital

'In 1914 I helped to make Mexico a safer place for the US oil companies. I helped to turn Haiti and Cuba into a patrimony of the

National City Bank in order to make a profit. In 1900 and 1912 I helped to prepare the ground in Nicaragua for the international bankers Brow Brothers. In 1916 I made way in the Dominican Republic for US interests. In 1903 I did all I could to make the US fruit companies at home in Honduras.'

(US General Smedley Butter, 1925).

In *Capital* Volume III, Marx explained how 'other conditions being equal the rate of profit . . . falls and rises inversely to the price of raw materials. This shows, among other things, how important the low price of raw materials is for industrial countries . . . It follows furthermore that foreign trade influences the rate of profit, regardless of its influence on wages . . . '.

Lenin analysed the emergence of monopoly capital, especially the oil companies and arms producers, over the last quarter of the 19th century and first decades of this century. He saw how capital over-accumulated within national boundaries driving down the rate of profit; how capital combined into monopolies and extended overseas in search of labour and markets to restore profitability. In the midst of the First World War, as capitals clashed in rival bids to assert their global domination, Lenin observed, 'Monopolies have stimulated the seizure of the most important sources of raw materials . . . the more capitalism is developed the more strongly the shortage of raw materials is felt, the more intense the competition and hunt for sources of raw materials throughout the whole world, the more desperate the struggle for the acquisition of colonies'. Thus the division and redivision of the world has been fought out between a handful of rich nations. The cost: over 100 million killed in wars this century, many times more killed by the robbery of their land and homes.

Today, transnational corporations control about half of the world's industrial production and over half its trade. 15 transnationals control the marketing of 20 key foods, fuel and raw material commodities; six account for more than half the world's oil trade. The bowl of cereal and cup of tea, the materials in our clothing and vehicles, the fuel in their tanks and in central heating, the equipment we work with and the furnishings about us are taken from the Third World by the transnationals.

Third World nations producing raw materials receive on average 15 per cent of the revenue raised from sales of their produce: the rest is shared out among the transnationals, their bankers, insurers, shipping agents, retailers, etc. Oil extraction costs can be less than a seventh of the retail price. When petrol prices were pushed up more than 50 per cent last autumn (1990) the extra profits were divided up between the transnationals and the producer countries. This is a price imperialism is prepared to pay to ensure that compliant monarchs and governments stay in their place. Should they be threatened by popular revolt, or should they rebel or 'overstep the mark', armed might is at hand to enforce the status quo. Britain alone has intervened militarily in the Middle East on 26 separate occasions since 1945.

General Schwarzkopf has served US corporate interests in a career of postings throughout the Middle East, South East Asia and Grenada. British forces are currently stationed in over 30 countries. In the past year they have added Colombia, Peru and the Philippines to their postings. They remain in the Gulf. The Middle East and the Gulf contain 66.3 per cent of all known oil reserves.

Guns for oil

'Whoever controls oil will control the world, for he will rule the seas with heavy oil, the air with refined oil, and the land with petrol and light oil. In addition, he will economically control his fellow-men because of the fantastic wealth he can win from oil ... Who has oil has empire.'

(Henry Berenger, merchant to the French government circa 1918)

Oil and guns have interlocked for over 100 years. John D. Rockefeller, one of the pioneers of the US oil industry, began his career supplying goods to the northern army during the Civil War. The profits made went towards the foundation of the Standard Oil Company in 1870. In 1873 the Russian Tsar allowed foreign interests to prospect for oil in the Caucasus. Two sons of Alfred Nobel, inventor of dynamite, were given concessions and joined by Rothschilds. Marcus Samuel, from London's

East End, traded Russian oil and in 1897 formed Shell Trading and Transport Company. To compete in the Far East with US Standard Oil, Shell merged with Royal Dutch. In 1906, Shell lobbied the Royal Navy to switch from coal power to oil. Winston Churchill, appointed First Lord of the Admiralty in 1911, distrusted Shell and its Dutch, hence possibly German, affiliation. With the Royal Navy's conversion to oil, the British government bought a 51 per cent stake in the Anglo-Persian Company (later BP) three months before the outbreak of World War One. At its end Foreign Secretary Lord Curzon boasted: 'The allies floated to victory on a wave of oil'.

Following the collapse of the Ottoman Empire, Britain and France carved out chunks of the Middle East for themselves. After much wrangling between Britain, France and the USA, Britain got control of all of Iraq in 1923 – at the expense of the Kurdish demand for statehood. Central to the disputes was Mosul in the Kurdish territory where oil reserves were suspected. A concession was granted to the Iraq Petroleum Company, controlled by the Anglo-Persian Company (BP). The Kurdish people rebelled and Churchill, now Secretary of State for Oil and War, initiated a strategy of '*air control*' in the Middle East, replacing ground troops with bomber aircraft which delivered 'collective punishments', including gas, on Kurdish villages.

During the 1920s and 1930s the RAF grew, at first in response to French aircraft development and then to combat German militarisation. In 1940 Britain was the largest aircraft producer in the world. The navy, airforce and increasingly the army, with the growing role of tanks, depended on oil-based fuels. Control of oil reserves dictated much of the strategy through which inter-imperialist rivalry was conducted before and during World War Two (the North Africa campaign, Nazi attack on the Soviet Union, the Far East war). The Vice Chairman of the US War Production Board claimed that 'the responsibility which rests upon the petroleum industry . . . is nothing less than the responsibility for victory'.

The transnationals and the weapons producers collaborate with military high command to direct imperialism's geo-political strategy. To produce today's jet engines, submarines, aerospace technology etc, large quantities of fuel and raw materials are needed. Over half of all direct US investment in developing countries in the past 20 years has been in oil extraction, mining and material processing. In the 1970s the US Lockheed Corporation, producers of Polaris and Trident missiles, joined Shell and Standard Oil of Indiana in developing equipment to extract strategic raw materials from the ocean bed. The arms and oil companies are interwoven in the heart of finance capital: Shell is bound through interlocking share ownership, directorships and banks with Lockheed, Rolls Royce and Hawker-Siddeley.

In the recent period BP's directors include a former Commander-in-Chief of UK Land Forces, the chairman of the Armed Forces Pay Review Body, a trustee of the Police Foundation, directors of Rolls Royce, Hawker-Siddeley, ICL, PowerGen, National Westminster Bank, Standard Chartered, P & O etc. They are part of the military-industrial complex in Britain. Together BP and Shell operate some 2,250 subsidiaries in over 70 countries.

The Saudi deal and the arms bonanza

In 1965 Britain was facing a balance of payments crisis and with the steady withdrawal of British forces from east of Suez, the sale of arms to 'reliable' local regimes was considered a lucrative means of controlling Middle Eastern oil. Increased world oil consumption was filling Arab coffers.

Between 1951 and 1971 40 aerospace projects were cancelled in Britain, including the Blue Streak missiles and the TSR2 supersonic bomber. British Aerospace exports fell by 50 per cent over 1958-64 while imports from the USA soared. The Plowden Report 1965 foresaw a world market for aircraft and missiles worth £15bn over the next decade. Labour Defence Secretary Denis Healey established the Defence Sales Organisation to promote arms sales. Healey explained: 'While the government attaches the highest importance to making progress in the field of arms control and disarmament, we must also take what practical steps we can to ensure that this country does not fail to secure its rightful share of this valuable commercial market'.

Britain and Saudi Arabia had collaborated since 1962 in suppressing a Nasserite revolt against monarchism in North Yemen. In 1965 the British Labour government in the form of John Stonehouse MP, Parliamentary Secretary to Ministry of Aviation Roy Jenkins, announced the biggest export deal Britain had ever achieved – £120m worth of weapons to Saudi Arabia. Victory over bids from Lockheed, Northrop and the French Dassault company had been achieved with bribes – standard practice in the arms business. The deal was tied to the proposed British purchase of $725m worth of F-111s from the USA – the £120m was intended to offset this enormous cost. Despite professed Labour Party policy of not selling arms that could be used in Vietnam, the Saudi deal also included equipment sales to the USA. Between 1964 and 1967, British exports of bombs, grenades, mines, guided weapons etc to the USA increased six-fold. Also in 1965, when US engagement in Vietnam was accelerating, Healey sent the SAS into Indonesia to assist in the mass murder of the largest communist movement in Asia outside of China and the Soviet Union. At least 700,000 people were killed and 200,000 imprisoned. Indonesia is a major oil producer.

Arms purchases by Middle East governments mushroomed after the Yom Kippur War in 1973. An October 1973 Arab Conference condemned the USA for giving Israel means 'to challenge the legitimate right of others' – ie weapons. Arab oil producers cut back supplies and oil prices rose ten-fold; their income rose from $7.2bn in 1972 to $57bn in 1977. By 1980 OPEC funds had reached $350bn. In that same year Third World countries spent $60bn on arms and defence, about half the weapons being bought by Middle Eastern countries. Between 1973 and 1987, of the major Third World arms purchasers, six of them were in the Middle East. Britain spends approximately five per cent of its GNP on the military each year, the USA seven per cent and the Soviet Union over eight per cent. UN figures for 1986 show Israel spending 19.2 per cent of its GNP on the armed forces, Iraq 32 per cent, Jordan 13.8 per cent, Iran 20 per cent, Syria 14.7 per cent, Oman 27.6 per cent, Saudi Arabia 22.7 per cent.

In 1984 Iraq spent $33.3bn on arms imports. Estimates put Iraqi arms purchases between 1980 and 1990 at $80-100bn. That compares with

Britain's arms expenditure of $69.5bn over the same period with a GNP eight times that of Iraq. In the 1970s the Shah of Iran had been the big arms buyer. In some years Iran consumed close to half of all US arms exports. Iran's total defence expenditure for 1975–76 was $10.4bn or nearly a third of its GNP. This was a sum greater than Britain's military expenditure for the year, which had more than five times Iran's GNP. Over 1973–83 US arms sales to Saudi Arabia were worth $35bn, to Iran $14bn and to Israel $11bn – the latter receiving many of the supplies gratis.

In 1991 the US intends to export $33bn worth of weapons, two-thirds going to the Middle East. Asia and the Pacific Rim are targeted as promising new future markets. Indonesia is already one of Britain's biggest arms buyers outside of the Middle East.

This macabre game results in death for hundreds of thousands of poor people. Arms provided to Israel bring orders from Iran; Iran's armoury warrants sales to Iraq; Iraq's military strength requires Saudi counter-strength and so on and on. The blend of weapons is adjusted as rival suppliers claim assorted victories and each new generation of weapons calls forth further rounds of orders and counter-orders. Thus the trade in death and destruction is by far the most valuable trade in the world, and its proprietors, the Grand Masters of War, unconstrained by any shred of morality or conscience, seated behind desks in New York, Washington, London, Paris and Bonn, serve only the Golden Calf of Profit.

APPENDIX TWO

THE SUEZ CRISIS 1956: A BLOW AGAINST BRITISH IMPERIALISM
EDDIE ABRAHAMS/TREVOR RAYNE
FRFI 64 · NOVEMBER/DECEMBER 1986

In October and November 1956 British, French and Israeli armed forces invaded Egypt hoping to overthrow the nationalist government of Gamal Abdul Nasser. The British government, headed by Conservative Prime Minister Anthony Eden, was particularly determined to regain control of the lucrative Suez Canal, nationalised by Nasser in July of the same year. Orchestrated by Eden, the invasion ended in humiliating failure. It marked a watershed in British imperialism's fortunes. Although over 1,000 Egyptians had been murdered British imperialism lost its dominant position in the Middle East. It was replaced by the USA which had for more than a decade been contesting British influence there.

Nasser challenges imperialism

At the end of World War Two, Britain and France had resumed their monopoly of influence in the Middle East. With Indian Independence in 1947 the post-war Labour government devised a scheme to transform the region into a bastion for British imperialism. Labour Foreign Minister Bevin put it thus: 'My whole aim has been to develop the Middle East as a producing area (in agriculture as well as oil) to help our own economy and take the place of India'.

In this scheme, control of the Middle East oil supply was of critical concern to British imperialism. The area held 75 per cent of known oil stocks outside the socialist countries and supplied 77 per cent of Europe's oil needs. British companies such as Shell and British Petroleum were amassing enormous fortunes in an industry oiling the wheels of capitalism and imperialism.

To secure and guarantee this oil, both from Arab nationalist movements and US imperialism which was aggressively challenging British dominance, the British government signed a number of treaties with dependent and pro-imperialist governments in the region. The Baghdad Pact, the Transjordan Treaty and the Portsmouth Treaty all secured legitimacy for full scale British invasions in the event of war and instability.

Egypt, and the Suez Canal in particular, was of major strategic importance. The Suez Canal, 'co-owned' by the British, brought in at least £20m profit annually. Two-thirds of all ships passing through it carried oil and one quarter of all British imports travelled through the Canal. At the beginning of the 1950s Britain still had 80,000 troops in Egypt and more than 60,000 British troops passed through the Canal annually.

The Egyptian people were not, however, prepared to tolerate British dominance and plunder for ever. Since the end of World War Two the nationalist movement had consistently grown stronger. In 1952, the pliant and pro-British King Faroukh was overthrown in a popular coup organised by Gamal Abdul Nasser and his Free Officers Society.

Nasser immediately set about challenging British power in the country. He demanded the removal of British troops and Egyptian control of the Canal. By 1954 most British troops were withdrawn to the Canal zone. In addition, Nasser refused to sign the Baghdad Pact. Instead, along with President Tito of Yugoslavia and others, he became a founding member of the Non-Aligned Movement in 1955 and opened diplomatic relations with China in 1956. Egyptian radio regularly broadcast its support for the Algerian National Liberation Front and for the Mau Mau freedom fighters conducting armed struggle against British imperialism in Kenya. In 1955 Nasser turned to Czechoslovakia for arms after the US and the British refused to supply them.

Nasser's government also embarked on an ambitious economic development programme with its plan to build the Aswan Dam on the Nile river. It would expand cultivable land by 30 per cent and double Egypt's hydro-electricty supply. In February 1956 the World Bank agreed to loan $200m for the project on condition that Britain and the US supplied $70m. But in July the US withdrew its funding. Nasser responded on 26 July by nationalising the Canal and declaring that its income would be used to finance the building of the dam. He declared that the Canal had been 'a source of exploitation and extortion . . . The Suez Canal was one of the facades of oppression, extortion and humiliation.'

British imperialism responds with war

Britain immediately made war preparations. Eden declared that, 'The Egyptian has his thumb on our wind-pipe' and called a secret meeting with French Prime Minister Guy Mollet and the Israeli government. They arrived at the secret Treaty of Sevres which planned for the Israelis to attack first. The British and French were then to move in under the pretence of keeping the two sides apart. They were to destroy the Egyptian air force, land troops in Egypt and take control of the Canal. They would then move on to remove Nasser.

The Labour opposition joined in the anti-Nasser campaign, whipping up a tide of racist chauvinism. Labour leader Gaitskell 'deplored this high handed and totally unjustifiable step by the Egyptian government' and stated: 'it's all very familiar. It's exactly the same as we encountered from Mussolini and Hitler in those years before the war.'

The TUC-controlled *Labour Herald* ran banner headlines screaming 'No More Hitlers'. The Labour Party, however, unlike Eden's Conservatives, were conscious of the frailty of Britain's imperialist pretensions. Their experience in Palestine had taught them that without US backing, British imperialism was no longer capable of playing an independent world role. They therefore opposed any military action against Nasser unless it was sanctioned by the US- dominated United Nations.

There was opposition also from within the ruling class that was reflected inside the Tory Party. Many heads of Shell and BP were appalled by the invasion. First the Canal was blocked so tankers had to be hired to take oil round the Cape, then Syrian soldiers severed the pipeline from Iraq to the Mediterranean, then serious anti-British demonstrations flared up across the Arab capitals and in Tehran. Suez jeopardised their position in the Middle East to the benefit of their US rivals.

Eden was, however, determined on war to teach Nasser a lesson and exercise British imperialist might. On 29 October, the Israeli military struck. On 1 November British and French planes bombed and immobilised the Egyptian airforce. Four days later their troops landed in Port Said to prepare for a final offensive.

Neither the British, the French nor the Israelis had reckoned on the resistance they experienced from the Egyptian and Arab masses. Imperialist ships in the Canal were sunk, blocking it off to any commercial or military use. Neither had the British reckoned with US opposition.

US imperialism sabotages British war effort

US imperialism, while prepared to work for Nasser's downfall, was opposed to any military action against him. The US did not want to risk destabilising the area and risking its oil supplies. On 1 November it therefore mobilised the United Nations to vote for its call for a ceasefire. When Eden disregarded this, the US turned the economic screws. The US Federal Reserve Bank started selling sterling, and in a day one sixth of Britain's gold and dollar reserves vanished as the British government tried to defend the pound. In addition, the US blocked British access to IMF funds and refused to supply any oil. The US Treasury Secretary declared, as if talking to a servant: 'You will not get a dime from the US government until you have gotten out of Suez.'

As a result, and humiliatingly, Britain was forced to declare a ceasefire the day after its troops landed in Port Said for its major offensive. By the end of December, British and French troops were forced to leave Egypt and in January 1957 Eden resigned as Prime Minister. The Suez Canal remained nationalised and Nasser continued in office until his death in 1970.

Suez 1956 marked the decisive eclipse of British imperialism as the dominant power in the Middle East. While continuing to play a counter-revolutionary role in the region – in Jordan, Kuwait, Cyprus, Oman, and elsewhere – it was a second fiddle to the US.

APPENDIX THREE

**REPRESSION AND TORTURE: THE BRITISH LABOUR PARTY AND
THE LIBERATION STRUGGLE IN SOUTH YEMEN**
BILL BOLLOTEN
FRFI 43 · OCTOBER 1984

The People's Republic of South Yemen is a small Arab nation of 33,600
square kilometres on the southern coast of the Arabian peninsula, and
has a population of 2 million. It was born on 29 and 30 November 1967,
following a bloody four-year guerrilla war. 129 years of British colonial rule were ended after a heroic struggle by the people of Aden and the
hinterland of South Yemen against the military might and terror of the
British armed forces and a succession of British-imposed schemes and
manoeuvres designed to deny the people their right to self-determination. The crucial phase of the armed struggle for independence (1963-
1967) took place when the British Labour Party government headed by
Harold Wilson was in power. It was under this government that the
most sustained repression and torture of Adeni and Yemeni patriots
fighting for independence took place.

British imperialism annexes Aden

In 1839 the British Crown annexed the territories initially for use as a
military and trading post. The occupation was fiercely resisted by 1,000
local warriors, who were only subjugated after three days of fighting.
Aden possessed a fine natural port and was also prized by the British for
its unique strategic position – it was able to service British trade routes
to India and the Far East and was valued for its role in developing British commercial interests in the Middle East. The economy of Aden
became utterly dependent on the fortunes of the imperialist money and
trading markets.

In the hinterland areas the British used the pre-existing tribal divisions to foster inter-tribal disputes. Literally hundreds of treaties were
concluded with puppet Sheikhs, Amirs and Sultans who acted like
tyrannical feudal barons. Up to 1940, the British spent not a penny on

any development in the hinterland where disease and poverty were rife. Yet millions were spent arming and bribing the tribal 'leaders'. In the rural areas of the hinterland, the land and the meagre sources of irrigation were owned by these feudal leaders. The majority of peasants existed in a state of perpetual bondage to them, and were forced to hand over to these exploiters between one fifth and two thirds of the harvest.

When the British left in 1967 the country had three Yemeni doctors and 940 hospital beds for one million inhabitants. Adul Fattah Ismail, a leader of the victorious National Liberation Front (NLF), commented in 1970:

'We have no schools in the rural areas in which to educate our children. We find no hospital to treat our sick. And when we ask ourselves why, we find that our enemy British imperialism wanted to keep our people underdeveloped, ignorant and diseased, so they could not resist or throw off the yoke of imperialism.'

If any resistance to the British colonialists did arise, the British resorted to 'aerial supervision' – the bombing of villages and homes as a brutal form of collective punishment.

After World War Two, Aden assumed a new importance for British imperialism. After important bases were lost in Palestine and Egypt, the 1957 Defence White Paper envisaged both Aden and Singapore as major military bases. In 1960 Aden replaced Cyprus as the Headquarters of the British Middle East Command. Installation and military building in Aden expanded very rapidly – Khormaksar RAF station was soon the busiest in the world. In 1954 a huge oil refinery had been built by BP to replace the Abadan refinery nationalised by the Mossadeq government in Iran in 1951. Aden had become a massive military base protecting British imperialism's interests in the oil-rich Persian Gulf and throughout the Middle East.

As the British base grew, so did the Adeni working class who very quickly became radicalised. In March of 1956 alone, workers fought 33 strikes involving 7,000 workers. In the second half of 1956, 18,000 workers participated in 44 strikes. By 1959/60 strikes began to paralyse the operations of the BP refinery. The British responded by arresting and gaoling labour leaders, deporting activists and eventually banning strikes.

The Adeni working class, while fighting for its own economic interests, was also in the vanguard of the struggle against British colonialism. They mobilised a movement to boycott the 1955 and 1959 bogus and gerrymandered Legislative Assembly elections which disenfranchised the majority of workers in Aden. It was rightly seen as a stooge body imposed by the British against the will of the Yemeni people. The Legislative Assembly was used to ratify the formation of a puppet 'Federation of South Arabia' merging the hinterland, dominated by reactionary, pro-imperialist Sheikhs and Amirs, with Aden. This manoeuvre, designed to isolate and encircle the nationalist movement in Aden, sparked off massive anger and led to the formation of the National Liberation Front (NLF).

The National Liberation Front

The nationalist movement gained further impetus from the September 1962 revolution in North Yemen which deposed the pro-British Imams. Militant nationalists from South Yemen launched the NLF in June 1963 to open a front in the south to combat British-backed counter-revolution against the Yemen Arab Republic of the North. The NLF was composed of Adeni workers, activists of the Arab Nationalist Movement, army officers and revolutionary youth and students. As the most consistent fighters for national liberation, the NLF drew its support from and represented the interests of the Adeni workers and the mass of poor and downtrodden Yemeni peasantry.

On 14 October 1963, in the Radfan mountains, the NLF launched its first armed attacks against British imperialist forces in what was to be a four-year long heroic struggle.

The British responded by encircling the Radfan area with huge numbers of troops who terrorised the Radfanis and burnt their crops. 1,000-pound bombs were dropped on villages in what became a six-month counter-insurgency campaign. Denis Healey, who was to become the Labour Minister of Defence the following year, commented that the 'troops have done their job magnificently'.

The Labour government in power

As the liberation struggle in Yemen entered its decisive phase, the Wilson Labour government was elected in October 1964. *The Economist* remarked at the time:

> 'Aden will be the first test by which the Arabs decide whether Mr Wilson's Government is truly of a new colour.'

In a matter of days the intentions of the incoming Labour administration were clear. In November, Healey stated that the policy of the government was 'to retain the base [Aden], in agreement with the Government of South Arabia, for so long as it is required to serve the interests we have in common.'

The pre-election claims of the Labour Party to promote 'friendship with the Arab world' were only for the gullible. The Labour government had no intention whatsoever of departing from Aden – they were as committed to defending the interests of imperialism as they had always been. One of its first acts, in the words of new Prime Minister Harold Wilson, was ' . . . preparing for the inevitable martial take-over, suspension of the constitution and a declaration of a state of emergency'.

The Labour government did not release the hundreds of political detainees, did not repeal the repressive labour laws banning strikes and did not allow the Adenis their rights to self-determination. The Labour government *did* step up repression to new frightening and brutal levels. Firstly the government appointed a new High Commissioner, Sir Richard Turnbull, who in the 1950s had led the repression against the Mau Mau revolution in Kenya. In 1965 the NLF was outlawed – suspected members could be detained without trial. Anyone convicted of assisting the NLF could receive ten years' imprisonment. Finally, as was to happen in Ireland, trial by jury was abolished.

Whilst stepping up repression against the working class and peasant forces, the Labour government was prepared to collaborate with feudal and bourgeois forces which it hoped to use as agents of its rule. It tried to cultivate political links with FLOSY (Front for the Liberation of South Yemen). FLOSY represented the Adeni bourgeoisie and the Sultans and two of its leaders, Al-Asnaj and Makawi, were later to emerge as bitter opponents of the revolution in South Yemen.

Labour government directs torture

The NLF, however, rapidly increased its base of support and was now capable of mounting attacks in Aden itself which were devastating for the 17,000 British soldiers both in casualties and morale. The NLF increased the number of its armed operations from 36 in 1964 to 286 in 1965, 510 in 1966 and 2,900 in 1967. By 1966 the whole of the Arab Special Branch had been assassinated by revolutionaries. Faced with the complete hostility of the people, the British could only obtain information through interrogation and torture. Reports of brutality and torture emerged as early as January 1965 – this was only *three months* after the Labour government came into office. Suspects were interrogated at Fort Morbut, where violent beatings and torture through the use of electrodes, the injection of drugs and disorientation techniques also took place. The detainees were then sent on to the regular prison at al Mansoura.

A British soldier, Corporal George Lennox, who served in Aden in 1964 and 1965 has described what he witnessed at Fort Morbut Interrogation Centre:

'Nearly every night after the state of emergency was declared and after a lot of suspects were being taken in, we used to hear, sitting in our Corporal's club drinking, a lot of screaming and shouting; really disturbing screaming, as if it was associated with someone being hurt . . . it was a common thing for us just to laugh and joke about it. "There's another cunt getting fucking done in" . . . I can remember one particular guy from the ____ Regiment – who was a boxer for them. And he used to come in and boast in the morning. He used to come in and say "Yeah, we thumped this wog last night and he's really screaming." '

On another occasion Lennox witnessed a beating:

'... I watched three soldiers ... drag out an Adeni detainee from the exercise yard. There was blood coming from the man's mouth and he was dressed only in a loin cloth round his waist. The three soldiers, standing about five yards apart began, in turn, to hit the Adeni. The first soldier was using a five-foot-long broom handle and beating the man about the head and prodding him in his midriff and genitals. He was then passed to the second soldier who hit him with a tin mug commonly used by the infantry. The third used his fists. The unfortunate wretch fell unconscious twice. He was then revived with a fire hose only to be beaten again.'

Just as was to happen in Ireland, the charge that the British were routinely torturing detainees was at first pompously denied. Observers from the International Red Cross and Amnesty International were refused access to detainees, although the latter published a report in September 1966 detailing brutality by the British. When Corporal Lennox spoke to the *Sunday Times* newspaper about the atrocities he had witnessed, he was himself detained, tortured and expelled from the British Army. Finally the Labour government appointed its own 'inquiry' into the torture allegations. The subsequent Bowen Report, while mentioning 'irregularities', was essentially, as Fred Halliday has aptly written, 'an exemplary Whitehall cover-up operation'. George Brown, the then Labour Foreign Secretary, in his introduction to the Bowen report, justified the torture at Fort Morbut, writing that it:

'had operated with considerable success, having provided information leading to the discovery of numerous arms caches and to the arrest of a large number of terrorists.'

In February 1966 the government announced that they would be abandoning the Aden base, while hoping that a neo-colonial Federal Government would continue to look after imperialist interests. Yet the Labour government maintained the presence of 17,000 British soldiers in Aden for a further 21 months. Under Labour, military expenditure in Aden had increased from £3.6m in 1963/4 to almost £14m in 1967/8.

Life for most Arabs in Aden became one of constant street searches and house raids, frequently accompanied by cowardly acts of bullying or vicious beatings from the British soldiers. One British battalion alone, in a period of six months, searched 35,000 Arabs and 8,000 vehicles in the course of which they captured only 12 grenades and six pistols. In the eleven months of 1967, when the British were still in Aden, British forces killed 119 Arabs and wounded 123.

In June 1967 Labour Foreign Secretary George Brown announced that Britain would not now withdraw until January 1968, and that Britain would supply arms to the hoped-for pro-imperialist Federal Government. Labour planned to station a military mission in Aden and provide air and naval support for a period after 'independence'. This move was applauded by the Tories. The Conservative ex-colonial Minister Duncan Sandys even said that while listening to George Brown he could have been listening to himself.

Soon, however, this plan by the Labour imperialists was in tatters. The Crater district of Aden was occupied by the NLF for 13 days in an historic uprising on 20 June 1967. The NLF released hundreds of prisoners, gutted the Legislative Assembly building and handed villas belonging to British officers over to the people.

The armed struggle was successfully brought to a conclusion on 30 November 1967 when the British forces were driven out of Aden and South Yemen was declared independent.

The People's Republic of South Yemen, born out of such determined struggle against imperialism, immediately declared its support for the revolutionary movements of the Palestinian people and continues to this day to provide consistent material support for the Palestinian guerrilla organisations.

On winning independence, the NLF leadership immediately tackled the problems left by colonial rule. In the early years of independence foreign banks and capital were nationalised, the landlords were expropriated and the land distributed to the toilers. State and co-operative farms were established that today account for over half of Yemen's agricultural production. A new public health service was introduced and the provision of education at all levels was vastly expanded. The number of students grew from 65,000 in 1967 to 400,000 in 1984. The social and economic position of Yemeni women has also been radically improved since the revolution.

Even after being thrown out of Aden, the British Labour government continued its counter-revolutionary activity. Only £3m of a £60m aid package promised by the Labour government ever materialised while this same government sponsored armed attacks against the newly named People's Democratic Republic of Yemen. Over the next 10 years British imperialism was to use and refine the lessons of repression and torture it learnt in South Yemen and apply them against the nationalist minority in the Six Counties of Ireland. The Labour Party in government was to be the driving force in this process.

ALSO AVAILABLE FROM LARKIN PUBLICATIONS

Counterattack No 1

THE LEGACY OF THE BOLSHEVIK REVOLUTION

Edited by Eddie Abrahams

'This polemical and incisive work offers . . . a valuable text for reflecting upon the ideological debates of the day'
Eloy Alberto Orego, *Granma International*

In 1917 the Russian Bolsheviks seized power and founded the world's first socialist state. That state grew into a union of states, the USSR, and survived against all the odds for 74 years. This book brings together a collection of articles which examine the legacy of the Bolshevik Revolution.

The collapse of the socialist bloc in Eastern Europe and the USSR was welcomed in the name of 'democracy' and 'reform'. In contrast this book reveals the bitter reality of the new capitalism which is savaging these countries, making millions unemployed, destroying entire welfare systems, putting an end to free education, health care and cheap housing which were taken for granted under the previous system.

The Legacy of the Bolshevik Revolution looks to the future with an examination of the current situation in Cuba. Here despite a massive economic and political assault by the USA and in the face of increasing hardship since the collapse of Soviet trade, socialism survives and attempts to meet the basic needs of the people.

First published July 1992
ISBN 0 905400 14 3
144pp, price £4.50 (+ 65p p&p)

Counterattack No 2

LABOUR:
A PARTY FIT FOR IMPERIALISM

By Robert Clough

'For a view of the Labour Party outside its red rose and double-breasted suit image, this is a valuable work' *John Pilger*

This is the untold story of the Labour Party: how it used the RAF to defend the British Empire against the Kurdish and Indian peoples; approved the use of battleships against the Chinese people to maintain the gains of the Opium Wars; used headhunters against Malayan freedom fighters; and later on tortured and interned Irish nationalists.

It is the story of its racism: its description of Africans as 'non-adult people'; its decades of connivance with South African apartheid; its continuous support for racist immigration controls.

It is the story of a left wing which was part of this corruption, and which constantly sanctioned such terror, because it saw its membership of the Labour Party as of far greater importance than the fate of millions suffering the iron heel of Labour imperialism.

It is the story of a Party which, representing a small, privileged section of the working class, has constantly betrayed the interests of the mass of the working class; unemployed workers, black, Asian and Irish people, all those engaged in a struggle against the British state – a Party which has made a mockery of the words 'freedom', 'democracy' and 'socialism'.

First published November 1992
ISBN 0 905400 15 1
192pp, price £4.95 (+ 80p p&p)

subscribe
to the
best communist
anti-imperialist
newspaper in Britain
FIGHT RACISM!
FIGHT IMPERIALISM!

Subscription rates:
- ☐ Britain (inc. N. Ireland): £4.50 for six issues, £8 for 12 issues
- ☐ EC/Europe air printed paper rate: £6 for six issues, £11 for 12 issues
- ☐ EC/Europe air letter rate: £7 for 6 issues, £13 for 12 issues
- ☐ Africa, America, Middle East, South Asia – air printed paper rate £7.50 for 6 issues, £14 for 12 issues
- ☐ East Asia, Australasia, Pacific air printed paper rate: £8.50 for 6 issues, £16 for 12 issues.
- ☐ Libraries and institutions: double individual rates

Make cheques/POs payable to Larkin Publications. Add £5 for foreign currency cheques. Overseas rates are given for printed paper reduced rate and are unsealed. If you wish your mail to be sealed please let us know and we will inform you of the extra cost.

I would like to subscribe to Fight Racism! Fight Imperialism!

NAME_____

ADDRESS _____

_____

_____

I enclose payment of £ _____ for _____ issues at _____ rate

Return this form to: FRFI, BCM Box 5909, London WC1N 3XX

Birdwatching
at Pulborough Brooks
through the Seasons

A guide to the West Sussex RSPB Nature Reserve

David Golds

S.B. Publications

Dedication
To Angela, for putting up with me through so many years.

First published in 2010 by S. B. Publications
Tel: 01323 893498
Email: sbpublications@tiscali.co.uk
www.sbpublications.co.uk

ISBNISBN 978-1-85770-354-2

Designed and Typeset by EH Graphics, East Sussex (01273) 515527

Front Cover: Upperton's Barn (the visitor centre) from the west
Back Cover: The summer meadows

Contents

Preface

It has been my privilege to watch Pulborough Brooks develop from a wildlife wilderness to an exciting nature reserve giving pleasure to over 100,000 visitors annually. I have witnessed this transformation both as a volunteer and, since 1995, as a part-time member of the reserve's staff. Much of my time has been closely involved in helping visitors to enjoy the reserve and, increasingly, devising and running bird-related courses as part of the events programme. Through talking to so many people during these activities I came to realise that there was a gap in the information available about the reserve that could usefully be filled, and this book is the result. I hope that it will be of value to a wide range of visitors and that it will encourage them to make the most of the seasonal changes that enhance the Pulborough Brooks' birdwatching experience.

ACKNOWLEDGEMENTS

This book is based largely on my own birdwatching at the reserve but it also relies very much on the records of bird sightings submitted to the RSPB over the years by visitors, volunteers and staff. It would have been difficult to write without these records and I am indebted to all the observers. Reference was also made to *The Status of Birds at Pulborough Brooks, West Sussex. Phillips and Callaway. December 2002* (an internally published report, now out-of-print). Apart from the use of the above data, there has been no direct RSPB involvement in the writing of the book, which is totally my responsibility.

All of the photographs are by David and Janet Shaw and I am extremely grateful to them for their help and for so generously donating these wonderful pictures.

My thanks are also due to all involved at SB Publications for their assistance. Not least, I must thank my wife Angela for her knowledgeable and observant companionship on our birdwatching walks.

Information for Visitors

Pulborough Brooks is an easy place to visit, the nature trail and hides being open every day of the year except Christmas Day. The visitor centre is closed on Christmas Day and Boxing Day, otherwise this opens daily.

The reserve is located on the western side of the A283 about halfway between Storrington and Pulborough. There are signs to 'RSPB Nature Reserve' at several major junctions in the area.

A bus service, Compass Bus route 100, which operates between Pulborough railway station and Burgess Hill (not Sundays and Public Holidays), stops at the reserve entrance on the A283 (timetables from Compass Bus 01903 690025 and www.compass-travel.co.uk).

In addition to the reserve and nature trail, described in a later chapter, there is a popular tearoom serving lunches, teas and light refreshments and a shop offering an excellent selection of natural history books, binoculars and telescopes, bird food, country clothing and gifts. The field study centre is the focus for the national curriculum-related field teaching programmes and is also the venue for some of the numerous and varied wildlife events for adults, families and children held throughout the year.

Enquiries can be made to pulborough.brooks@rspb.org.uk or by telephoning 01798 875851. The postal address is RSPB Nature Reserve, Wiggonholt, Pulborough, West Sussex RH20 2EL. More information including recent bird and other wildlife sightings can be obtained by visiting www.rspb.org.uk/pulboroughbrooks.

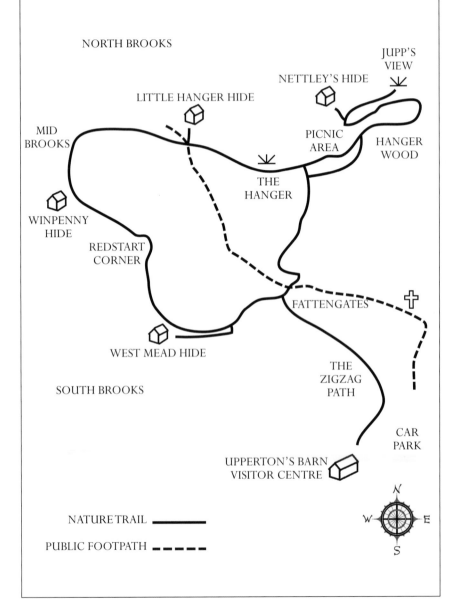

MAP OF THE RSPB PULBOROUGH BROOKS
NATURE RESERVE

NORTH BROOKS

JUPP'S VIEW

NETTLEY'S HIDE

LITTLE HANGER HIDE

MID BROOKS

PICNIC AREA

HANGER WOOD

THE HANGER

WINPENNY HIDE

REDSTART CORNER

FATTENGATES

WEST MEAD HIDE

THE ZIGZAG PATH

SOUTH BROOKS

CAR PARK

UPPERTON'S BARN VISITOR CENTRE

NATURE TRAIL ————

PUBLIC FOOTPATH ‑ ‑ ‑ ‑

N W E S

Introduction

As a place to watch birds, Pulborough Brooks compares well with other nature reserves throughout the country. Its reputation is such that it is one of the most visited of all Royal Society for the Protection of Birds (RSPB) reserves.

During the year, visitors are offered the opportunity of seeing over 70 bird species that breed habitually and over 150 that are regularly recorded. Some of these occur in nationally and regionally important numbers. With birds in this abundance, coupled with the excellent visitor facilities, Pulborough Brooks is, unquestionably, a first-class place to go birdwatching. Twitchers, far more so than ordinary birdwatchers, may lament that, due to its geographical situation, it does not consistently attract rare birds in the same way as some places although, as these pages will show, rarities are far from unknown.

This book is intended to help everyone, whether regular visitor or newcomer, keen birder or general country lover, to enjoy birdwatching at Pulborough Brooks. The aim is to provide as much information as possible about when and where you are likely to see and hear the reserve's birds.

Although there is a chapter covering each quarter of the year, it is ultimately not the calendar but a host of seasonal factors that govern bird activities such as migration and breeding. Consequently, various aspects of behaviour sometimes take place earlier or later than the 'normal' times forecast in the text.

For the maximum convenience, each quarterly chapter is designed to be read independently from the others and, therefore, a small amount of repetition about the various locations is inevitable.

Every effort has been made to be realistic about the chances of seeing particular birds and not to raise false hopes through overoptimism. Having said that, anyone with even a little experience of birdwatching knows just how unpredictable birds can be. Although birds that you confidently expect to come across sometimes fail to materialise there is, surprisingly often, the compensation and excitement of seeing a species that you did not anticipate. What is certain is that the more often you are able to come to the reserve, and the longer you spend at each visit strolling quietly around the nature trail, and watching patiently from the viewpoints and hides, the more birds you will see.

Whilst the focus is on the relatively common and regularly occurring species, mention is made of many of the more unusual birds that have passed through over the years. Some, at least, of these will eventually visit the reserve again and be seen by vigilant birdwatchers with the good fortune to be in the right place at the right time. More practically, where a species is described as having been recorded at migration time, but only relatively occasionally, it is always worthwhile checking carefully at the spots where it has occurred because there is no reason why it should not, one day, be found there again at that same time of the year.

As far as identification is concerned, all the information required will be found in the numerous field guides (obtainable from booksellers) to the birds of this part of the world. Sound guides in various formats are available to assist with learning songs and calls.

The text uses the British (English) vernacular names that are in everyday use, rather than the International English names (which appear in one form or another in some field guides) such as 'great cormorant', 'barn swallow' and 'winter wren'. Other than in the 'Guide to the Reserve', local usage has been adopted in dropping the words 'hide' and 'viewpoint', reference being made, instead, simply to 'Nettley's', and so on.

When the status of a species is given, for instance 'scarce', this relates to its standing at the reserve, which is not necessarily the same as the national status.

Visitors are invited to enter significant wildlife sightings in a register at the visitor centre. It is hoped that as many birdwatchers as possible also routinely input *all* of their records (not just those from Pulborough Brooks) to BirdTrack (www.birdtrack.net), both for their own benefit and to help national organisations collect data vital to their mission to conserve birds. In addition, descriptions of unusual species for Sussex, as defined by the Sussex Ornithological Society (SOS), should be submitted to the Recorder of that organisation on a record form obtainable from him or the SOS website (www.sos.org.uk).

Although this book concentrates on its birds, Pulborough Brooks is a nature reserve, not just a place for birds. Its diverse habitats also support, amongst other wildlife, over 100 species of flowering plants in the ditches, more than 35 species of nationally important invertebrates, half of Britain's dragonfly species, 30 butterfly species, four reptile species, five species of amphibian and 19 mammal species.

The area covered is that part of the reserve to which visitors are regularly admitted, including the nature trail and places in and around the visitor centre. It does not extend to other parts of the Arun Valley managed by the RSPB because public access to them is very restricted, being limited normally to a few public rights of way. Also not included is the land adjoining the car park, which is undergoing enormous changes, with the RSPB undertaking a long-term project to restore much of it to heathland. In years to come, this promises to be as stunningly beautiful, in its own way, as the rest of the reserve, supporting its own flora and fauna including nightjars, woodlarks and, perhaps, tree pipits and Dartford warblers.

A Brief History
of Pulborough Brooks

Man's activities on the Arun floodplain, of which Pulborough Brooks is a part, can be traced back as far as agricultural settlements of c2500 BC. It is probable that the valley had become an estuary in the mid-Iron Age but changes to sea levels meant that, in the early part of Roman rule, the view from the hills would have been of a rich and fertile valley. Later in Roman times, further sea level variations resulted in the transformation of the view to that of an extensive swamp.

As history advanced, villagers were able to graze their cattle on the meadows, take advantage of fish and wildfowl for the kitchen and gather naturally occurring materials such as reeds, rushes and osiers for thatching, seating and basket making. There is evidence from the fifteenth century of improvements being made to the ditches for drainage purposes. More extensive work was carried out in the early nineteenth century and, by the middle of that century, various ditching and embanking schemes had achieved a drainage structure that lasted until modern times. By skilled and intensive use of the ditch system, farmers managed the land as water meadows, periodically flooding and draining the meadows at various times of the year. One operation was designed, in part, to ensure that rich silt in the flood water was deposited on the ground, thereby adding valuable nutrients to the meadows. By coincidence, this system of agriculture, coupled with natural regular winter flooding, not only provided a livelihood for local people but also produced the ideal habitat for wintering waterfowl, breeding waders and other ground nesting birds, and an abundance of other wildlife including both terrestrial and aquatic plants and invertebrates.

With the increasing cost of labour, water meadows fell out of use, but the basic structure of river and ditches remained largely unaltered until the implementation of a major flood relief scheme, completed in 1967. This involved the canalisation of the river, which included the raising of flood embankments along its course, and improving drainage. As a result, the regular seasonal flooding ceased, denying the thousands of waterfowl their traditional winter home on the brooks. The effects of the scheme also made possible significant alterations to agricultural management which, together with the drying out of the soil and pools, resulted in dramatic declines in breeding waders and every other facet of wetland wildlife. During the 1970s and 1980s the situation continued to deteriorate and was not helped when much of the farmland at Pulborough Brooks became derelict in 1985, heralding a further drying out of the fields and the spread of rank vegetation.

This, then, was the state of affairs when the RSPB became interested in the possibility of acquiring the site. The Society had to convince itself that the expenditure of the substantial sum required to purchase the land would be a wise use of its resources. Although, by that time, there were very few birds present, examination of ornithological records dating back to the 1950s demonstrated the historical importance of the locality for birds. Surveys of other aspects of the natural history, and investigations into the prospects for effective hydrological control, led to the conclusion that the place had great potential for the restoration that would bring the birds and wildlife back. As a result, it was agreed to buy Pulborough Brooks and the purchase was completed in 1989. This was a momentous decision, being the first time that the RSPB had bought a major new site where the birds that were the objective of the conservation measures were not present. The reserve was opened to the public in December 1992.

The size of the reserve at that time was 171 ha (423 acres) of which lowland wet grassland covered 121 ha (299 acres). The remainder consisted of arable fields, dry permanent pasture, woodland, hedgerows and scrub.

Restoration work commenced almost immediately upon acquisition, the crucial factors in the management of the wet meadows being grazing, mowing and the ability to manipulate water levels.

A large number of water control devices were installed in the 15 km (9 miles) long ditch system to make it practicable, in all normal conditions, to manage water levels in order to achieve various degrees of flooding, in different sections of the meadows, at each season. As a result, in the winter large areas are covered in shallow flooding to provide feeding and roosting opportunities for the visiting and resident waterfowl. North Brooks is flooded much more extensively than Mid and South Brooks. Flooding is greatly reduced after the winter to permit grazing (and to provide for ground nesting birds) but levels are maintained in the permanent pools at suitable heights for breeding birds. In the autumn, levels are lowered to expose areas of mud where passage waders can feed.

A cattle grazing regime was introduced, designed to produce a variety of vegetation structures. In the summer, grazing is supplemented by mowing, and hay crops are taken from a number of meadows.

Overall, the control of water and vegetation creates, season by season, a range of habitats suitable for birds to breed, feed and roost.

The RSPB's commitment of money, labour and expertise was rapidly rewarded, with all wintering birds showing noteworthy increases and some, for example teal and pintail, being present in greater numbers than before the canalisation of the river. Within five years of purchase, the reserve became nationally important for wigeon, gadwall, teal, pintail, shoveler, white-fronted geese, Bewick's swans, ruff and (on migration) whimbrel. The reserve now supports a large proportion of the Arun Valley's wintering waterfowl and breeding waders.

Pulborough Brooks was designated a Site of Special Scientific Interest (SSSI) in 1999, and the increase in wintering birds as a result of RSPB management led directly to the designation of 528 ha (1304 acres) of the Arun Valley as a Special Protection Area (SPA) and RAMSAR Site (for wetlands of international importance) by December 2000.

In the years following the establishment of the reserve, the RSPB has been successful in acquiring a considerable amount of additional land in the valley. Most of this is further south on Amberley Wildbrooks but some adjoins the original boundaries. The Society now owns or manages some 475 ha (1,174 acres) in the Arun Valley.

Guide to the Reserve

Distances

As an aid to judging distances around the nature trail, the following are the average walking times between major features. Remember that, in reality, it will take *much* longer because you will be spending time sitting in the hides and stopping frequently along the trail to watch birds and enjoy the superb views.

Visitor Centre to Fattengates -	5 minutes
Fattengates to Nettley's hide -	11 minutes
Nettley's hide to Little Hanger hide -	9 minutes
Little Hanger hide to Winpenny hide -	6 minutes
Winpenny hide to West Mead hide -	7 minutes
West Mead hide to Visitor Centre -	10 minutes

The Car Park

By whatever means you have travelled to the reserve, whether by car, bicycle, bus or one of the public footpath routes from Pulborough, you will commence your visit by passing through the car park. This may sound like an uninspiring start, but far from it. As well as the surfaced sections, the car park and adjoining areas have extensive stretches of rough grass and are virtually surrounded by trees and bushes, all providing good habitats for a variety of birds.

The Courtyard

Beyond the gateway leading from the car park to the visitor centre is the courtyard, which has a lawned area, ornamental plant borders and, most importantly, the bird feeding station. This attracts many birds, some lingering for a while, others paying more fleeting visits, and a long and rewarding time can be spent here enjoying close views.

Around the far side of the building is the gate giving entry to the nature trail when the visitor centre is closed. Beside that gate, and a pond, is the access to a 'waterwise' garden, the play area for children and a wildflower meadow.

The Visitor Centre

The visitor centre, Upperton's Barn, was reconstructed, to largely the same external design, from the semi-ruined threshing barn purchased by the RSPB at the same time as the land. It incorporates a tearoom, shop, toilets and field study centre, together with the reception area that is the first point of contact for all visitors.

From the large main windows there are breathtaking views over the reserve and much, much further (some of the more distant landmarks are easier to find through binoculars). The fields fall away to the flat meadows of Mid Brooks and South Brooks and thence to the river Arun, which flows south past Amberley Wild Brooks, through Arundel and into the English Channel at Littlehampton. For such an important feature of the landscape, the river is curiously difficult to see and, even from the altitude of the visitor centre, the water is hidden at low tide by the banks. When the tide is higher, the glint of water is visible in several bends of the river's course. In places, there are glimpses of both the railway and the main A29 road, which share the valley floor with the river.

To the north west (right) is the conspicuous tower of Pulborough church. The next settlement to the south is the hamlet of Hardham, with its tiny, bell-turreted church. In a line just to the right of the church, but ten miles distant, the tall, slender mast, visible in clear conditions, is at Bexleyhill between Lickfold and Henley. Further south along the valley, the village of Coldwaltham is identifiable by the pyramidal cap of the church. In the far background are the wooded South Downs above Bignor, Barlavington and beyond.

Part of Upperton's Field, in the foreground, has been used for a number of years to assess how a range of experimental management techniques can help to reverse the national decline in farmland birds.

The First Section of the Nature Trail

After a short step from the visitor centre's northern doorway, and past the viewing area by a large pond, the nature trail bends left and heads resolutely downhill. This gently curving path is fancifully known as 'the zigzags', a throwback to the first years of the reserve when the only route here was, indeed, of that configuration. The zigzag path still exists as a grassy track, mainly to make the incline easier for wheelchairs.

On the left of the path you will see a wide belt of native trees and shrubs, some of the thousands planted during the reserve's early years. This feature is repeated by the side of several other sections of the trail and on the northern side of the entrance road. The hedge-line beyond the grass on the other side of the path is the reserve boundary, whilst a little further away tiny Wiggonholt church hides among the trees. The church, which has no patron saint, consists of a single room and was built for the use of the shepherds who worked on the brooks. It merits a visit and can be reached by a public footpath starting from the car park.

Fattengates

At the foot of the hill is the locality known as Fattengates. Here there are mature deciduous trees, a spruce plantation, scrub and a large pond. Immediately after the pond is a junction where you can either turn left and follow the rest of the trail clockwise, or right and do the walk in the reverse direction (both ways return to this point). Note that the book's quarterly chapters presume that the anticlockwise route is chosen.

The Nature Trail from Fattengates

Assuming that the right-hand turn is taken at the junction, your way soon passes through a pair of gates. Between the gates you cross the public footpath that runs from the car park, by way of Wiggonholt church, across the reserve and thence to the river and on to Pulborough. There is a small pond on the right, by the second gate, which is just within the boundary of the reserve. The trail continues through the trees and bushes with, quite soon, a small viewing place, which is handy for scanning the fields on either side of the path.

The next objective is a pair of field gates, one on either side of the path, that on the right being a convenient location from which to check the field for birds, whilst the one on the left affords distant views of the valley. Beyond this cattle crossing is a fork, where you should bear left only if you want to go directly to the Hanger viewpoint and Little Hanger hide, so missing out Jupp's View and Nettley's hide.

Hanger Wood

The right fork will take you into Hanger Wood and down through the trees to the spot, nearly at the altitude of the brooks, where you turn right to go to Jupp's View or bear left for Nettley's hide.

North Brooks

There are principally four places for watching North Brooks. Jupp's View is an open platform, almost down at the level of the nearby pools, from where a large swathe of the brooks can be observed. The vista from Nettley's hide is very similar but the western end of the hide also gives a view of the scrubby edge of the wood where it adjoins a marshy corner of the brooks.

From Nettley's hide you have to retrace your steps through the wood as far as the spot where you are able to bear right onto a path through the picnic area. After a short distance this path merges with the main trail, which soon takes you to the third vantage point, the Hanger viewpoint, situated a few paces down its access path. One of the benefits of the panoramic view from this lofty location is that birds can be seen out on the brooks which, from the lower level vantage points, are hidden by vegetation. On the other hand, those birds are considerably further away and so this is a situation where a telescope is often an advantage.

The trail from the Hanger viewpoint, which is bordered by tall trees and bushes, leads to Little Hanger hide, reached by walking down a short side path. Back virtually at the same height as the meadows, you can here experience a different perspective of North Brooks and some of the pools. As at the Hanger viewpoint, the surrounding trees, scrub and grassy places offer varied bird interest.

Birdwatching from any of these sites has the considerable advantages of the light coming from more or less behind and of being reasonably well sheltered from the prevailing wind. Conditions are drastically different in the winter if the wind is blowing from a northerly quarter, when the birdwatcher's protective clothing and his enthusiasm for the task in hand may be tested to the full.

From whichever of these locations you chose to look over North Brooks you will see the large village of Pulborough in the distance. The various coloured buildings and the prominent tower of the parish church can be useful reference points when helping others to locate a bird seen on the rather featureless meadows. The reserve's northern boundary is, for some distance, the river Storr, the banks of which can be discerned about half a mile before the first buildings in Pulborough.

Mid Brooks and South Brooks

Unlike North Brooks, there is no high ground along this edge of the brooks and so there are no elevated points from which to watch. There are, though, two hides, Winpenny and West Mead, each providing views across Mid Brooks towards South Brooks and the South Downs. Winpenny hide is close to the river Arun, here the western boundary of the reserve, the floodbank being clearly visible from the windows. Because the hides face south and west the sun can make watching difficult in the afternoon and, in the worse conditions of a low sun, birds appear from West Mead hide mainly in silhouette. In compensation, some wonderful sunsets have been enjoyed from that hide.

Again in contrast to the North Brooks' section, there are no woods and glades to wander through, and Little Hanger, Winpenny and West Mead hides are linked by a single track. Notwithstanding this, it is a route that is far from devoid of interest and not just a means of getting from one hide to another. Directly after Little Hanger hide the nature trail passes through two gates to cross the route of the public footpath across the reserve. It then gradually descends to about the same elevation as the brooks.

Up until here, the trail has been enclosed between high trees and bushes but now the character changes to a much more open aspect. In some parts the brooks are separated from the path by trees, in others by hedgerows. On the left, fences or hedges segregate visitors from the pastures of, firstly, the field called Winpenny Brook and, later on, Fattengates Field.

Roughly halfway between Winpenny and West Mead hides the pathway bends sharply to the right. This is Redstart Corner, so called because of the attraction of nearby fences and hedges to migrating redstarts, particularly in August. A short way further on a gap in the hedge on the right offers views across the meadows towards the riverbank.

West Mead hide lies just off the trail and is approached over a wooden bridge. Thereafter it is but a short walk back to the junction at Fattengates where a right turn will take you up back up the hill to Upperton's Barn, the visitor centre.

The brooks in flood

The visitor centre

Wood Pigeon

Marsh Tit and Great Tit at the feeding station

Pintails

Shelducks

Peregrine Falcon

Little Egret

Snipe

Canada Geese

Shoveler

Little Grebe

Redwing

Kestrel

January to March

At the start of this period birds may be contending with the very worst of the winter weather, yet a few weeks later they will react to the onset of spring. Numbers of wintering waterfowl gradually decrease as birds fly away to breed, although there is compensation for their loss in the excitement of seeing the first summer migrants. In January, there will only be relatively few birds to delight your ears with song but, as time passes, they are augmented by the voices of more and more species. Barn owls start to visit prospective nest sites early in the year and it is not long before several smaller birds show evidence of nest building.

Although you might be tempted to hasten away from the car park towards the main part of the reserve, a leisurely stroll around the perimeter can be a pleasing start to the day.

Some of the birds which start to sing regularly several months in advance of spring will be in voice, amongst them wrens, dunnocks, robins, song and mistle thrushes, goldcrests, marsh, coal, blue and great tits, chaffinches and greenfinches. A much less usual addition to the list of singers was a siskin in March 2008. The loud whistling of nuthatches, the chattering from magpies and the gruff calls of rooks add to the sound picture, as do the alarm notes produced by many birds, with those of blackbirds often in the fore. These alarms could be a response to the occasional presence of a kestrel, merlin or peregrine or the more regular threat posed by sparrowhawks.

Groups of long-tailed tits, which are sometimes members of mixed parties potentially containing chiffchaffs, goldcrests, treecreepers and coal, blue and great tits, make a habit of moving through the trees, feeding as they go. Another tit, the marsh, lives hereabouts but is a less frequent sight.

This is an excellent spot for woodpeckers. Green woodpeckers like to feed on the expanses of grass bordering the entrance road and, even when they are not visible, you will readily hear their distinctive laughing calls.

The much sought-after lesser spotted woodpecker is seen in trees around the car park as often as anywhere on the reserve. January is undoubtedly the best time to try for lesser spotted woodpeckers but February also offers opportunities, a significant feature of both months being the lack of foliage which otherwise easily hides these sparrow-sized birds. Considerably more abundant is the great spotted woodpecker and it is often possible to locate several, either by their explosive calls or from the drumming, which commences almost from the start of the year. Favourite places for drumming are various resonant branches high in the great oak near the courtyard pond. This woodpecker habitually probes the bark of trunks and boughs in its quest for food, and has also been seen exploring the oak rails of the low fencing that edges the parking area.

Very early, or late, in the day the hooting of tawny owls is a common sound from the adjacent woods. Much less frequently, little owls are seen by the entrance road. A number of other species have made random appearances on, over and around the car park. There has, for instance, been a single sighting of the scarce grey partridge and twice, in January and February, woodcocks have flown over, no doubt on the move between the feeding areas and their woodland roost. Early in 2003 a stonechat regularly perched not far from the entrance gates. Other car park scarcities are siskins and, in the conifers at the back, common crossbills. It was from here in March 2007 and 2008 that several ravens, an uncommon species for the reserve, were observed flying over.

Signs of approaching spring, and the breeding season, grow as the days lengthen. Watch for birds, large and small, collecting sticks, twigs and vegetation for nest building, coal tits and other small birds chasing each other through the perimeter trees and robins displaying their red breasts to rivals. Listen for the blackbird to add his rich voice to the increasing volume of song.

Come March, and spring migration is getting underway. The most obvious sign of this, which you can hardly miss, is the song of chiffchaffs, the majority of which will be new arrivals from the south. Another migrant, the wheatear, is in short supply this early in the year but has appeared on grassy places, including those near the car park.

The garden in the courtyard is populated by scores of birds taking advantage of the peanuts, sunflower seeds, mixed seed and other food provided on the ground, on bird tables and in hanging feeders. Some feed entirely on the ground but many move between there and the feeders, depending on food availability and the severity of competition from the other birds.

Great spotted woodpeckers like the feeders and quite often fly across from the woods. Conversely, the lesser spotted woodpecker is normally a very scarce visitor to the feeding station and it was remarkable in 2006 when one came every day for ten days in January and again on a couple of days in February.

Blue and great tits are seldom absent and coal and long-tailed tits drop by, as does the odd marsh tit. This latter species looks very similar to the willow tit, but that is extremely scarce at the reserve and it is almost certain that a bird of the same general appearance seen here will be a marsh tit. Nuthatches know that an easy meal is to be had, and usually have to share a feeder with numerous greenfinches.

Birds feeding on the ground range in size from pheasants to the tiny wrens that disappear beneath the stone troughs in search of insects. Moorhens scuttle to and from the pond to snatch a seed or two. Pied wagtails and blackbirds are often around and, occasionally, there is a mistle thrush. Song thrushes tend to seek somewhere rather quieter to feed and are best looked for on the grass beyond the play area. Chaffinches can be present in large numbers and need to be looked at carefully as, just sometimes, there can be a brambling amongst them. Very irregular visitors to the feeding station include house sparrows, goldfinches, siskins, lesser redpolls and reed buntings.

As so often, a guaranteed concentration of small birds, as here, is irresistible to sparrowhawks, which appear from nowhere to make dashing low flights through the courtyard in an attempt to catch a feathered bite to eat.

A sustained watch from the visitor centre window, the tea terrace or the viewpoint at the start of the nature trail, coupled with an element of luck, could result in the sighting of some birds of prey. Sparrowhawks are active around the field and common buzzards - one, two, three or even, as on one February day, nine - are seen occasionally, usually high in the sky. Although a hunting kestrel is not uncommon, it is much more of a challenge to catch a glimpse of a merlin, probably in rapid pursuit of a skylark or another bird of similar size. Rarer raptor sightings from here have been red kites, a hen harrier and the odd peregrine.

Most wetland birds, such as those on the water by West Mead, are far too distant to watch with ease, even through the telescope, but little egrets tend to stand out rather well. Shelducks are also pretty obvious and they have ventured even closer, into Upperton's Field, where lapwings also gather from time to time. Snipe are known to use the field, although they are normally impossible to see until they fly. However, with all of these species, it is far better to look for them later on, from the hides.

You will certainly see pheasants, up to about twenty, on and around the field but there are few records of another game bird, the grey partridge. As well as accommodating scores of wood pigeons, the field also provides foraging for a much lower number of stock doves. Black-headed gulls, which you are much more likely to see on the water later in your walk, have also congregated here in large numbers. One or two herring gulls, far from a regular sight, have flown over.

Late in the afternoon, a barn owl now and then chooses to hunt for small mammals around the edge of the field, by the conifers at Fattengates or over the rough grass towards Wiggonholt church, all within sight of the visitor centre. In some years, barn owls breed in a box located high inside the roof of the visitor centre, or in a box fixed on a tree away down at the end of the field, in which case they may start visiting those sites from early in the year. When coupled with the fact that the boxes are also sometimes used for roosting, it is always worth checking for activity around dusk. In the case of the roof box it is important, to avoid disturbing the owls, to watch from the car park and never from the tea terrace. You can easily and safely see the area around the box in the tree from several places near the visitor centre, from the trail to Fattengates and from the field gate near West Mead.

Until 2008, another of the reserve's resident owls, the little owl, was not shy of showing itself during the day and it has long been worth scanning carefully through the trees at the bottom of the field to see if one was roosting there. Alas, the local population of this popular species has plummeted, with breeding and roosting no longer taking place at the traditional sites. Whether this is a temporary state of affairs or a more permanent change remains to be seen.

Upperton's Field is a first-rate feeding site for green woodpeckers and there can be two or three, or even more, present at the same time. It also attracts a wide range of birds of which some - skylarks, meadow pipits, starlings, chaffinches, goldfinches, linnets, yellowhammers, reed buntings - can at times be in large flocks. Other species, including pied wagtails, dunnocks, blackbirds, song thrushes, mistle thrushes and greenfinches may be present in smaller numbers. It would also be attractive to corn buntings but their numbers have fallen to the extent that they are now very unusual here. Frustratingly, many of the birds that drop in to the field to feed are lost to sight in the vegetation as soon as they land. It is usually not long, though, before something alarms them, and they fly to nearby trees and bushes where they are easier to watch.

On some days, flocks of fieldfares and redwings assemble to feed on Upperton's Field. There can be scores in these flocks and, on one occasion, 200 fieldfares were counted. Also in large flocks will be members of the crow family, especially the mixed gatherings of jackdaws and rooks. Magpies and carrion crows are invariably in smaller numbers. Late March could be the time for one of the uncommon visits by newly arrived wheatears.

Jays can be seen periodically in the trees around the tea terrace, which have also, on rare occasions, been the location for lesser spotted woodpeckers and treecreepers.

Birds use the pond outside the main window for drinking and bathing. The first hint of this activity may be a shower of water droplets over the plants at the edge. The nearby brambles and gorse are an attractive habitat for dunnocks and, sooner or later, one or two are almost bound to appear. Every so often, the tall plants and fence posts around the pond become perches from which stonechats, generally a male and female, drop down to catch insects. When mallards take up temporary residence they cruise around the pond, and roost in the vegetation.

Over the years, a number of scarcer species have been seen in the vicinity of the visitor centre. Into this category fall lesser redpolls and common crossbills, which are less than annual, a black redstart (March 2003) and a willow tit (January 1995).

Walking down the hill, on the first part of the nature trail, you will again hear and see many of the birds associated with the field in front of the building. Some will be flying to and from the field, others perched in trees and bushes. The crowing calls of pheasants are an everyday sound and you may see several sparring with each other by the path. Listen for the calls and drumming of great spotted woodpeckers, coming more often than not from the trees over by Wiggonholt church. A lesser spotted woodpecker could be perched in any of the trees but, as always, a large element of luck will be needed to find one. Green woodpeckers, often first located by their calls, feed hereabouts, sometimes on the path itself.

The bushes are a possible place for bullfinches, as well as for the ubiquitous long-tailed, blue and great tits. Less common, but still seen from time to time, are goldcrests (even firecrests on red-letter days), goldfinches and reed buntings. One of the few recent corn bunting observations was from this path in January 2003. Especially in January, fence posts along the way are favourite perches for a pair of stonechats. In several years up to a dozen lesser redpolls have spent time in the trees by the side of the zigzag path which, much less frequently, have also provided a perch for a siskin.

As the weeks pass by, more and more species will start to sing and so, on the way down the hill, listen for the songs of wrens, dunnocks, robins, chiffchaffs, chaffinches, greenfinches, linnets and yellowhammers. Almost always, the rather less melodious calls of rooks drift across from the region of the church.

From late afternoon onwards, the rough grass adjacent to the trail can prove to be a good foraging area for a barn owl and once, during a March day, a short-eared owl hunted over the ground towards the church.

Keep your eyes open from mid-March for early migrants. Both chiffchaffs and spotted flycatchers have been reported on this section of the path and, in one year, there was a yellow wagtail.

Pause just before the pond at Fattengates to check the edge of the conifer plantation for any movement in the branches. A close look through your binoculars may reveal the cause to be one or two of the goldcrests and coal tits that frequent these trees. Sometimes they emerge to flit around in the blackthorn scrub, where they are easier to watch. Even if these birds are not in view you may well hear them calling and singing. Wrens feed and hide in the brambles but blackbirds and song thrushes are more visible, foraging as they do in the leaf litter at the path's edge. Other common birds that like this habitat include dunnocks, robins, long-tailed, blue and great tits and greenfinches. The denser bushes will almost certainly be harbouring several bullfinches. Common crossbills have occurred in the conifers, although very infrequently.

Lesser and great spotted woodpeckers have been seen in the deciduous trees here but more probable are nuthatches and treecreepers, the nuthatches often drawing attention to themselves by calling loudly. A yellowhammer can sometimes be found perched in one of the trees or bushes. In March 2001, Fattengates was the scene of one of the reserve's rare willow tit sightings.

From late in the afternoon this can be a good area to see barn owls, should they decide to hunt over the rough grassland. Tawny owls have been seen and heard here at all hours and, on a January day, one chose to roost in a conifer in full view of the path.

Do not neglect to look at the pond because, whilst never teeming with birds, once in a while it has attracted some interesting species. Apart from the common moorhens and mallards, there have been one-off sightings of water rail, kingfisher and grey wagtail.

A quiet interlude by the pond gives an opportunity to hear a variety of bird noises, with the range increasing as the weeks advance. The gentle sound of wood pigeons is frequently in the background as are the more urgent calls of green woodpeckers. Rooks regularly fly over, calling loudly.

Every now and then, the voices of wetland birds, amongst them grey herons and Canada geese, are heard as they, too, pass overhead. Almost always, wrens, dunnocks, robins and chaffinches will be singing, to be joined in time by a song thrush and, maybe, a linnet. Although the odd chiffchaff has been seen here in the winter, several will be singing their unmistakeable tune around Fattengates when migration gets underway during March. In addition to chiffchaffs, other early summer migrants have included isolated instances of wheatears and spotted flycatchers. Departing winter visitors pass through on into March and fieldfares, redwings and, less reliably, bramblings are all possible.

Whilst enjoying identifying the variety of birds that spend time in this area do not be surprised to catch a glimpse of a sparrowhawk, for whom one of those same birds could end up as a meal.

After you leave Fattengates it is hardly possible to walk any distance along the lane without hearing and seeing pheasants. In addition, the nearby fields have also been the source of a few of the very infrequent red-legged partridge records. Once or twice, the fields have been hunting grounds for both barn and little owls but this is not something you should count on. Far more certain are the calls of green woodpeckers, which resound from near and far.

On occasions, the fields bordering the path contain feeding flocks of fieldfares and redwings which, depending on the vagaries of the season, are either spending the winter in the area, or passing through on migration. Towards the end of March, early swallows can be seen every so often, taking advantage of the shelter afforded by the lane to hunt for insects. As the same month progresses there will be no difficulty in seeing and hearing the chiffchaff, another summer visitor, and you will normally hear several singing from trees, both close by and further into the woods, especially by the cattle crossing just before the fork in the path.

Dunnocks, robins, blackbirds and song thrushes fossick around in the leaf litter by the side of the path. Other species, including mistle thrushes, chaffinches (with, sporadically, bramblings), greenfinches, goldfinches, linnets, yellowhammers and, occasionally, reed buntings find food in the fields. The trees and hedges are scoured for insects and any remaining seeds by goldcrests, long-tailed, coal, blue and great tits, all betraying their presence by calls and, as spring approaches, songs. At this time of the year bullfinches, of which you will probably first become conscious by their calls, can be easily watched eating buds in the bushes. Unobtrusive treecreepers climb the trunks of nearby trees, demanding your keenest attention if you are to spot them. Much more conspicuous are the jays, which have a propensity to fly from the hedges in alarm at your approach.

The many birds to which Hanger Wood is home attract your attention by their calls and, as the days lengthen, their songs as well. Wrens, dunnocks, robins, goldcrests, long-tailed tits, blue tits, great tits, treecreepers, chaffinches and bullfinches are typical. Eventually, from somewhere nearby, a song thrush will start singing and there is always a background of sounds from wood pigeons and, often, rooks. By the end of March chiffchaffs will be singing all the while. Other, non-woodland, noises such as those from Canada geese and teal arise from down on the brooks or from flocks flying overhead.

Sparrowhawks and tawny owls both occur here but are difficult to see amongst the trees. The density of the wood also means that it is easier to locate the great spotted woodpeckers by their calls than visually. Another hard to see species, this time due to its small size, is the firecrest, which has inhabited the wood once or twice in January and February.

The first weeks of this quarter are part of the winter period when the maximum quantities of birds congregate on North Brooks. Later on, numbers start to diminish as many species head back to the places where they will breed but, whatever the date, you will find much of interest here.

In most years there will be a little grebe or two, either feeding in the ditches or, when the water is deep enough for them to dive, out on the flooded meadows. In a very few years, deeper water has also attracted the great crested grebe, a much scarcer visitor. Several cormorants often loaf in the centre of North Brooks, with some showing their breeding plumage as early as January. The cormorant is not only common but also easy to see, unlike the bittern which is a rare winter visitor and very secretive. The likelihood of seeing one should not be totally discounted, however, as was proved in January 1993 when a bittern was watchable from Nettley's.

Back at the easy-to-see end of the spectrum are little egrets, of which up to three are seen from time to time, and grey herons, which are always to be observed fishing patiently in a ditch or pool. Another very sizeable bird, this time a rarity, was the white stork in March 2003. The common crane, also large, is classified as a very rare vagrant at the reserve and so the second ever record, at the end of March 2007 (and on into April), was a noteworthy event. It coincided with a period of persistent east winds and the appearance of several cranes in south east England. This was bettered by the visit for two days in March 2008 of three cranes, which was itself followed by more records of the species in April and May.

Also difficult to miss are the resident mute swans, of which there can be up to a couple of dozen. The other swans to look for at this time of the year are the Bewick's swans, migrants from Siberia. You will need to plan your visit carefully to stand a chance of seeing these because, although sometimes using the brooks to rest and bathe during the day, they mainly exploit the flooding as a night-time roost. It is best to arrive early and station yourself at a good viewpoint, such as Nettley's or the Hanger, in order to see the herd leave the roost, which usually happens between approximately 7 am and, at the latest, 9 am. As an alternative, from about 4 pm onwards, watch for birds to fly into the roost. Be aware that there are other areas in the valley where the Bewick's roost and so they cannot be guaranteed to use Pulborough Brooks on any particular night. Overall totals fluctuate from winter to winter, up to the all-time maximum of 147. The adults are normally accompanied by varying numbers of dusky-grey immatures.

As far as geese are concerned, it would be surprising if there were not at least a few (and often very many more) greylag and Canada geese. Almost every year sees a small number (up to the mid-teens) of white-fronted geese, with January the most likely of the three months. Dark-bellied brent geese are abundant on nearby coasts and harbours but unusual here, although a very few have been noted in January in some years. The odd barnacle goose (of feral origin in the majority, if not all, cases) appears irregularly as do one or two Egyptian geese (definitely feral).

Of all the birds on North Brooks, it is the dabbling ducks that predominate. Early in the year, wigeon and teal can run into thousands and mallard, pintail and shoveler are counted in hundreds. Despite the onset of migration, substantial numbers of these ducks often remain in March. Gadwall are usually around, but in very low numbers. The most favourable time to look for a garganey is during April and May but some return from Africa much earlier and there is one record of a bird on 4 February, and others from the end of March.

Apart from the dabbling ducks, a handful of shelduck inhabit the brooks and occasionally one or two mandarin ducks may show themselves. A few diving ducks, mainly pochard and tufted duck, are often present and deep water, caused by exceptional flooding, brings in larger numbers particularly of the former. In January and February 2001 up to four individuals of another diving duck, the scaup, were here and goldeneye have visited in several years. Less common records are of a smew or two, and a male goosander, which was visible from Nettley's one day in January 2005.

Unusual ducks, varying in status from wild to escapes, include Carolina wood duck, an American wigeon (January 2002), a green-winged teal present for several days in February 2005, a ringed teal and a pochard x tufted duck hybrid. Another bird which has never been common is the ruddy duck and none has been recorded since 2002.

In addition to sparrowhawks, the most frequent birds of prey are kestrels and peregrines. These have a liking for perching in trees and so, as well as scanning the sky, it is always worth focussing your attention on the tall willows visible from the Hanger. Up to two common buzzards are possible and there is sometimes at least one merlin in residence. Hen harriers have been seen in each month but marsh harriers are very uncommon. February 2006 saw a red kite soaring over the Hanger and there was a further instance in the following month.

There have been one or two sightings of grey partridges on North Brooks and once, in March, a red-legged partridge was near Little Hanger. Pheasants are plentiful here, as is the case throughout the reserve.

Moorhens and coots are always on the brooks, sometimes rather a lot of them. If a water rail decides to emerge from cover (a notable event) it will almost always be near Nettley's, often in the ditch right under the front windows. Little Hanger has also produced a few records of this renowned skulker and they have been heard from Jupp's View.

The most abundant wader is, without doubt, the lapwing. Despite the increasing effects of migration back to where they will breed, for much of the period there will be at least several hundred and even later in March there can still be scores. As spring approaches, their song-flight display is a spectacle to look forward to with keen anticipation. Other wading birds occupy the brooks at various times, some more reliably and in greater numbers than others. In a few years, one or two oystercatchers and avocets, not regular Pulborough Brooks birds, have appeared. Annually, little ringed plovers start to arrive from mid-March, at a time when two or three ringed plovers may be occupying the same habitats. Golden plovers, hardly ever more than a handful, are difficult to locate on the ground but they seem to enjoy the company of lapwings and are much easier to recognise in the air when a mixed flock takes flight. Although, locally, coastal areas are the dependable places to look for grey plovers and sanderlings there were two of the former in March 2002, and a sanderling was reported from Little Hanger in January 2004. Another species that inhabits the same coastal and estuarine haunts, often in vast flocks, is the dunlin and here you will often find just a few searching for food on pool margins and mud.

A winter speciality of the reserve is the ruff and up to a dozen, sometimes more, are present quite regularly in most years. Snipe, from a few up to a score or so, are seen (more in some years than others) mainly from Nettley's but also from Little Hanger. Jack snipe will almost certainly be somewhere out on the brooks but are exceedingly difficult to see. The same can be said of woodcock, not least because of their generally solitary and crepuscular habits. Having said that, there have been woodcock sightings from Nettley's twice in March, a view of one in flight from the Hanger in January and, early one morning in the same month in 2006, one flew past Jupp's View.

Black-tailed godwits are often present in each month, but particularly February and March. Numbers are usually up to the mid-teens but in early

February 2007 there were over fifty, with almost as many at times in the following month. These totals were far surpassed in February 2008 when there were scores on many days with a maximum on 4th of about 235. The low counts of curlews, normally amounting to no more than one or two individuals each month (but not annually) was exceeded in 2006 when there were seven or eight birds throughout February and up until the middle of March.

During the quarter, common redshanks, scarce in the winter, start to return with a noticeable increase in March, when their calls become a feature of North Brooks. Recorded only in a few years, and then always in March, is the spotted redshank. Similarly less than annual are greenshanks (again always in March), green sandpipers (any month) and common sandpipers (February and March).

You will almost always come across gulls, some in flight and others on the ground. The most frequently encountered are black-headed gulls, many of them in breeding plumage by late February, and common gulls. Both species can be in flocks of well over a hundred. Very infrequently one or two individuals of other gull species turn up, with lesser black-backed, herring and great black-backed the most likely. A very few Mediterranean gulls have been recorded in each month, but not yearly. There have been sporadic sightings of single little gulls in this quarter, the most recent dating from between mid-February and mid-March 2007. A yellow-legged gull, a rare vagrant, was reported in January 2007.

A barn owl quartering the brooks can never be guaranteed although it is always worth scanning from the Hanger late in the day, or earlier if severe cold or very wet weather may have interfered with hunting during the preceding nights. More likely is the daytime sight of one or two short-eared owls hunting over the brooks, but only in those winters when there is a relatively high population of these birds in this country, and the meadows are supporting a profusion of small mammal food. Irrespective of population levels, little owls have never been very frequent on North Brooks, with only the odd sighting from the northern boundary.

Birds that winter in the area include fieldfares and redwings, liable to be seen in anything from small groups or large flocks, either on the brooks or around the Hanger, and bramblings, which have been observed, infrequently, near Nettley's, Little Hanger and Jupp's View. Goldcrests are a year-round feature and can be found regularly in the trees and bushes. On the other hand, the firecrest is primarily a winter bird at Pulborough Brooks and, probably in more years than not, one can be located, with patient searching, near Nettley's or Little Hanger or somewhere between the two. In a minority of years a few siskins have spent some time in the trees near Little Hanger and, almost equally infrequently, lesser redpolls are seen near Nettley's. In January 2003 a twite was reported, also in the vicinity of Nettley's.

The view from either of the hides can, with luck, include a kingfisher. Of the three months, January is the most preferred when one, or even two, birds appear from time to time. Grey wagtails, smart birds but not quite as colourful as the kingfisher, are scarce here but there have been a handful of sightings from the hides. These vantage points offer a chance of seeing stonechats, often a pair, perched on the top of vegetation (Little Hanger is, at times, particularly good for them, as is the Hanger). Likewise, reed buntings use the tops of stems as a lookout, and sometimes sing on the island in the pool outside Nettley's. One of the more surprising North Brooks events was when two ring-necked parakeets flew over in February 1992. However, this was far outshone by the bearded tit, which appeared outside Little Hanger in January 1999.

When in and around the hides keep your ears and eyes open for woodpeckers. Lesser spotted woodpeckers have been found several times in January in the trees near both hides but the odds of coming across one are slim. The prospects for great spotted woodpeckers are much better, with the whole of the wooded area between the two hides a promising habitat. In January the first drumming is heard, against a background of green woodpecker calls and wood pigeon sounds. To see a green woodpecker in this part of the reserve, try looking from Little Hanger onto the neighbouring grass.

March is the time to start searching the sky for the first returning hirundines. Whilst there is variability from year to year, sand martins, swallows and house martins tend to appear in ones and twos from about the middle of the month.

Further interest arises with the arrival of the first warblers, although there is on occasion room for discussion as to whether one or two of them may have stayed throughout the winter. Certainly, chiffchaffs have been observed near Nettley's and at the Hanger in January, but there is a noticeable increase of genuine migrants as March goes on, with song from at least the middle of the month and sometimes as early as late February. The trail between Nettley's and Little Hanger, including the Hanger, are the best places to look and listen. Blackcaps start to be noticed from late March, often around Nettley's and the Hanger. There can also be a few willow warblers in much the same places.

Other incoming migrants that have been spotted are a whinchat, from Nettley's on 20 March, a ring ouzel on 28 March, also from Nettley's, and a tree pipit on 27 March on the way to Little Hanger.

The mixture of habitats around the trail between Nettley's and Little Hanger - woodland, scrub, hedgerows and rough grassland - is excellent for a wide range of birds, many of which you will have already encountered at various points along the trail. As winter turns to spring the amount of song increases with wrens, robins, blackbirds, song thrushes and chaffinches amongst the more prominent voices. Of the several tit species to be heard and seen the small parties of long-tailed tits are as delightful as any. Treecreepers climb trees around Jupp's View, the Hanger and both hides, especially liking the large oak to the left of Little Hanger. Goldfinches and linnets are quite likely to be perched high in the trees but bullfinches, commonly up to three and occasionally as many as seven together, prefer the cover of the hedges and scrub.

Until 2006 perhaps the most desirable (for birdwatchers) bird to have been seen in this part of the reserve was the willow tit at Nettley's in January 2000. Then, extraordinarily, for the whole of January, February and up to 11 March 2006 a hawfinch (part of an influx to this country) took up temporary residence. It could be watched frequently between the Hanger and Little Hanger and, on 19 February, the hawfinch spectacle extended to the picnic area, where two males and a female were seen.

There is always the prospect of all sorts of bird sights and sounds in the course of a quiet amble through the picnic area between Nettley's and the Hanger. Dunnocks and other small birds like to forage in the bracken and under the tables. Wren and robin song and vigorous disputes between male blackbirds are early signs of the impending breeding season. Common calls are those of chaffinches and blue and great tits and, sometimes, you may hear a goldcrest or treecreeper. A chiffchaff, no doubt an overwintering individual, was here once in early February but this species can be reliably seen, and heard singing, in the nearby trees often as early as the beginning of March. Some blackcaps also spend the winter in this country, one being seen nearby in mid-January. There have been sporadic reports of blackcaps in March including one of a bird singing at the end of the first week. Pairs of bullfinches are frequently in the bushes and one of the roving flocks of goldfinches sometimes puts in an appearance.

One-off or scarce sightings in and around this picnic site include red-legged partridges (March), a woodcock (February), a barn owl (February), a willow tit (March), firecrests (February and March) and reed buntings (March).

The trail between Little Hanger and West Mead provides food and shelter for many birds, some residents, others seasonal visitors. Wrens, dunnocks and robins are typical inhabitants of the hedges and their songs and displays will be in evidence from early in the quarter. Another bird that sings long before spring is the skylark and the Winpenny region is a good place to listen. Chaffinch and great tit song can also be expected and, sometimes, that of goldfinches. It is just possible that you may hear a chiffchaff singing at the end of February but, in any case, you will be able to listen to them in March almost anywhere along this stretch of the trail.

As well as the time for chiffchaffs, late March is the occasion to start looking for other early migrants, the most likely on this part of the trail being blackcaps, of which there have been several in some years. There have been isolated occurrences of whinchat and, both near West Mead, wheatear and willow warbler. Winpenny was the location in March 2000 for a tree pipit.

Now and again, mainly in January and February, you may come across some of the wintering songbirds. Bramblings and lesser redpolls have favoured trees near West Mead and Winpenny and the latter has also been a site for siskins.

Members of the thrush family tend to be well represented. Especially in January there can be large numbers of blackbirds all around the trail, many probably winter visitors from abroad. At times they are seen harassing song thrushes attempting to feed by the path or in the adjoining fields. These fields are also feeding places for mistle thrushes and, at least until the middle of March and sometimes later, small flocks of fieldfares and redwings. If disturbed, the latter two seek sanctuary in the tops of the trees beyond Little Hanger and near West Mead. The same trees conceal jays, which fly out in alarm if approached too closely, and, exceptionally, great and lesser spotted woodpeckers. Nuthatches and treecreepers also make infrequent appearances.

The fields and meadows by the path are foraging areas for several species including carrion crows and their allies, the magpies, jackdaws and rooks. These are difficult to miss, unlike green woodpeckers which disappear into hollows and behind tussocks with surprising ease for such colourful birds. Noisy groups of starlings are rarely absent and they have formed flocks of over a thousand. In contrast, meadow pipits are unobtrusive but they are always around and there can be up to forty or so together.

January and February are the normal months for stonechats and they, usually a male and female, are often to be found perched on posts and wires anywhere between Little Hanger and West Mead. This is a favourite haunt in any month for parties of long-tailed tits, which move hurriedly through the hedgerows, calling as they go. Less conspicuous, but often present, are the goldcrests that search for food in the scrub. In several years, especially in January and February, the much less common firecrest has been seen in similar habitats, often near the hides. Bullfinches, at times as many as eight together, forage deep in the bushes, most reliably in the vicinity of West Mead. Yellowhammers, sometimes singing, are regularly observed along this section and small flocks of linnets add to the variety. You are most likely to see reed buntings from the hides, though one or two in the trailside vegetation are possible. They have been heard singing from the middle of February.

In many places away from the reserve, collared doves and house sparrows are relatively common. At Pulborough Brooks they are scarce and any appearances are cause for comment. One of the former was at the Pig Run (page 72) on a late March day and an individual of the latter strayed to the Winpenny area in the middle of February.

There have also been some remarkable sightings of birds which are very uncommon anywhere, not just at the reserve. In March 2003 a bittern was between Winpenny and West Mead and, astonishingly, in an earlier March, a stone-curlew was flushed from a meadow in the same area. It was to be nine years before another stone-curlew was located, again on this side of the reserve. January 1996 was the occasion on these meadows for one of the very rare visits of a great grey shrike and, ten years later, in the same month, there was a hawfinch (probably the same individual referred to earlier at North Brooks) near Redstart Corner.

Slight deviations from the trail will take you into the two hides, the first of which is Winpenny. Many of the species likely to be seen from this hide are the same as those from West Mead but, in a lot of cases, the views will be more distant. However, this is not always so and much depends on the prevailing conditions, especially water levels.

If the water in the pools is deep enough, or there is abnormal flooding, any of the West Mead dabbling ducks could be present, otherwise the most probable of the family are mallard and wigeon. Wigeon, maybe in hundreds, take advantage of the excellent grazing available on Mid and South Brooks and particularly enjoy cropping the riverbanks. A singular event for Winpenny was the presence of two goldeneye in January 1999.

Whooper swans are a reserve rarity but there are one or two December and January records, including one of a bird flying along the river in January 2006. Bewick's swans are not observed from here very often and are best looked for on North Brooks or from West Mead.

Some winters are very good for short-eared owls and among their daytime hunting areas are the meadows by the river. Winpenny is then the place to be to study their typically wavering flight as they patrol over the rough grassland, sometimes pausing to perch on a post.

Should a kingfisher decide to fish in this area (unfortunately not a happening that can be promised) then it is far more likely to be outside here than West Mead. The ditch running away from the windows on the southern side is a favourite location. Grey wagtails are very infrequent but have been seen from this hide in January.

Ospreys migrate over the reserve irregularly, in very small numbers, and then usually in the height of spring, or during the late summer. An exception was the bird spotted from Winpenny, flying north, late in March 2007.

Coming to West Mead, you will find that little grebes are fairly regular in most years, with March usually the most productive month. Only seldom, though, have great crested grebes visited. Cormorants are rarely reported from these brooks but you can expect a grey heron on almost any day. Little egrets, in ones and twos, are recorded from time to time and a vagrant cattle egret was here early in February 2007.

Most of the time, any swans you see will be mute swans, which are often around in small numbers. It is, however, advisable to be careful with swan identification because, in some years until about the middle of March, Bewick's swans spend a little time on the pool during the day. Greylag and Canada geese are far from uncommon and, in most years, there are a small number of white-fronted geese, often only staying for a short time and not necessarily easy to spot. A dark-bellied brent goose was at West Mead for one day in March 2004 and a pink-footed goose stayed for an equally short time in February 2008. Odd geese, probably feral or escapes, have included barnacles, Egyptians and a swan goose. In the same category, there has also been a black swan.

A few shelduck are possible but the majority of ducks will be wigeon and teal and, periodically, you can expect hundreds of each. Proving that even a wigeon is not necessarily exactly what it might seem at first glance was the appearance, in January 2006, of an American x Eurasian wigeon hybrid. Mallard also produce an array of hybrids but most of those on view will be the genuine purebred articles. Gadwall and shoveler should give less cause for confusion, as should pintail, although you would only expect the latter at times of deep water. A few pochard and, especially in March, tufted duck almost complete the cast of ducks, except for the goosander which was here in January 1999 (two goosanders were seen flying over in March 2002).

Both hides are good places from which to scan the sky for raptors. Annually, in each month, a lone hen harrier may drift across the landscape but marsh harriers are very infrequent. One or two sparrowhawks and kestrels are sighted daily and there is often a peregrine and, in some years, a merlin. Common buzzards, perhaps soaring above the distant hills, are not unusual. A red kite was over the brooks one day in February 2005 and again in March the next year.

You can expect to see several moorhens and coots but skulking water rails are much more of a problem although, every now and then, they have shown themselves in the ditches around West Mead.

A nice surprise in March would be a wader returning from the south earlier than average, a role that has occasionally been filled late in the month by little ringed plovers and wood sandpipers. Over-wintering golden plovers are usually in low figures, while lapwing numbers gradually decrease from a high of several hundred as the weeks go by. In some years, there have been a few dunlins in each month. Ruff counts are variable, up to about twenty, with January and February often the most prolific times. Skulking jack snipe are known to be on the brooks but they are very rarely seen, other than when flushed by people working out on the meadows. In comparison, common snipe are comparatively simple to see, although they hide amongst dead rushes with accomplished ease, with West Mead producing considerably more sightings than Winpenny. Towards the end of the quarter the cries of redshanks start to be heard again and you will probably see several individuals. Less frequent waders include woodcocks and curlews (both recorded very sporadically in the odd January and February), uncommon January instances of greenshanks and green sandpipers and, in February, common sandpipers. Black-tailed godwits are also irregular on this part of the brooks but, occasionally, there have over 40.

From time to time common gulls are numerous, otherwise black-headed gulls are the most abundant of the gulls. Very random visitors have been lesser black-backed, herring and great black-backed gulls.

There is the probability that green woodpeckers and pied wagtails will be feeding on the ground not far from the hide and a careful look through binoculars into the middle distance may reveal a stonechat, alternating between perching on top of a stem and dropping down to pick up food. Not surprisingly, the bird that often occurs in the greatest numbers is the wood pigeon, which typically gathers in large flocks.

In February and March there is an outside possibility of seeing a water pipit from West Mead, one or two having turned up here, just for a few days, in several years. Much more certain amongst the migrants are sand martins, a very small number of which are noted in many years from about the middle of March. One of the reserve's infrequent stopovers by a ring ouzel on passage was at West Mead late in March 1998.

Barn and little owl sightings are very uncommon but cannot be entirely discounted. Nevertheless, they are rather more probable than any repeats of the red-throated diver of February 1996 and the March 2001 spoonbill.

In the time since you left the visitor centre it may well be that the mix of birds which you saw on the outward walk will have changed. For that reason it is prudent, unless you are short of time or desperate for a hot drink in the tearoom, to pause again at Fattengates and then complete the circuit with a leisurely stroll back up the hill, birding as you go.

North Brooks in spring

The nature trail in spring

Robin

Grey Heron

Song Thrush

Reed Bunting

Chaffinch

Tufted Duck

Black-headed Gull

Coot with chicks

Blue Tit at the feeding station

Redshank

Blackbird

Linnet

Moorhen

Wren

April to June

This is the quarter when the summer migrants arrive in force, some staying to breed, others just pausing for a few hours or days on journeys which will take them to nesting places a great deal further north. Although most of the winter visitors will have departed, some may still be around, the precise numbers and species depending on a diversity of factors. Above all, it is the time when song is at its peak and you will hear an enormous range of bird voices that change as the habitat, and the birds which make it their home, varies from woodland to grassland, from hedgerows to wetland and so on. Breeding gets to be the birds' main concern and as time progresses the sight of parents taking food to their nests and fledglings becomes common, as do the insistent calls of the youngsters. As midsummer approaches the songs of many species diminish, to the disappointment of anyone who did not make the most of birdsong earlier in the season.

If you have arrived by car it is sensible to watch from inside the vehicle for a time, especially when there is not a lot of human activity. Birds are not disturbed by people sitting quietly inside parked cars and many, including mistle thrushes (perhaps with juveniles) and chaffinches, will come close to cars while searching for food and others, like robins, perform courtship and threat displays unaware of the occupants sitting close by. It is also a frequent event for robins and other birds to perch on wing mirrors in the hope of receiving a few crumbs. Watch, too, for birds flitting around in the trees and bushes near where you are parked.

A gentle stroll around the car park can be very rewarding, especially for birdsong. Warblers arrive during the first part of the quarter and several species sing in this vicinity. Probably the most certain to be heard is the chiffchaff but the scratchy song of the whitethroat is also almost assured from the bushes along the road towards the visitor centre. Blackcaps and garden warblers sing from trees close to the car park and can often be located and watched fairly easily. April is a particularly good time to listen for singing willow warblers and, although they are more plentiful in some years than others, they have sometimes sung from the birch trees that border the grass on the northern side of the entrance road.

Incongruous though it may seem, the car park is often the first place that you will hear the sought-after song of the nightingale. Admittedly, this may be in the distance, although individuals have been known to pour out their songs far closer, from the bushes right by the main entrance gate, in competition with the noise of traffic on the main road.

There are many other birds to hear and, even if you are unable to identify all of them, the songs will give enormous pleasure. During your circuit of the car park you are almost certain to hear wrens, robins, dunnocks and chaffinches, with blackbirds and song thrushes being moderately dependable performers. The songs and calls of tits, mainly coal, blue and great, are a constant element augmented, from time to time, by the twittering of goldfinches. In the background, the gentle sounds of wood pigeons are often accompanied by the distant calls of rooks. More strident noises come from pheasants, which you will meet all around the reserve. About the middle of April, listen and look for the first cuckoo of the year.

The drumming of great spotted woodpeckers is a feature of spring and, with a little patience, you may be able to see one hammering away, perhaps on a bough of a large oak. They also reveal their presence by short, sharp calls. You are much less likely to come across a lesser spotted woodpecker, but they have been seen around the car park at this time of the year. If you arrive early in the day, you will probably disturb a green woodpecker or two from their foraging on the grassy borders of the entrance road. If you are around *really* early, at first light, there is the chance of hearing a tawny owl hooting from the adjacent woodland, and a barn owl hunting by the roadside cannot be entirely ruled out.

The crow family is well represented by rooks, which sometimes feed their young by the wayside, jays, magpies, jackdaws, and carrion crows. On the heels of the unexpected sighting of ravens in March 2007 another was located nearby during the following June and one flew over the visitor centre in April 2008. Other users of the car park include pied wagtails and the occasional marsh tit and yellowhammer. You will probably locate bullfinches in the bushes and, in the trees, nuthatches (often very vocal) and treecreepers, by their calls.

In addition to the warblers, other summer migrants which have visited here, albeit very rarely, are redstarts and spotted flycatchers (one of the latter was perched on the roof of the visitor centre on a late April day). A few winter visitors, such as bramblings and siskins, could still be around in early April and it was in that month a few years ago that one of the reserve's scarcer breeding species, the red-legged partridge, was glimpsed in this area.

Your attention may be drawn to the sky by the sound of birds passing above, such as a noisily honking flock of Canada geese but, in any case, keep an eye on what may be happening overhead. Circling common buzzards are possible or even one of the infrequent, but almost certainly increasing, red kites. There is also the prospect of a soaring sparrowhawk although this species is most likely to be seen swooping through the trees in its quest for small birds.

The courtyard feeding station draws in large numbers of birds, some to hang on the feeders, others to eat food scattered on the ground. A lot are typical of many gardens - pied wagtails, wrens, dunnocks, robins, blackbirds, coal, blue and great tits, chaffinches, greenfinches and, occasionally, goldfinches. Occurring less usually in the average garden are the pheasants, strutting around pecking at the ground, moorhens scuttling back and forth from the pond and great spotted woodpeckers and nuthatches visiting from the woods for nuts and seeds. Marsh tits, occasionally accompanied by young, sometimes use the feeders. Less than annually, a few siskins and bramblings remain to feed in April. There are two April records of reed buntings and also one of a passing merlin. Even some of the summer visitors like nightingales and blackcaps have been seen in the surrounding bushes but they are more likely to be heard singing from outside the confines of the courtyard.

If you listen at dusk in the late spring and summer it is just possible that you may hear the distant churring of a nightjar. Happily, the prospects of seeing and hearing these strange birds around the car park and visitor centre are increasing as the result of the ongoing work to restore heathland.

Every spring and summer, visitors see a wide variety of birds from the visitor centre windows, the tea terrace and the viewpoint next to the nature trail door. Shelduck sometimes fly around the wood on the left of the field and, once in a while, there have been mandarin ducks in the same area. Less exotically, a mallard or two may be on the pond just in front of the main windows. The pond is also a breeding place for moorhens.

The extensive view of the sky gives a good opportunity for locating any birds of prey that may be around. There is a chance of sparrowhawks, at least one or two common buzzards, kestrels and, usually from mid-April, hobbies. An occasional peregrine is possible and, on a day in May, a lucky observer was looking out at just the right moment to see an osprey. There has been just one sighting (in April) of a marsh harrier.

The airspace is also home to swifts, which can return as early as late April but generally arrive in the middle of May, and sand martins, swallows and house martins, which start to appear in the latter part of March. It is exciting to scan the sky both here and as you walk around the reserve for these signs of spring.

You can seek other summer visitors in the immediate surroundings of the centre. Whitethroats are never far away and have bred in brambles right outside the main window, so it is not unusual to see one perched and singing on the gorse or scrub. In May you will often need to go no further than the door to the nature trail to hear a nightingale singing from fairly close by. Lesser whitethroats, garden warblers and blackcaps have also been found close to the building and a spotted flycatcher was near the tea terrace once in June.

In April, spend some time searching Upperton's Field through binoculars just in case there are any migrant wheatears. At the same time, check for anything else of special interest, bearing in mind that the field has, every now and then, been a brief stopping point for whimbrels, whinchats and yellow wagtails. From early April, listen for the cuckoo and watch for one in flight or perched on a fence post.

Tempting though it can be to concentrate on birds newly arrived in this country, there is still the prospect of coming across the last of the winter visitors. Although most fieldfares leave in early April, a score or so sometimes feed on Upperton's Field during the month. In some years a few siskins, lesser redpolls and common crossbills remain in the area during April.

Of the resident birds, some are often present in large numbers, notably the wood pigeons, jackdaws, rooks and carrion crows that gather on the field. Also feeding there can be a flock of starlings and a few stock doves, as well as goldfinches, linnets and yellowhammers. A rarity is the house sparrow, but one or two do find their way close to the building. Another scarce bird, the red-legged partridge, has very occasionally been visible from the window.

In past years, the solitary oak tree at the foot of the field has been a regular breeding place for little owls but, as mentioned in the previous chapter, there has recently been a marked reduction in numbers, at least locally, and they did not nest in 2008. Hopefully, at some time in the future, they will again use this site when there should be, throughout the quarter, the opportunity of seeing one, perhaps two, of the owls perched on the tree or an adjacent fence post. There would once more be the hope in June of seeing juveniles as well. When circumstances are favourable, the large window in the visitor centre is an ideal little owl viewpoint, particularly if advantage is taken of one of the telescopes provided for visitors to use.

Barn owls are also quite regular breeders hereabouts, sometimes using a nestbox at the far end of the field or, more often, a box located in the roof of the visitor centre. When barn owls breed in one of these places you are likely, by standing in the car park or the first portion of the nature trail (where you will not cause disturbance to the birds), to see the adults flying to and from the nest at dawn and dusk. Whenever possible, live CCTV pictures of nesting barn owls are transmitted to a screen in the visitor centre. If a box in the roof is unoccupied by barn owls, a corner of its cavernous space is often used by relatively tiny pied wagtails to build their nest.

The main window is also a place from which to look for great spotted woodpeckers in the trees around the field and for green woodpeckers feeding on the ground. The trees near the tea terrace are occasionally places in which to find nuthatches and treecreepers. Probably the most unusual sighting from the visitor centre was the Sandwich tern that flew over in May 1998.

Your walk down the hill will be memorable for the number of different species singing. At the start of the quarter some, like wrens, dunnocks, robins, blackbirds and song thrushes will already be in full voice but others will not join them until later. A good example is the nightingale, which does not sing until mid-April but from then its loud and extraordinarily varied utterances can be heard from near and far, both by day and night. The amount of song from nightingales, in common with some other birds, tends to diminish significantly after a few short weeks.

As April progresses, an increasing number of warblers commence singing and this part of the trail is a wonderful place to hear and see some of them. Whitethroats are a certainty all the way from the visitor centre and lesser whitethroats, though fewer, also occur on this section. Garden warblers are heard, as are blackcaps, with the latter probably the easier to see, especially when they sing from the tops of the dead elms. In June, these same trees are places where, every so often, swallows choose to feed their fledglings. The unmistakable notes of chiffchaffs sound from almost everywhere and, in some years, there are willow warblers here. Much less usual was the grasshopper warbler, observed by the zigzag path in early May 2002, exactly the same time as one sang, for a tantalisingly short spell, from over in Upperton's Field in 2007.

Another summer visitor, the spotted flycatcher, most likely to be seen on autumn passage, is in decline as a breeding bird both at Pulborough Brooks and nationally. Despite that, there have been a few May sightings on the path from the visitor centre and, in 2005, one was noticed carrying nesting material. There has been a single example of a pied flycatcher, also in May.

You are bound to see and hear the great tits and blue tits inhabiting the trees and bushes by the path and also the small family parties of long-tailed tits that occasionally flit through the branches. Normally easy to see while singing, often from prominent perches such as the dead trees near the corner, are chaffinches, greenfinches, linnets and yellowhammers. A very small number of lesser redpolls and common crossbills are infrequent April visitors to the nearby trees. The bushes beneath always hide one or two bullfinches although these are often difficult to see.

The path and its wide, grassy, borders are good feeding places for quite a few birds and you will possibly come across pheasants, wood pigeons, pied wagtails, mistle thrushes, magpies, carrion crows and green woodpeckers. The calls of great spotted woodpeckers float across from the distant trees and, from time to time, one may fly over in typically undulating fashion.

As always, it is wise to keep an eye on the sky, not only for swifts and swallows but also for birds of prey. Common buzzards, kestrels and hobbies are possibilities and, very occasionally, even a red kite or two. Uniquely, in June 1993 a very rare vagrant red-footed falcon was perched on a tree guard in the hedge.

During an evening visit, if you are really lucky, you stand a chance of seeing a barn owl hunting over the rough grass towards the church.

To an extent, the birds at Fattengates continue the theme established on the walk so far. Wood pigeons feed and coo, green woodpeckers call and search for ants, whilst wrens, dunnocks, robins, blackbirds, song thrushes, blue and great tits, chaffinches and greenfinches sing. The warblers are again represented by lesser whitethroats, whitethroats (which are plentiful and sing from, amongst other places, the birches by the path), garden warblers, blackcaps, chiffchaffs and, occasionally, willow warblers.

The variety of trees in the vicinity, while not great in quantity, encourage a few of the birds that live in and around woodland. A tawny owl has now and again been visible from the path, roosting in the conifer plantation. The same trees attract goldcrests, whose thin songs often drift over on the breeze. There are occasional sightings of great spotted woodpeckers in the deciduous trees, and there have been very rare reports, in April and June, of their lesser spotted cousin. There can be nuthatches, often very vocal, high in the trees and, less frequently, you may happen upon a treecreeper climbing a trunk. This is a good site for bullfinches, with always up to two. Just as with all the other breeding birds, they will almost certainly be accompanied by young in the later part of the quarter.

Another feature here is the pond, which usually has a moorhen or two and sometimes mallard. There are a few April records of mandarin ducks and an isolated one of a rather unexpected kingfisher. When looking at the pond, listen in case a lapwing is calling over Upperton's Field behind you, or there is the distant sound of a cuckoo.

The undoubted high spot of Fattengates at this time of the year is the song of nightingales. Not only can singing be heard extremely well here but also it is among the best places on the reserve to try to see one of these elusive creatures. In May, if a nightingale decides to break cover and sing in the open, the dead branches between the pond and the 'no entry' gate to the plantation are favourite perches. Otherwise, turn right at the junction immediately past the pond and try to find a singing bird in the tangled branches under the trees. By June, adults will be feeding their young and this can give another opportunity of catching a glimpse of a nightingale, although by late in the month song will have diminished to a few isolated phrases.

Siskins and common crossbills have been seen in April but they are rare and far from annual. Fattengates also has one-off records of an April redstart and of a pied flycatcher in May.

After Fattengates, the green lane gives opportunities for listening again to songs already heard, or catching up on others that you may have missed. You could well come across wrens, dunnocks, robins, blackbirds, song thrushes, lesser whitethroats and possibly willow warblers. In the unlikely event that you have not, so far, heard a chiffchaff it is as certain as anything that there will be at least one singing from the trees by the fork, just beyond the cattle gates, with a blackcap also a real prospect.

The sounds of long-tailed tits from high in the oaks may attract your attention and, at the end of May, they could have fledglings with them. Great and blue tits also search for food amongst the leaves and, although the foliage may deny you a view of them, chaffinches, greenfinches and goldfinches are probable songsters. Vocally considerably less accomplished are the bullfinches that inhabit the thick hedgerows on either side of the path.

Jackdaws, rooks and carrion crows feed in the fields, where there can still be a few migrating fieldfares and redwings early in April. A less than usual bird by the lane was a spotted flycatcher in May 2005, although the rarity prize for this part of the reserve must surely be awarded to the black stork, which flew over early in May 1998.

The seasonal sounds of wood pigeons, cuckoos, green woodpeckers, wrens, robins, blackbirds, song thrushes, garden warblers, blackcaps, goldcrests, blue tits, great tits, jays and chaffinches are all features of Hanger Wood. A different, non-woodland, call drifting up from the brooks could be that of the redshank, and this should whet your appetite for what is in store when you reach North Brooks.

On the way down the slope you may see treecreepers, which breed here, climbing up a trunk or along a branch. Other breeders have included tawny owls (juveniles were seen in 1995 and 1999) and marsh tits. The turtle dove is, sadly, a bird in severe national decline and it no longer breeds at the reserve, although it has been seen on three or four occasions in this area. Other uncommon sightings have been pied flycatchers (April) and up to two spotted flycatchers.

Wetland birds on North Brooks range from those that are resident all the while during the quarter, through others on passage and only around for a short time to, now and again, some of the rarer species. The presence of some birds depends on factors such as water levels, which vary according to the weather. The dates of arrival and departure of passage waders is affected by a variety of external causes.

The great crested grebe is a scarce bird here and so the presence of two in April 2007 was something of a surprise. On the other hand, little grebes, usually no more than one or two (there have, exceptionally, been five on the same day) are sometimes to be seen, diving in any deep water that has formed or in the ditches. At the other end of the size scale, a few cormorants like to idle their time away on low banks between the pools. Grey herons, up to ten but normally fewer, patiently hunt for food, standing so still that they can be difficult to spot, especially when they stand in ditches with no more than heads and necks visible.

On some days up to eight little egrets, rarities in the UK until recent years, can be seen, and a vagrant cattle egret was here in May 2007. Still a very rare vagrant, a night heron was feeding on these brooks in April 1992. Another rare, but possibly increasing, visitor to this country (there was successful breeding in the UK in 1999 and 2008) is the spoonbill and individuals have been on this part of the reserve in April 1995 and 1996, May 2002 and for much of May and June 2006, when there were up to three. In 2008, a spoonbill was present for about a week from the end of May.

The ever-present mute swans, sometimes over twenty, are usually prominent and, if they have bred successfully, there will be cygnets. Greylag and Canada geese also breed in many years and may be parading their goslings in view of the hides. As is the case throughout the year, almost any feral or escaped swan, duck or goose can turn up. In some years, one or two barnacle geese appear, as do Egyptian geese. A bar-headed goose was seen in April 2004 and ruddy shelducks (presumed feral) were on site for most of April 1995 and at the end of May 2006. Similarly, a red-crested pochard has paid a brief visit.

Shelduck, anything up to thirty or so, are easy to see and may have ducklings. Mandarin ducks, often no more than one or two are, in contrast, difficult to observe but also breed in some years, when a family may be seen out on the water or, more probably, hidden closer to the shore amongst the long vegetation. In April, a variable number of wigeon, from a few score to perhaps two hundred, remain from the winter thousands, although numbers drop very quickly through the month as the majority fly away to breed. Every so often a very few stay for the summer and these have been known to nest. Teal show similar trends and, of the small numbers that remain, a few pairs usually raise young. There can be up to sixty mallard and you will see their ducklings in each month. Of the other ducks that winter at the reserve, shoveler can still number about one hundred in April and thereafter a few are around each month. Only up to half-a-dozen pintail are likely in April with, on the odd occasion, a singleton remaining in the subsequent months. You will see no more than about six gadwall, which are only irregular breeders. Pochard and tufted duck both require deep water in which to dive for food and are therefore uncommon in the spring and summer. Nevertheless, a few of both species have been seen in April and May and tufted ducks were observed with a brood on North Brooks in 2002. For much of April 2006 a scaup, which is a rare visitor, was in temporary residence. Ruddy ducks have not been seen since 2001, when two were attracted by deep flooding. April and May have produced scarce sightings of single goosander on passage.

The duck that many birdwatchers hope to see is the garganey, which sometimes stays in very small numbers to breed but, more often, is just a temporary visitor on migration from Africa. The beginning of April is the time to start looking in earnest (there is a very early record of one on the second day of February) even though in some years they do not arrive until the end of April and well into May. Whilst there have been as many as five together, it is safer not to expect more than one or two at a time.

The brooks provide good feeding and breeding habitat for moorhens and coots. You will always see at least a few and, at times, numbers of both can rise into the thirties. On the other hand, the water rails that live here are seen only extremely infrequently.

The sightings of the very rare vagrant common crane that had commenced at the end of March 2007 continued into April, when this large bird was clearly visible on several days. Even more excitingly, on one day there were two individuals. These events were to be broadly repeated in 2008, when views of two individuals in early April and two circling in the sky one day in the middle of May followed confirmed reports of birds in March. June of the same year saw a brief visit by a white stork.

The potential for wading birds is great, and the more frequently you are able to visit, the more species you are likely to be able to add to your tally. Oystercatchers are not everyday waders here but up to two have occurred in several years, including 2001 when a pair nested near to the reserve. An even less frequent visitor is the black-winged stilt, which came for a few days in April 2005. Also unusual, and continuing the black-and-white theme, was an avocet's brief appearance in April 2005. This was destined to be repeated in the following April and in early June 2007.

Little ringed plovers are seen mainly in April and May and less often in June, with generally two or three at a time, rising at most to six or so.

Ringed plovers also appear but they are much more irregular than their close relation. Two other plovers, which are very infrequent, are the golden plover, recorded no more than once in May and June, and the grey plover of which an occasional one or two are seen during the quarter. You are certain to see and hear the lapwings that breed on the meadows. Only a few, some with young, will be present until June when the wintering population starts to build and numbers can increase to over 100. Rarities for the reserve were the little stint (classified as a rare passage migrant) in May 2001 and, even rarer, the three Temminck's stints (very rare passage migrants) here in early May 2008 and the pectoral sandpiper (a very rare vagrant) which dropped in right at the end of June 2002. Only marginally less uncommon were the three curlew sandpipers, present for a couple of days in May 1996, and the two that followed in May 2007.

April and May are good months to see dunlin and there can be ten or more, though usually less. Ruff cannot be relied on with the same certainty but normally a few can be seen, at least in the first two months. This is not the best time of the year to see snipe, with just a few visible in April. That is also the month of this quarter's only jack snipe record.

You should, with luck, be able to find a black-tailed godwit or two because, in these three months in most years, there can be sightings of anything from singles to handfuls and once, late one May, an incredible 40. Some individuals may be in their striking breeding plumage. Bar-tailed godwits are much scarcer with the only records being of odd birds in May 2000, 2001 and 2006. Another of the larger waders, the whimbrel, is likely to pass through in small numbers from mid-April. Its confusion species, the curlew, is an almost yearly visitor to North Brooks and has been seen, however briefly, in each month.

Redshanks, often in good numbers, are always to be seen and heard and several pairs breed in the majority of years, so look out for the chicks. The migratory spotted redshank uses the brooks in most years to break its journey, almost always in April and May. Although there are seldom more than one or two, they may, if you are fortunate, be in their stunning summer plumage.

Also on the move are several other waders. In some years the best month for greenshanks is June, in others April, although they often appear in each month, and there have been up to eleven on the same day. Green sandpipers are seen at much the same times, in smaller numbers and often from Little Hanger as well as Nettley's. Another regular visitor, predominantly in May, also in April and June, is the common sandpiper, typically alone, exceptionally up to three. The wood sandpiper does not come here every year but has been seen in each month of the quarter. Briefly in May 1995, and again in early June 2007, birdwatchers had the opportunity of seeing a turnstone, a wader that would more typically be expected on the coast.

The most usual gull is the black-headed gull, the handful that normally loafs far out on the brooks occasionally increasing to several score. A change takes place with the passing weeks as they gradually acquire the dark heads that are in the minority at the beginning of the period. Common gulls are anything but common, with only an occasional one or two. Lesser black-backed gulls are also infrequent, though not quite as scarce as herring gulls. In some years a little gull, usually alone, sometimes two or more, may drop in for a short stay. This is the norm and so it was remarkable in 1993 to have three little gulls in residence between April and July. Early in April 2007, there was one of the very few visits by Mediterranean gulls when two birds were present for a day. A few days later two very rare vagrant yellow-legged gulls flew in for a few hours.

Springtime, especially April, used to be the time when there was at least a prospect of black terns but none was seen from 1998 until the long barren spell was broken by the welcome appearance of two individuals in early May 2008. An isolated occurrence was the presence of a common tern in April and May 1999.

Wildfowl, waders and gulls are not the only birds that use the pools and meadows and a scan around may reveal several other species. Readily visible are wood pigeons, stock doves, rooks, carrion crows and starlings, all on the lookout for food. Early morning, especially from mid-April and during May, is a good time to search for cuckoos, which have a tendency to perch on posts while looking for nests in which to lay their eggs. The same time of day, and the evening too, in May and June, can yield views of a hunting barn owl. This is not the best time to hope for a kingfisher but, very infrequently, one is glimpsed outside Nettley's. Almost whenever you look there will be pied wagtails flitting across the mud in pursuit of insects and, in April 2008, there was a white wagtail. In June, flocks of goldfinches move around looking for seeds. The reed buntings that breed out in the tussocky places show themselves periodically, usually when perched on the top of a plant. The corn bunting is no longer a breeding bird, which is the same sad story of so many other places, and was last heard singing in 1990 on the far side of North Brooks.

As well as the passage waders, other birds make a temporary stop on the brooks during migration, none of them in large numbers. Yellow wagtails are seen, if at all, in April and May, except in those years in which a pair or two stay to breed when, of course, they may also be seen in June. Whinchats, which have bred very irregularly in the vicinity, pass through intermittently in April and May. Wheatears are more reliable, normally moving through in April or early May and most often visible from Little Hanger. Excitingly, in May 1998, there was a red-backed shrike in one of the meadows.

The skies over the brooks offer a fair selection of birds of prey, some more common and frequent than others. In May 2002 there was a honey buzzard, and red kites have been observed sporadically in each month. Marsh and hen harriers are rare, and even more so was the Montagu's harrier of May 1999. Sparrowhawks and kestrels are widespread, common buzzards (sometimes several) are in the sky from time to time and, sooner or later, a peregrine can be expected. Ospreys fly along the line of the river on migration, so in the spring it can pay to keep an eye in that direction and, indeed, also somewhat closer in case of a repeat of the incident on one April evening when an osprey flew directly over North Brooks. Normally, any wintering merlins will have departed and there are only outside odds of finding one in April or May. By late April, the hobbies will be arriving and from then it is usual to see up to four and occasionally more. While concentrating on the sky it is, on most days, impossible to miss the displays of aerial hunting performed by swifts, sand martins, swallows and house martins, potentially in flocks of a hundred or more.

The trees, bushes and open spaces around the hides and viewpoints offer prospects for adding many more birds to your North Brooks' list, including an almost certain six warblers (and there have been more). You will be very unlikely to have come across a sedge warbler so far on your walk but, from early in April, there is every prospect of finding one, or even two, singing and visible right outside Nettley's. Jupp's View, the Hanger and Little Hanger are other nearby places to look and listen for sedge warblers. There is normally not too much danger here of confusing their song with that of the reed warbler, which breeds in comparatively low numbers on parts of the reserve remote from the nature trail. Very infrequently, though, a reed warbler is seen near Little Hanger. The Hanger, and to a lesser extent, Little Hanger, are locations to listen for lesser whitethroats in April and May. Those, plus Nettley's, are also excellent spots to hear whitethroats. April and May are good times to stand at the Hanger or near Nettley's to listen to, and practice separating, the similar songs of garden warblers and blackcaps. There is no mistaking the chiffchaff's song, which is heard over the entire Nettley's and Hanger region from the start of April to the middle of June. At the Hanger it is not unusual for a chiffchaff to sing from the branches right above your head. Willow warblers are less common, although you may come upon one in April between Nettley's and Little Hanger. Not many wood warblers pass through on spring migration but the odd few have been reported in April and early May from Nettley's, the Hanger and Little Hanger, including two instances of singing. In several years, lone grasshopper warblers have been seen and heard on North Brooks during June but they qualify as very scare visitors.

The vicinity of the hides is another place where, on a couple of occasions in May, turtle doves have been seen. The trees in the region of both hides are used by great spotted woodpeckers and, very rarely, lesser spotted woodpeckers. Nettley's has been the location for a very few sightings of the tree pipit, another scarce bird. Towards the end of May 2007, a spotted flycatcher was singing at Jupp's View.

The area around the Hanger and towards Little Hanger is splendid habitat for nightingales and at times, until the beginning of June, their loud voices are often on the verge of drowning out the songs of wrens, robins, song thrushes, whitethroats, garden warblers, blackcaps, chiffchaffs and chaffinches, amongst others. Long-tailed tits seem to like the trees in the neighbourhood of the Hanger and similarly Little Hanger, where there may occasionally also be a stonechat perched on the vegetation. Goldcrests are, every now and then, seen and heard singing near Nettley's and at the Hanger. The environs of both hides and the Hanger have, almost annually, been the temporary location for spotted flycatchers in each month. Pied flycatchers only occur infrequently. Trees near the hides provide feeding opportunities for nuthatches and treecreepers, whereas bullfinches prefer the thick cover beneath. Very rarely a yellowhammer has been seen near Nettley's and, equally rarely, marsh tits have appeared near Little Hanger. In 2006, the slope below the Hanger was the venue for the conclusion of the astonishing influx of hawfinches, which continued from the preceding months. Up to five individuals were at the Hanger in the first days of April, until the final sighting on 11 April.

The picnic area, in the glade above Nettley's, is a pleasant place to sit for a while to listen for blackcaps, bullfinches, garden warblers, whitethroats and lesser whitethroats. There is the possibility of a willow warbler and, once in May, a couple of tawny owls were there. In April 2006 a firecrest was a temporary resident in the surrounding area. Probably the picnic area's most outstanding event was the visit by a golden oriel in June 1995.

Continuing the quarter's dominant theme of birdsong, the walk between Little Hanger and West Mead gives further opportunities to hear a variety of songs and sounds. It is worthwhile making a short diversion to the right, down the public footpath (the area known as the 'Pig Run') which crosses the nature trail at the gate by the turn-off to Little Hanger, and leads eventually to the river. From the brambles low on the track's bank a sedge warbler sometimes sings in full view, rising and falling in its brief display flight. The song of a garden warbler may be easily traced to the higher scrub, where the performer will often remain concealed. Almost certainly, you will hear whitethroats, chiffchaffs, dunnocks, greenfinches and, hopefully, a willow warbler. Watch out, too, for a cuckoo and, infrequently, a reed warbler.

In 1991, there were two outstanding sightings in this locality. Late in May, an alert and observant birdwatcher noticed in the distance a bird constantly dropping from a post in pursuit of invertebrates. It took him but a moment's inspection through binoculars to realise that he had found the reserve's first and only woodchat shrike. A few days into the following month, one of Pulborough Brooks' scarce, vagrant, hoopoes was by the side of a nearby ditch.

Retracing your steps from the gate at the bottom of the track, you rejoin the nature trail.

The first section heading towards Winpenny gives another opportunity to hear some of the sounds from the Pig Run, although rather distantly. It is also another favoured site for singing nightingales, and sometimes a lesser whitethroat's distinctive rattling song is heard. The field to the left of the path is much used by green woodpeckers, magpies, jackdaws, rooks, carrion crows and noisy family parties of starlings. Sometimes a song thrush feeds near the hedge.

All the way to West Mead the hedges and low trees help to support populations of wrens, dunnocks, robins, whitethroats, long-tailed, blue and great tits, chaffinches, greenfinches and reed buntings. Much of this stretch of the trail is good for yellowhammers, which sing their characteristic ditty from towards the tops of the trees. Situated, as you now are, adjacent to Mid and South Brooks, and under the flight path from there to North Brooks, it is not surprising that the calls of wetland birds like grey herons, shelducks, lapwings and redshanks are frequently heard from afar or overhead.

Periodically, passage migrant whinchats, definitely not an everyday bird, are seen near Winpenny. A house sparrow, even less common at Pulborough Brooks, was found near Winpenny once in April. Stonechats, occasionally with juveniles, are regulars, both there and near West Mead. Over the years, the trail near both Winpenny and West Mead has been the location for a small number of red-backed shrikes (very rare vagrants). Spotted flycatchers were, on one June day only, in the trees near West Mead. Some of the irregular appearances by grasshopper warblers have been in April, near the hides. In late May 1997 there was not only one rare and thrilling golden oriel close to West Mead but also another near Winpenny.

A point midway between Winpenny and Redstart Corner has, in some years, been another place to hear and see a sedge warbler. Redstart Corner itself is worth checking for goldfinches, linnets and reed buntings. August and September is really the time to expect redstarts but there was an isolated visit in April and May in one year. April is also the month from which there are a couple of tree pipit records, and in the middle of May 1993, one was singing on South Brooks. There is the slight potential in April for coming across a wheatear on grassland in this part of the reserve and West Mead was, on a single occasion, the location for a ring ouzel.

Of the two hides, West Mead will probably be the most productive for birds, especially if the nearby pool is holding a substantial amount of water. Of the many species that can potentially be seen from both hides, a lot are usually more frequent, and easier to watch, at West Mead and so, to avoid repetition, they are dealt with later, in reference to that hide.

Winpenny provides an alternative perspective of Mid and South Brooks and is also close to the river Arun. Although, due to the high banks, the river cannot be seen it is the route followed in flight by some unusual (for the reserve) birds such as the common terns seen once in April and once in June and the solitary little terns that have occurred in April and May. Equally rare are Sandwich terns, though there have been very sporadic April and May sightings of singletons. Ospreys also favour the river on passage and have appeared, very occasionally, in May.

Good views of waders depend on the amount of water and exposed mud in front of the hide and whether the narrow strip of water towards the nearest part of the riverbank can be seen through the vegetation. In any case, the opportunities are usually better from West Mead. This having been said, Winpenny has a major claim to wader fame with the distant views of a stone-curlew in April 2007.

In June 2007, the unusual sightings of ravens, which started in March, continued with observations on two days of a bird over South Brooks (another had flown over North Brooks at the end of May).

The likelihood of encountering a kingfisher is not great in this quarter but Winpenny, in May or June, offers as good an opportunity as anywhere.

At West Mead pool, little grebes have become familiar birds in recent years and, moreover, they bred here for the first time in 2002. Increasingly evident, too, are little egrets, with sometimes several out on the meadows. Almost always, a scan over the brooks will reveal a few grey herons, mute swans and greylag and Canada geese.

Most of the ducks on show will be mallard, often with ducklings, plus there may be a few wigeon, gadwall and, in April, pintail. Mandarin ducks and shoveler can be on and around the water, although rather irregularly. If you are really lucky, you will be in the hide in April or May at a time when a garganey makes one of that species' unpredictable visits. When the water is deep enough, a few tufted duck often take up residence. Remarkably, the pool was the location for a green-winged teal for just over two weeks from mid-April 2000. A regular sight, both on the water and the adjacent meadows, are shelduck, probably with ducklings. Their relative, the ruddy shelduck, is a rare, probably feral, visitor that was last seen here in May 2006. Other birds not qualifying as truly wild have been the very occasional Egyptian and barnacle geese.

Watch the sky for birds of prey, both from the hides and the trail. Marsh harriers are infrequent but have been seen in each month. Hen harriers are even less likely. A one-off, and notable, event in May 1999 was the presence of a Montagu's harrier. Common buzzards, occasionally several, take to the air every so often. A merlin would be very unusual this late in the season, although one or two have still been here in May. Kestrels and sparrowhawks are always about and there have been a couple of April instances of red kites in this area. The latter part of April, sometimes earlier, heralds the return of hobbies and in May, the peak time, several can be in the air at once. The same two months are also the most reliable for seeing a peregrine or two.

You will undoubtedly find a few moorhens as you look around, and possibly one or two coots. Unfortunately, it is highly improbable that there will be a black-winged stilt, as in April 2005 when the bird seen from Nettley's moved across to this part of the reserve.

Little ringed plovers are a feature from April until at least early June. On occasions, there have also been several ringed plovers, so care needs to be exercised in identification. Another of the plovers, the grey, is all but unheard of on these brooks. Lapwings, however, are virtually guaranteed and bring their chicks to the muddy fringes from nests in the meadows. June is often the month when lapwing numbers show a noticeable increase. There is the prospect of a dunlin and, in April, the very remote possibility of a jack snipe, and rather better odds on a handful of common snipe. Intermittently, there may be black-tailed godwit, but this is unusual. Although a curlew is not totally unknown here at this time of the year, any bird of that general appearance is much more likely to be one of the whimbrels, which pass through between mid-April and mid-May. The sounds of redshanks are frequently heard from the three or four birds that are probably now in residence. From early April and throughout May, greenshanks drop in for a while, normally in ones and twos and only sporadically more. Typically, green sandpipers appear each month as singletons, with higher numbers possible in June. Despite their name, common sandpipers are few and far between, although not as sparse as wood sandpipers. Unusual members of the wader fraternity that have favoured this part of the reserve with a visit include the oystercatcher pair during their nearby nesting attempt in 2001, and the very rare vagrant marsh sandpiper, here for just two days in May 2002.

April has been the month for sightings of two large white birds - a white stork in 2003 (there was also one in the previous June and July) and a spoonbill in 2001. A spoonbill was seen again in May and June in both 2006 and 2008. As well as gracing North Brooks in the spring of 2008, three common cranes spent a little time in the middle of May on Mid Brooks.

Gulls will most probably be the regularly visiting black-headed species, although lesser black-backs have appeared infrequently, as have common gulls. There will inevitably be a few wood pigeons and perhaps stock doves and twice, in May and June, a turtle dove has been near West Mead.

In those years when barn owls nest in the visitor centre, or the box in the trees at the bottom of the field, West Mead is the place to sit in the evening in the hope of seeing adults flying back to the nest box with prey captured out on the meadows or further afield. It is worthwhile scanning the field boundaries in case an owl is perched on a fence post. Evening, too, is the time when there is the outside hope of coming across nightjars hunting for insects around the edge of the brooks.

In addition to barn owls, should little owls reoccupy their traditional nesting place not too far from West Mead, there is the prospect of seeing that species in the locality. As with all owls, so much depends on where they are nesting or roosting, the availability of food and the weather, that nothing can be guaranteed from one year to the next. Unusually, there was a short-eared owl in April 2000 and again in June 2001, and a long-eared owl was on the edge of the brooks in May 1997.

From here, it is often possible to see and hear birds that thrive in open grassy areas like green woodpeckers, skylarks and meadow pipits. Scarce passage tree pipits have very occasionally been in the neighbourhood of the hides. Another, even scarcer, passage migrant, the water pipit, has appeared outside both hides in April in a limited number of years.

Various wagtails are possible, the most regular of which is the pied. Yellow wagtails have been observed from the hides in each month and, very rarely, there have been juveniles in June. On no more than the odd occasion, grey wagtails have been here in May.

The final part of this section, from just beyond West Mead to the junction at Fattengates, is a return to nightingale country and time to pause to listen to this renowned songster again.

North Brooks in summer

South Brooks and the distant South Downs

Mute Swan with cygnets

Black-tailed Godwits

Pied Wagtail on the visitor centre roof

Long-tailed Tit

Nuthatch at the feeding station

Barn Owl at the visitor centre nestbox

Juvenile Great Spotted Woodpecker

Cormorant

Greenfinch at the feeding station

Lapwing

Spotted Flycatcher

Goldfinch

Male Pheasant

Female Pheasant

July to September

Small birds, sometimes in family parties, will still be visible during the first few weeks. Once they have discharged their parental responsibilities, they become much more difficult to see, to the extent that, at times, you might be persuaded that they have all deserted their usual haunts. In fact, because they are moulting their feathers, our song birds are doing their best not to be seen so that they do not fall easy prey to a predator. Having completed their moult they become more straightforward to see again and some species, including warblers, can be observed feeding avidly in preparation for migration. Song is much diminished, with only a few species continuing to sing dependably. Barn owls may still be taking food to the nest in the early part of the quarter and hobbies are frequently to be seen hunting for martins, swallows and dragonflies. It is a prime time to look out for passage migrants, especially a variety of waders and other birds that are not regular inhabitants of the reserve.

Woodpeckers - green, great spotted and even lesser spotted - are all possible in and around the car park. Green woodpeckers value the grassland on either side of the entrance road as a productive site to search for ants. They are easily disturbed, upon which you will probably glimpse them disappearing in characteristically undulating flight towards the cover of the trees. Whether visible or not, the green woodpecker habitually makes its presence known by the loud, laughing, call and this is as likely to be heard here as anywhere on the reserve. Also most probably initially located by their calls are the great spotted woodpeckers. These will almost certainly be high in the trees, perhaps the dead elms at the start of the public path to Wiggonholt church, but sometimes they are seen at lower levels, on fencing and fallen branches. The other woodpecker, the lesser spotted, is a totally different proposition, with sightings being rather rare. Nevertheless, they have occurred in each month of the quarter in the surrounding area.

Of the relatively few species still singing hereabouts, robins and wrens are the most probable performers. Blackbirds and blackcaps have both been heard in July, as have yellowhammers, several of which every so often sing along the length of the entrance road. Some species have a late burst of singing in the autumn and, around the car park's wooded edge, coal tits are amongst the potential candidates. Whilst song, as such, is at a low ebb there is a constant chatter of calls from many birds, against which the loud sounds from nuthatches stand out.

Watch the trees for a while and you may see and hear some of the parties of birds, including blue and long-tailed tits, which form at the end of the breeding season. Tiny goldcrests can be expected in any of the trees. Feeding groups of linnets are sometimes to be found and, occasionally, a colourful jay will fly low over the car park. In July 1999 a family party of woodlark, a species which may be on the increase locally, gathered on the western side of the entrance road. Late in the quarter, flocks of house martins feeding in the sky are a sign of autumn passage which, in some years, has also been indicated by the presence of redstarts, blackcaps and spotted flycatchers.

In the courtyard, the hanging feeders are regularly patronised by tits, mainly blue, great, and coal (marsh tits are less frequent) together with nuthatches and greenfinches. Dunnocks, robins and chaffinches pick up food scattered on the ground and, at quiet times, green woodpeckers peck on the grass in and around the play area. During the first weeks of the period you can anticipate that many of these birds will have juveniles with them. There will also be youngsters among the groups of long-tailed tits that pass through, often not staying for very long. Another juvenile, but far less common, was the cuckoo that once stayed around for a few days at the end of July.

The roof of the visitor centre is a favourite place for pied wagtails, and the ridge a perch for carrion crows. It was also a temporary stopping place for two migrating tree pipits early on a September morning. Very infrequent visitors to the courtyard have been song thrushes, spotted flycatchers, house sparrows and, to this pond and those at the other side of the building, grey wagtails.

You can have a reasonable expectation of encountering a great spotted woodpecker around the visitor centre; a lesser spotted woodpecker would be a considerable surprise at this season. The surrounding trees provide perches for jays and mistle thrushes and, once in a while, a treecreeper will ascend one of the trunks. Common crossbills are unusual visitors but in 1997, an especially good year for them, there was a small flock in the vicinity of the centre. Another productive year was 2008 when flocks appeared in this country from mid-June, a movement reflected in the sight of small groups, usually in flight, near the car park and visitor centre in August and September. Siskins come to the reserve in the winter and up to ten have flown over late in September, the month in which they sometimes arrive.

Time spent checking the sky from the visitor centre windows, or the viewing places outside, can be rewarded by views of birds of prey. Sparrowhawks are common and are usually engaged in the low-level ambush of small birds, although they can come into view high above the field. One or two soaring common buzzards are very possible, albeit in the distance, and at times there can be up to seven together. A kestrel is likely on any day, but not until September will there be the chance of a merlin. Every month holds the real hope of a hunting hobby or two with September, when up to four have been reported, the best of them. Unusually (at least until there is further increase in the species' West Sussex population) a red kite flew over in September 2005.

The field itself is a valuable source of food for a range of species and, in many cases, the number of individuals increase as autumn approaches. Pheasants, stock doves, wood pigeons, green woodpeckers, jackdaws, rooks, carrion crows and starlings are some of the more obvious but there is a host of smaller birds that tend to disappear in the vegetation and so require more persistence to view. Included in this latter group are skylarks, meadow pipits, pied wagtails, chaffinches, greenfinches, goldfinches, linnets, yellowhammers and reed buntings. Moorhens and snipe are two more species that, now and again, forage on the field, and the odd bullfinch has also occurred there. There is one record of a red-legged partridge.

Early in the quarter, in those years when they nest in the visitor centre, barn owls may still be seen around the building in the evening and owlets have been observed emerging from the box late in the day. At any hour, one or two little owls often perch on and around the oak tree at the foot of the field, if they have been nesting there (in step with the decline in the species, for the first time in many years this site was not used in 2008).

The lower part of the field has been the location in August and September of a few migrating wheatears. Other birds preparing to depart for the winter and seen round about, infrequently and in small numbers, have been tree pipits, spotted flycatchers and yellow wagtails. More frequently, you will see swallows and house martins, potentially in large flocks.

Some unusual sights from the visitor centre include the greenshank that flew over once in September, the ravens observed in September 2002 and August 2008, and the hawfinch at the foot of the field in August 2001.

The brambles and birches on the way down the hill to Fattengates are cover for several warblers. These are not necessarily easy to see as they flit quickly from leaf to leaf and you will most often find them by their sounds. Whitethroats will be in the majority with five or more possible and, in July, the prospects both of song and of family parties. Chiffchaffs and perhaps a willow warbler or two are other potential inhabitants of the foliage. Especially from August, examine the elder bushes for lesser whitethroats, garden warblers, blackcaps and even, as was once the case, a sedge warbler. Also indicative of seasonal movements are possible glimpses of a few redstarts, whinchats, stonechats, spotted flycatchers (there have been up to six in September) and pied flycatchers.

Other summer visitors that have been seen or heard from time to time include cuckoos (almost always juveniles), swallows (from time to time bringing food to fledglings perched on nearby trees) and, also now and then accompanied by youngsters, nightingales. At the very end of September 2007 an early redwing, a winter visitor, was here. In the distant sky a hobby, another summer visitor, may be hunting. Otherwise, birds of prey are normally limited to sparrowhawks and kestrels, although a red kite was seen from here at the end of July 2004.

You will hear the calls of great spotted and, especially, green woodpeckers. When there is not too much disturbance the latter have a liking for feeding by the path. Lesser spotted woodpeckers have been seen, but infrequently.

Despite the main season for song having ended, some birds will still be singing. Wrens, usually invisible in the undergrowth, can be heard throughout the period and robins only have a lull round about July time. August is usually a quieter period for several species such as song thrushes and great tits and the amount of song from greenfinches, goldfinches and yellowhammers is destined to decrease as the weeks go by.

The slender, dead, elm trees to the right of the path as you go down the hill are favourite perches for birds such as pied wagtails, chaffinches, greenfinches and linnets. Members of the crow family are usually in evidence, with the dead elms affording opportunities for magpies, rooks and carrion crows to pause and survey their surroundings. Jays, which you will probably hear long before you see them, are also possible.

Watch for the small groups of long-tailed tits as they move restlessly through the foliage. The denser bushes are the regular habitat of at least two bullfinches. Less often, a meadow pipit or mistle thrush makes an appearance and there have been limited glimpses of marsh tits. July 2003 produced two unusual reports, one of a common crossbill and the other of a corn bunting.

In common with the walk down the hill, the area approaching the path junction holds the promise of warblers. Whitethroats are the most abundant but lesser whitethroats are also possible. There have been a few August records of garden warblers and blackcaps (up to four), and willow warblers are seen in both July and August. In July, a chiffchaff may still be singing from somewhere in the trees. The wood warbler is a scarce passage migrant at the reserve but Fattengates has the distinction of several July and August sightings of up to two. As proof that birds turn up in unexpected habitats at migration times a reed warbler, having emerged from its reedbed breeding territory somewhere, was observed here late one August.

Other species embarking on southward migration are the flycatchers and from mid-July to early September spotted flycatchers, at times as many as half a dozen together, use the trees hereabouts as good sites from which to launch their short flights in pursuit of insects. Less regularly, there have also been one or two pied flycatchers. Another bird to check for here is the nightingale, but most will have departed by August. This is a further place that has attracted cuckoos in July and August. Exceptionally, there have been redstart sightings nearby in August and September and one of a wheatear at the end of August.

The deciduous trees have produced a small number of sightings of lesser spotted woodpeckers, and great spotted woodpeckers have also been seen. Healthy numbers of common tits can be anticipated, but much less expected was the very scarce willow tit in late September 2003. Nuthatches attract attention to themselves by their routinely noisy calls and at this time of the year a search in the direction of the sound can reveal a family party. Observation of the conifers will sooner or later result in the sight of a goldcrest, maybe singing. Only in infrequent years, 2008 being an example, will there be a few common crossbills or, as in September 2005 and 2007, siskins. Very rarely, a tawny owl has been found roosting in the trees.

The pond is relatively unfrequented by birds but a moorhen can sometimes be there and, very infrequently, it has attracted grey wagtails in August and September.

Two nightjars were found feeding at Fattengates on an August evening in 1995 and there was another as late in the season as 29 September in the same year. This activity could become a regular feature if habitat improvements result in an increase in the number of nightjars breeding locally.

The green lane after Fattengates can be very good for warblers, with the greatest numbers often in August. Lesser whitethroats, whitethroats, garden warblers, blackcaps, chiffchaffs and willow warblers are seen in the trees and hedges. The odd burst of song may be heard from some, particularly lesser whitethroats, and you will almost certainly hear chiffchaffs well into September.

Especially during the last half of the quarter there is the possibility of coming across various migrating birds, both in the trees and bushes edging the lane and in the surrounding fields and their boundaries.

Amongst these have been yellow wagtails, redstarts, spotted flycatchers and, once, a tree pipit.

The lane is inhabited by an array of resident birds. Blackbirds and song thrushes peck about on the ground at the edges of the path and the field margins, whilst goldcrests and parties of long-tailed tits look for food at a higher level. Flocks of goldfinches pass overhead to land and feed in the fields, and bullfinches call from the thick shrubs. The area around the path fork to Nettley's can be a good place to meet up with blue tits, greenfinches, chaffinches, nuthatches and jays. Among the scarcer birds recorded around the green lane have been a tawny owl in August, a firecrest in July and, in an adjacent field, a grey wagtail.

Great spotted woodpeckers frequent the trees in Hanger Wood, and there have been a few September visits by lesser spotted woodpeckers. Those other woodland specialists, nuthatches and treecreepers, are often out of sight, deep in the wood, but they do appear from time to time on trunks and limbs closer to the path. For much of the quarter, the wood can be another place to find spotted flycatchers. Marsh tits probably live nearby, but in very small numbers, and you would be extremely fortunate to find one.

Now and then during this period you will hear bursts of song from great tits and wrens, and do not be surprised, in September, to come across a singing chiffchaff. Other common sounds are the contact notes of long-tailed tits, the laughing calls of green woodpeckers and the raucous cries of jays.

On North Brooks, little grebes are not a regular sight although occasionally one or two exploit ditches that have deep water, or swim and dive in the pool outside Nettley's. Far more reliable are the cormorants, which congregate to rest way out in the middle of the brooks. Anything up to about half-a-dozen little egrets visit periodically. Their relative, the grey heron, is always around in numbers ranging from one up to over twenty, often including juveniles. Mute swans, too, are constantly on site and potentially in even greater abundance. For a sheer mass of birds, and noise, little surpasses the flocks of greylag and Canada geese which, when they decide to visit the brooks, can arrive in their hundreds.

In addition to those regular geese, North Brooks periodically has its share of members of the wildfowl family that are obviously escaped or feral, together with others of more uncertain origin which could be argued to be genuine wild birds. Within these categories fall the barnacle and bar-headed geese that are sometimes seen. In September 1998 there was a red-breasted goose, and two or three Egyptian geese make sporadic visits. As with geese, ducks are notorious for escaping from captivity and almost anything can appear at any time. An instance was the Chiloe wigeon, which dropped into North Brooks in September 2000.

Without too much searching, you will probably find at least a half a dozen shelduck and young. On the other hand, mandarin duck families (there may be one or two) are much more secretive, keeping largely to the pool margins and swimming into the cover of emergent vegetation.

Towards the end of the quarter, the number of most dabbling ducks increases noticeably as they start to arrive from other parts of the northern hemisphere. Initially, they will be in their dull eclipse feathers but, as time goes by, the drakes gradually become more colourful until, eventually, the full glory of their breeding plumage in which we know them in the winter is revealed. A few teal will undoubtedly be seen in the summer and, from about the middle of August, numbers start to increase perceptibly. This beginning of the winter influx is a week or two later in the case of wigeon (which are only present in the summer now and again) but by the end of September several hundred of each species will have arrived. The mallard is another all the year round duck, the population of which rises to a hundred or so during the quarter. Compared with the preceding species, pintail and shoveler exhibit a much slower build-up to what can, nevertheless, ultimately be impressive winter volumes. Gadwall are infrequent and only ever present in small numbers.

A dabbling duck in the process of migrating to Africa is the garganey. So few pass through that when one does appear it is very much a day to remember. Sightings are possible every month and usually involve single birds, but there have been as many as six at once.

Of the diving ducks, there is the outside chance of a tufted duck, as it is an irregular breeder. Pochard are almost unheard of at this season, an exception being the three that were reported one day in August 2005.

Among the best spots from which to see the North Brooks species mentioned so far, the two hides, Jupp's View and the Hanger are also the places to go to look for this period's exciting range of other wetland birds. If a water rail makes a rare appearance it will most probably be in August or September and outside Nettley's or, less likely, Little Hanger. Coots and moorhens are much more willing to be watched and the latter can be abundant - once, over fifty were counted.

Depending on conditions, especially the extent of the feeding areas of wet mud and shallow water, you have the prospect of amassing a long list of waders. Little ringed plovers, normally ones and twos and less often up to six, are found mainly in July and August. Ringed plovers are infrequent, as are golden plovers. Seldom absent are lapwings and several hundred can spend their day on the brooks (often in company with starlings).

Stints are few and far between, with the little stint the most frequent. Even these are not annual visitors but when they do drop in, usually in August and September, there are generally up to three. In September 2001, there was an extraordinary record of ten. Another good year for the species was 2008 when up to six were on view for the whole of the second half of September. The other stint which has been here, Temminck's, is a real rarity having been noted in this quarter only early in August 2000, when there were two individuals, and at the end of August and beginning of September 2007 when there was a singleton.

If, as is probable, none of these irregular waders are on view there is compensation in locating a ruff. These only occasionally arrive earlier than August and thereafter you can often see from one to a handful for the remainder of the quarter. During your scanning for a ruff you could easily find up to a dozen or more dunlins.

Snipe become increasingly noticeable in August and September. The hides, especially Little Hanger in years when the ratio of water to mud in the nearby pool is favourable, are the best places from which to look. In addition, you may find a small number feeding quite close to Jupp's View. More often than not, only a few snipe are seen together, except at times when scores congregate in a good feeding place. There have been July and August reports of jack snipe but it would take great good fortune to chance upon one.

Each month, up to about a dozen or so black-tailed godwits may be probing the North Brooks mud some, at least, still with vestiges of their striking breeding plumage. On the other hand, bar-tailed godwits are very infrequent visitors indeed. During the first part of the period you should hear, and perhaps see, a few redshanks around the edge of the pools. Rarely, there may also be a spotted redshank. In most years, several passage greenshanks pause for a time with, now and again, up to nine or ten together.

This is the season for green sandpipers and there are often several (once as many as twelve) to be seen. In addition to watching from the hides, it is worth looking at the pools adjacent to Jupp's View where a green sandpiper may decide to feed on the muddy fringes, and even preen and loaf out in full view. Common sandpipers, normally one, occasionally two and, unusually, three or four, are visitors from the middle of July to late August or early September. Nettley's is the usual place from which to see common sandpipers and sometimes Little Hanger can be profitable as well. The prospects of coming across a wood sandpiper (rarely more than one, although there have been four) are rather less and, again, July and August are the most probable times and Nettley's the favoured hide.

A couple of scarce, non-annual, visitors are the curlew sandpiper, recorded in August and September, and the pectoral sandpiper, which has been seen from the end of June into July and in September (for instance, one could be viewed during the last week in September 2008). A further unusual wader record was that of a single avocet in August 2004, to be surpassed by six at the end of the same month in 2007. Exceptionally, lone whimbrels pass through in July, and the same month in 2005 brought a curlew to the brooks.

Gulls are unlikely to be present in other than small numbers, nevertheless several species are possible. The most numerous will be black-headed gulls, the heads of which will gradually be changing to the mainly white of their non-breeding plumage. One or two common, lesser black-backed and herring gulls can be picked out from time to time.

Terns, which do not feature prominently on the Pulborough Brooks list, have been represented by common terns in July 1998 and August 2008, a flock of Arctic terns that flew south over North Brooks in September 1992 and a little tern, seen from Nettley's in July 2000.

Absorbing though the wetland species are, you will find many other birds, some more common and frequent than others, both on the brooks and in the surrounding trees and scrub.

The most regular birds of prey are sparrowhawks, usually seen from Nettley's and the Hanger, and kestrels which, although often alone, occasionally have juveniles with them. If a marsh harrier is going to be seen it will probably be in August or September, although this is not an annual event. Hen harriers are not frequent, either, with September the best month. More plentiful are common buzzards with, now and again, up to three in the sky. A few migrating ospreys have occurred in each of the three months and, even though they can normally be expected to follow the course of the river, two paused to perch on North Brooks in September 2005. Another species destined to migrate to Africa is the hobby and one or two are often visible. In September, there is a greater prospect of seeing several hobbies in flight at once. Also in September, and even from the middle of August, you just might see the first merlin of the season. A hunting peregrine could, at any time, be the cause of a major panic amongst birds out on the brooks.

A few stock doves can, now and then, be found feeding in similar parts of the brooks to the large flocks of wood pigeons. A cuckoo from Nettley's is not impossible in July, and it is worth a look from the same hide early or late in the day just in case a barn owl is hunting over the meadows. Another owl, a tawny, was once near Jupp's View at the end of September. In August 2008 two ravens, an unusual but possibly increasing species in the district, were in the air.

The brooks are a profitable feeding area for several of our smaller birds, including skylarks and meadow pipits. Pied wagtails, sometimes ten, twenty, thirty and more, are common and, in some years, there have also been a few white wagtails in June and July. Despite grey wagtails occurring in the locality, only a few have been seen on North Brooks, all in August.

The reed buntings that live out on the brooks are seen surprisingly seldom and then usually when one perches on the top of a clump of grass or rushes.

Given that a large slice of luck is always necessary to meet up with a kingfisher at Pulborough Brooks, you do have some hope of achieving this in July, and more so in August and September. Nettley's, where they have fished close by in the pool, is one place to sit and watch. Another is Jupp's View, where a kingfisher may flash past or perch on an overhanging branch. Most records are of single birds but on some notable occasions, four or five kingfishers have been in view at once.

The grassy slope between the Hanger and Little Hanger is a feeding place for green woodpeckers, which are most easily seen in flight. Great spotted woodpeckers are fairly common high in the trees but at this location there have only been an infinitesimal number of sightings of lesser spotted woodpeckers, all in August.

Varying quantities of swallows, sand martins and house martins can often be observed feeding in the air above the brooks. Numbers can increase dramatically as migration gets underway and swallows are sometimes counted in thousands during August. During September, all of these hirundines come and go in their scores and hundreds.

The longer the quarter wears on, the greater the prospect of coming across other birds on, or preparing, for migration. Yellow wagtails, from small handfuls up to fifty, are seen in the fields and meadows, often keeping company with cattle, mainly in the latter part of August and in September. Whinchats (there have been eight at once) can be watched from Nettley's and Little Hanger, principally in August and September and, every now and then, you may find a redstart perched on a post or fence wire in similar locations. Mid-August and September are the most likely times when the search for a wheatear feeding somewhere on the grass could result in success.

You will find warblers, some more abundant than others, in the environs of the hides, the Hanger and the picnic area. A star bird would be a grasshopper warbler, which has sung near Nettley's and Little Hanger but, unfortunately, the last instances were as long ago as July and early August 1997 and July 1999. Occasionally, a sedge warbler is seen and, in one year, song was heard in September. A reed warbler would be a surprise, although there was a July sighting near Nettley's. The scrub around the Hanger and Little Hanger attracts lesser whitethroats. Several common whitethroats are often quite widely distributed in the same habitat and, in July, you can come across family groups. A garden warbler may show itself around the Hanger, Little Hanger and near the picnic tables, and these are also the places where several blackcaps can be expected, especially from late August into September. A willow warbler would be an unusual occurrence although chiffchaffs are relatively common, especially in September when they sometimes sing. There have been very occasional reports of wood warblers near Nettley's and at the Hanger in August and September.

Any of the wooded areas bordering North Brooks give excellent opportunities for watching spotted flycatchers. Start looking in the middle of July and then concentrate on their main period in August and the first half of September, when there can be anything up to about ten individuals. Much scarcer pied flycatchers have been seen near Nettley's and the Hanger in August and September.

It is a matter of chance whether you encounter the nuthatches and treecreepers which will be somewhere in the trees. You are virtually certain, though, to happen upon the blackbirds, jays, starlings, chaffinches, greenfinches and linnets which can be almost anywhere. Goldfinch flocks, small early in the period but increasing to perhaps over a hundred individuals in September, range over a large area, searching for seeds. August and September have the promise of bullfinches in the scrub around Little Hanger and the Hanger. A visit to the Hanger is also a good opportunity for listening and looking for goldcrests and, in the middle of September, a firecrest was seen at Jupp's View. Common tits are all over the place and in September the great tits may well join robins in song. Marsh tits are decidedly uncommon but have been seen once or twice. Stonechats start to occur regularly in August and September and several are possible near Nettley's, at the Hanger and, occasionally, around Little Hanger.

Quail have been known to be present on the reserve only in an extremely limited number of years, and then always identified by their call rather than visually. It was, therefore, a remarkable incident in August 1995 when a quail was flushed on the approach to Nettley's. Not until 2008 was there more evidence of this species with calling heard, mainly from the bank of the Arun, in the first three weeks of August. There was also an incident of a bird being flushed, this time from the southern part of the brooks.

Rather than passing through the two small gates near Little Hanger that give ongoing access to the nature trail, a short walk down the track to the right after the first gate could be worthwhile. The scrub hereabouts provides a habitat for a range of birds including blue tits, starlings, lesser whitethroats and goldfinches. From August whinchats are on the agenda, with six having been seen at the same time on one occasion. The willow trees are places for chiffchaffs to feed and, in September, one may be singing spasmodically. In August, a spotted flycatcher is possible and there is one record of a wood warbler from the same month. Very infrequently, in September, there have been grey wagtails here. Snipe will be in the nearby meadows and, from time to time, a few take off and fly overhead, calling harshly.

Whilst any of the hedges and trees on the way to West Mead can conceal a few common birds such as wrens, robins, whitethroats, chiffchaffs, long-tailed tits, goldfinches and yellowhammers, the most rewarding place to watch can be around Redstart Corner. Here, in August, there is a reasonable prospect of seeing the bird after which this location is named. When redstarts are present (there have been up to four at the same time) they are generally to be found watching for insects from perches on either the hedge or fence running in a northerly direction across the field from the corner. It was here that a very scarce black redstart was seen for a day in August 1997, a repeat of the visit by the same species to the Winpenny area for over two weeks from late September, four years previously.

Especially in August, the areas around Winpenny and Redstart Corner are possible places for whinchats, several spotted flycatchers and a very few pied flycatchers. Redstart Corner has also produced a firecrest in August. Just occasionally in August or the first half of September, a wheatear may spend some time near Winpenny or West Mead. It was between Little Hanger and Winpenny that the reserve's first wryneck was discovered, early in September 2008. Throughout the quarter, you may find one or two stonechats by the path between Winpenny and West Mead. A meadow pipit is another one to look for and there could be a lesser whitethroat along the way and, perhaps, a reed bunting. An oddity hereabouts in September 2001 was a ring-necked parakeet.

From West Mead to the junction with the route back to the visitor centre there are large trees in which there can be spotted flycatchers, nuthatches and treecreepers and, in the scrub, both garden and willow warblers are occasionally spotted. There is a single record, from August, of a lesser spotted woodpecker in these trees.

As far as several species are concerned there is little advantage in watching from Winpenny rather than West Mead because they can occur anywhere on the brooks. Cormorants, never many, are in this category, as are grey herons and, at times, substantial flocks of greylag and Canada geese. Lone marsh harriers are recorded in August and September but hen harriers are scarce. Sparrowhawks, kestrels and common buzzards are observed regularly, typically in flight. Peregrines are not very frequent and red kites are less so but, for much of the quarter, hobbies are an almost guaranteed sight for anyone who is prepared to watch patiently and, now and again, several birds can be up at the same time. Sand martins, swallows and house martins will be in the air, hawking for insects or themselves being chased by hobbies, in any of the months. Large flocks of swifts come and go up until August, after which the odds of seeing a swift are slight. A few common gulls and adult and immature black-headed gulls loaf on the brooks now and then.

In addition to the above, Winpenny has the potential for some waders, although it must be said that it is normally not as productive as West Mead. Towards the end of August and in September a few snipe are quite possible. From early in July, a small number of green sandpipers may be feeding around the edge of the pool over towards the riverbank and, a little later in the month, there could be one or two common sandpipers as well. There has also been a wood sandpiper here. Another wader that turns up once in a while on these brooks is the ruff and, in August 2007, there was a curlew.

When an ever-elusive kingfisher makes one of its sporadic visits to the nearby pools and ditches it is almost assured to be seen from Winpenny, rather than West Mead. Late in September 2003 a short-eared owl passed over South Brooks. Particularly exciting birds at Winpenny have been the ospreys, seen on two August days migrating along the course of the river, and the honey buzzard which flew over in September 2000.

At West Mead, little grebes breed on or around the pool in some years, and you can then easily watch family parties and, over time, the development of the chicks. Occasionally, one or two little egrets spend some time on the brooks and are then usually visible from this hide. More often than not, when a grey heron comes to search for food in the ditches it will be a long way off and difficult to see, but every so often one will fly in and stand at the edge of the water.

Of the ducks on view, both shelduck and mallard may have broods. In September, teal can increase to over 100 but if there are any shoveler at all there will be no more than one or two. A high spot for duck watchers occurred in July 2002 with the visit of two garganey. Diving ducks are not usual, but both pochard and tufted duck have occurred in July. Moorhens and coots, probably with young, are common.

There will almost always be lapwings, from a few up to a hundred or so, around the pool and there may even be a chick or two. Towards the end of August and in September, West Mead is frequently the best of all the hides from which to search for snipe, and several often conceal themselves in the rushes quite close to the windows. For most of the quarter there are good prospects of greenshanks, green sandpipers and common sandpipers appearing on at least some days. Black-tailed godwits are most frequent in August, when there can be up to eight. Ruff are possible but they are few and far between. It is not every year that curlew sandpipers use the reserve during their migration so it was a significant event in August 2002 when the adjoining brooks hosted up to nine individuals. Waders which, over the years, have made no more than the odd summer visit to this part of the reserve are little ringed plovers, ringed plovers, golden plovers, dunlins, spotted redshanks and wood sandpipers.

The grassy areas stretching away from West Mead are good feeding places for green woodpeckers and their young and also, from late July through to the middle of September, yellow wagtails, of which there can be anything from one up to twenty or more. Pied wagtails may be located feeding anywhere on the ground.

In the evening, it is worth lingering by the field gate at the end of the path from West Mead and looking over towards the hill. If barn owls have nested at the visitor centre, or in a nest box to the south of the hide, there is a strong probability, certainly during the early part of the period, of seeing the parents taking prey either to the nest or to fledged owlets hidden in the trees. If little owls have bred at the edge of the hill it is not unusual to see them in flight or perched on a tree or post.

Whatever the time of day, it is worth taking a breather once or twice on the walk back up the hill to the visitor centre and pausing to scan the bushes, the field and the sky.

Fallow deer and a glimpse of West Mead hide

Flocks of wintering ducks on North Brooks

Kingfisher

Greylag geese

Mallard

Great Tit at the feeding station

Rook

Green Woodpecker

Lapwings

Jackdaw

Wigeon

Teal

Dunnock

Carrion Crow

Bewick's Swan

Pochard

October to December

At the start of this quarter the southward migration of summer visitors, especially house martins and swallows, is still in evidence. Even more noticeable is the build-up of dabbling ducks, culminating in the spectacular mid-winter peak. The return of the Bewick's swans is eagerly awaited and other winter visitors, including fieldfares and redwings, start to make an appearance. The behaviour of many birds is altered by severe weather, making some bolder and easier to watch at the same time as encouraging less usual species to visit the reserve and causing others to move away in search of more favourable conditions. A cheerful phenomenon in the depths of winter is the resumption of singing by a few birds.

Some of the birds that live around the car park will draw themselves to your attention by their calls, varied examples of which are those of green woodpeckers, blue tits, nuthatches, jays and chaffinches. Great spotted woodpeckers will be calling as they move through the trees and by the time December comes they will be drumming as well. At much the same time the first song thrush melodies join those of the robins, which will have sung throughout the quarter.

Blackbirds like to forage in the leaf litter and, occasionally, there may be a noisy flock of fieldfares or a redwing or two. In October 2005 a ring ouzel, their much scarcer relation, foraged by the entrance road. Woodlarks, still uncommon at the reserve, have been seen once or twice in and around these parts in November and December.

In the trees and bushes long-tailed, coal, blue and great tits search for food. Seen less often are treecreepers, which concentrate their feeding activities on climbing up the tree trunks and along the boughs. The trees also attract another bird, much in demand by birdwatchers, the lesser spotted woodpecker, which despite being at its most visible in November and December, still manages to elude all but the most single-minded, or fortunate, seekers. Very irregular visitors are siskins, which have occurred in each month, and lesser redpolls, which have occasionally been watched around the car park in October, at times in mixed flocks with siskins. In even shorter supply is the house sparrow, just one having been seen, on the grass near the entrance road.

A sparrowhawk is the most probable bird of prey here, and there have been occasional sightings of common buzzards, kestrels and merlins. Early in the morning tawny owls call from the woods and, every now and then, one is seen flying to its roost.

This might not be the most obvious place on the reserve to expect waders but woodcocks roost during the day in the surrounding woodland and there are several November and December records of birds flying over the car park, probably on their way to feed on the brooks.

Seasonal weather and shortages of natural food can bring even more birds than usual to the courtyard feeding station. Total numbers vary as the day goes by but there are always some birds to watch, except when they wisely disappear for a while in response to the arrival of a hunting sparrowhawk.

Depending on the species, birds will be taking food from the feeders or from the ground, with some exhibiting sufficient versatility, or determination, to do both. Regular visitors include pied wagtails, dunnocks, robins, blackbirds, coal tits, blue tits, great tits, chaffinches, and greenfinches. Occasionally, a mobile party of long-tailed tits will pause briefly on the feeders. Willow tits, never common, have not been seen here for some years and anything that looks similar is more likely to be one of the sporadic marsh tits. There can be no mistake, though, in the identification of the great spotted woodpeckers and nuthatches, which come in from the woods to take advantage of the food provided. This is another place where a lesser spotted woodpecker has appeared in front of people who just happened to be around at the right time.

Wrens will not be far away but seldom emerge from cover and, equally difficult to see, a goldcrest sometimes flits through the nearby trees. There are one or two records of firecrests in this locality. Very erratic callers at the courtyard are house sparrows and, usually not seen earlier than November, are bramblings and lesser redpolls. In November 2003 a mealy redpoll was identified near the visitor centre. The common crossbills that arrive in some winters have also occurred here and in 2008 a siskin was twice heard singing. One-offs include a grey wagtail, a hawfinch, and a blackcap.

The visitor centre window, the tea terrace and the viewing platform just outside the exit to the trail are good points from which to scan the extensive panorama for birds in flight. One or two (on the odd occasion up to five) common buzzards are quite possible, although they may be flying at considerable height and distance. A kestrel, hovering or perched, is more usual and, if you are lucky, a merlin flashing across the field in pursuit of small birds is a good winter sight. Another seasonal hunter here is the peregrine and periodically one or two appear in the sky above the brooks. Early October is normally the latest time in the year to see a hobby, the majority having already departed by then. The hen harrier is another raptor that is spotted from time to time, but usually not before November.

In October migration is in the air, quite literally, in the form of some quite large flocks of swallows and house martins. Other migrants that have been seen, very infrequently, on the field in October include whinchats and redstarts. All of those are moving south but, from the middle of the month, you may witness the arrival of birds from across the North Sea in the shape of fieldfares and redwings, which settle on the field to feed.

Depending on the current choice of conservation management, the field can attract many birds to feed, at times in ones and twos and at others in flocks running into scores. Into this category fall skylarks, meadow pipits, pied wagtails, chaffinches, greenfinches, goldfinches, linnets, yellowhammers and reed buntings.

Some common birds that are normally not particularly easy to locate in the setting of the field due to factors such as their low numbers, small size or timidity, are wrens, dunnocks, robins, blackbirds and song thrushes. Rather bolder are the mistle thrushes that form small flocks in October and disperse into ones and twos thereafter. Stonechats do not seem to mind being watched and, now and again, at least one, and probably two, will perch on posts and plants.

Pheasants, sometimes over twenty, like to feed on and around the field. Wood pigeons, often in great abundance, are regular visitors, whereas stock doves appear less regularly and in far lower numbers. This is a likely place to spot green woodpeckers (there can be as many as five or so) probing in the turf for invertebrates. Other, perhaps unexpected, patrons of this land are snipe, although they generally remain invisible, at least until they fly. The crow family can be conspicuous, with the largest congregations consisting of rooks and jackdaws, almost invariably together and periodically in flocks exceeding a hundred. A few jays, magpies and carrion crows also drop in for a feed. Less anticipated was the raven, which flew over in October 2008.

Even though a barn owl has been observed over the field, this is not a common event during the current season. In some years, there is a greater prospect of locating a little owl, probably perched on a tree or post in the middle distance. Scarce woodlarks have been recorded, very sporadically, during this quarter. Another bird with the same status, the red-legged partridge, has occurred just once.

Some unusual flyovers have been red kites in October and November, siskins in October, a curlew in December, two goosander in December 2002 and a juvenile Arctic skua in November 1993. Who knows what a continuous period of watching from this visitor centre vantage point might reveal?

The walk down the hill provides an opportunity of finding birds perching in the trees, or searching for food on the ground or among the bushes. In October it is quite possible to find a few swallows gathered in the trees. The brambles provide cover for wrens, which often only reveal their presence by making alarm calls as you walk by. Dunnocks get into similar places but are more inclined to come out onto the birch trees where they can be seen. There will always be a few blackbirds foraging by the side of the path and in some winters numbers increase noticeably. Pheasants emerge from the fields to feed on the ground, where they are readily visible. This is one of the parts favoured by stonechats and occasionally one or two are found perched on top of the vegetation. Goldcrests are quite common, albeit tricky to see, unlike the family parties of long-tailed tits that habitually show themselves during their restless movements from place to place. You will occasionally encounter small groups of meadow pipits.

The trees are used by many birds as perching places for anything from a few seconds up to a more prolonged stay. Keep an eye on the bare branches for magpies, starlings, chaffinches, greenfinches, linnets, yellowhammers and, not so often, lesser redpolls. A lot of these can also be seen, but not necessarily so easily, on the bushes and hedges that are additionally the domain of several bullfinches. Much less reliable are the irregular visits by bramblings and siskins.

This is not the time of year to expect a great chorus of birdsong but, nevertheless, it is good to listen for the few species that can still be heard. For the whole of the period you can confidently anticipate hearing the songs of robins and wrens, but only during early October can you hope to enjoy a chiffchaff singing, perchance a little half-heartedly, from one of the birches. Exceptionally, back in the courtyard, a siskin was singing once in the middle of October. In December, if not a trifle before, song thrushes will be singing from nearby and, without a doubt, several other places around the trail. Great tits, encountered almost as frequently as blue tits, also start to sing late in the year.

Calls characteristic of each species will give away the positions of other birds such as migrant fieldfares and redwings, and resident nuthatches, green woodpeckers and great spotted woodpeckers. The call of the lesser spotted woodpecker has resulted in a few October and November sightings from this path.

A hovering kestrel is the bird of prey that you will come across most frequently. A sparrowhawk is another possibility. There have been isolated instances of peregrines and red kites. A barn owl hunting over the rough grass towards Wiggonholt church is not an event that happens every winter, but it is something to bear in mind during the late afternoon.

Unexpected sightings on this first section of the trail have included a reed warbler and a willow warbler, both in October, a firecrest in November and a woodcock flying over in December. Pride of place in the extra special category must surely go to the yellow-browed warbler, a vagrant from Siberia, which flitted around in bushes close to the path in November 1999.

Most of the bird interest around Fattengates, at the foot of the hill, is centred on the trees and scrub but the pond is worth a glance, just in case there are repeats of the exceptional records of water rails, kingfishers and grey wagtails. If anything is on or around the water, though, it is much more likely to be a moorhen.

The brambles and bushes are occupied by wrens and robins (both of which should be singing), dunnocks, blue tits, great tits, chaffinches, bullfinches, and the goldcrests that venture out from the conifer plantation. Amongst the birds to look and listen for in the trees are great spotted woodpeckers, lesser spotted woodpeckers (as undependable as ever), fieldfares, redwings, treecreepers, jays, jackdaws, lesser redpolls (in some years) and common crossbills (in even fewer years). At times in December there will be a song thrush using one of the trees as a song post. Tawny owls are seen and heard, irregularly, in November and December. There is an outside chance of a barn owl making an evening hunting trip over the adjacent grassy areas.

Also seen in the area, but far from regularly, have been meadow pipits, pied wagtails, stonechats, reed buntings and over-wintering blackcaps and chiffchaffs. Others of erratic attendance include firecrests, a few siskins, and the black redstart that was nearby towards the end of 2000. Unquestionably, the most unusual event here was a Lapland bunting flying over in December 1990.

After Fattengates, there are plenty of trees along the path to harbour birds, and where there are trees on the reserve there is always at least a limited prospect of finding a lesser spotted woodpecker. Considerably greater are the odds of seeing some fieldfares and redwings perched high in an oak, after having flown up from the surrounding fields. The bare branches are explored by goldcrests, long-tailed tits, blue tits, great tits and an occasional treecreeper. Blackbirds like to forage along the side of the path, flying up and calling in alarm whenever they are disturbed. The hedges are home to bullfinches, sometimes half a dozen, which you will usually locate by their calls.

Green woodpeckers feed in the fields on either side of the path and frequently divulge their position by calling loudly when taking flight. Equally loud are the calls emitted by pheasants, jays, jackdaws and carrion crows. This is another good place, during the later part of the quarter, to hear a song thrush giving an early burst of song to join that of the wrens and robins.

If the field on the right has been cultivated to produce seeds, individuals and small flocks of many of the same species that use Upperton's Field may be in the neighbourhood, amongst which can be meadow pipits, pied wagtails, chaffinches and linnets. Out of the ordinary records from the adjacent fields are a couple of brent geese on a December day, a woodcock in the same month and a jack snipe.

Goldcrests, regulars in and around Hanger Wood, are best detected by the high-pitched calls, which they give as they work their way through the twigs and branches. Occasionally at this time of year there has also been a firecrest here. Dunnocks like to shuffle about in and under the low scrub, whilst bullfinches prefer to conceal themselves in the bushes. The sounds of blue and great tits are often part of the background, as are the contact notes from parties of long-tailed tits and the calls of great spotted woodpeckers and jays. The trees are used by fieldfares and redwings as high-level perches, and by nuthatches and treecreepers as places to explore for food. In common with so many locations around the reserve, wrens and robins will be singing. There have been occasional records of lesser redpolls, and rare sightings have included a grey wagtail, a mistle thrush, a blackcap and a willow tit. In 1999 a tawny owl was seen in the wood in October and November.

As far as sheer numbers of birds, and the range of species, are concerned this is the quarter when North Brooks comes into its own. Although there is much of appeal in the habitats on the higher ground, the principal attraction is the spectacle of birds on and around the water. Some of these will be in impressive numbers and others, of no less interest, in smaller quantities. When little grebes are present they fall into the latter group, with single birds the norm and eight (the record) the exception. Great crested grebes also occur mainly as singles, usually at those infrequent times when there is widespread deep flooding. A few cormorants are often highly visible perched, with wings outspread, on posts, or on the mud. Several grey herons are likely and, every so often, a little egret may fish in the same areas.

It would be almost unprecedented for mute swans not to be in view, and there can be twenty or so. Bewick's swans are less certain. Small numbers, usually accompanied by juveniles, arrive in the Arun valley in the middle of October or during the subsequent weeks. On some nights they will choose to roost on the North Brooks floods, flying in from about 4 pm and leaving again from roughly 7 am, hardly ever remaining until mid-morning. There is no way of knowing on which nights the swans will use North Brooks but, when they do, a late afternoon or, especially, dawn visit is a rewarding experience.

Greylag and Canada geese are seldom absent and anything from one or two to several hundred are possible. A very small number of white-fronted geese come to the area every winter and occasionally find their way to the reserve. Dark-bellied brent geese, plentiful on nearby coasts, are unusual visitors here and then only as single birds, except for the remarkable flock of 45 in October 1999. A special event in November 1993 was the visit of two pink-footed geese. In addition to the geese discussed so far, there are now and again the inevitable strangers, almost always of escaped or feral origin. For example, there have been barnacle geese, a lesser white-fronted goose, a red-breasted goose, a blue-winged goose and Egyptian geese. A black swan is yet another sporadic and improbable sight. In all likelihood, a few resident shelduck will be in evidence but once there was a ruddy shelduck again, almost without doubt, a feral bird.

Other than in very icy conditions, the brooks are inhabited by hundreds of dabbling ducks all going about their daily business of feeding, roosting, bathing, preening, courting and loafing. It will not be far into the quarter before all have moulted into their full and colourful breeding plumage, with the exception of some drake shoveler, which take longer to emerge from eclipse. Each species has its distinctive call, all of which make their contribution to the brooks' winter atmosphere.

Wigeon, frequently counted in thousands, spend much of their time grazing in tight flocks on the grass between and around the floods. Also totalling at least a thousand are teal, which like to feed in the shallower water. Up to several hundred mallard are not unusual and, when the water is deep, the normally low number of pintail can swell to a similar level. Of the other regular winter dabbling ducks, shoveler are seen in scores but mandarin duck and gadwall seldom in more than ones and twos. In November 1998 there was a surprisingly late garganey. Species of escaped, feral or dubious origin have included a Carolina wood duck, an American wigeon and a red-crested pochard.

Unlike the dabbling ducks, diving ducks are never numerous, their presence being reliant on water that is deeper than the average, sometimes coupled with the vagaries of bird movements. Pochard are the most frequent and may be encountered from singletons upwards to, exceptionally, over ninety. Almost as frequent, but never as many, are tufted duck. There are seasonal, but not annual, records of goosander, generally one or two but on occasions up to six. Far less is the incidence of red-breasted merganser, there having been sightings in only a few winters. The list of rare visitors includes a scaup in December 2000, a long-tailed duck in the same month in 1993 and a goldeneye, also in December (2004). There have been no records of ruddy duck since 2000.

Moorhens, capable of appearing anywhere from out on the floods to up in the branches of low willows, and coots are always around. Far less predictable are the water rails which are seen throughout the quarter, usually alone but sometimes in twos and threes (and once with a juvenile) from Nettley's and Jupp's View.

For one night in December 1993 the brooks provided a roost for the reserve's first common crane. This is never a common bird in the UK at any time and it was not until 2007 that there was another visit by this exciting species.

You will see and hear hundreds of lapwings, both on the ground and, in impressive flocks, in flight. Up to twenty to thirty golden plovers can be found, often associating with the lapwings and most apparent when a mixed flock takes to the air. Grey plovers are very unusual, having been here on only two or three occasions. The reserve is nationally important for ruff, although numbers vary periodically from just a few up to about thirty. Nettley's, and to a lesser extent the Hanger and Little Hanger, are the best places from which to look for snipe, of which there can be scores at this time of the year (in October 2002 there were 200 on North Brooks). No matter how many there are, they will not necessarily be obvious because they spend a lot of time, very well camouflaged, in the rushes. The odd jack snipe has been seen from Nettley's, despite this species as a rule only showing itself when accidentally flushed. Black-tailed godwits, singles or a few, occur in each month. Bar-tailed godwits are scare in the extreme. Dunlins occur every now and then, usually between one and six (exceptionally twenty). That even smaller wader, the little stint, is very uncommon but the numbers recorded in September 2008 were maintained through October, when there were up to six, and there were still one or two until early December. In the same year, the scarce, non-annual, pectoral sandpiper remained from September until the middle of October. A few redshanks have been seen in each of the three months. Green sandpipers, always singles, are typically observed from Nettley's or Jupp's View in October and November. Common sandpipers occur during the quarter, almost always in October, in ones, twos and threes. The list of waders seen only very infrequently on North Brooks during this quarter contains avocets, curlews and greenshanks. The star turn as far as unusual wader visitors goes was indisputably the grey phalarope, which performed its characteristic feeding actions in clear view of Nettley's for nearly two weeks at the beginning of November 2005. Another sought-after wetland bird was the bittern seen from Little Hanger in December 2005.

Black-headed gulls ordinarily make up the bulk of the gull population, sometimes with gatherings running into hundreds. A few common gulls are often seen but only on the odd occasion do they approach the hundred mark. Lesser black-backed, herring and great black-backed gulls hardly ever occur and then, generally, in low numbers. As so often, though, there are exceptions such as November assemblies of about 350 lesser black-backed gulls and some 20 herring gulls. There have been two or three records of little gulls, both in the October and early November period. In December 2000, an observer looking from Nettley's discovered a yellow-legged gull.

The brooks are a source of food for many birds, some dependent on wetlands, others equally capable of exploiting different habitats. Wood pigeons seem to be quite at home feeding on grassy areas alongside wigeon. In similar places, a few stock doves are seen now and then. With luck, you may happen on a kingfisher, or even two, quite close to Little Hanger, Jupp's View or, more likely, Nettley's. Stonechats, one, two or perhaps a family, are sometimes seen pausing on vegetation during spells of feeding and, likewise, the odd whinchat is possible in October. Carrion crows will come to peck around at the edge of the pools and starlings, all but invisible when down in the long grass, emerge to enjoy a vigorous bathe in the wet flushes. Flocks of goldfinches, now and again containing over a hundred birds, descend every so often on seed-bearing plants like teasels and thistles. Similarly, linnets feed on low plants far out on the brooks and scores have been observed coming in to roost below the Hanger. A few meadow pipits, reed buntings and a grey wagtail cannot be entirely discounted. During October varying numbers of sand martins, swallows and house martins hawk for insects over the meadows.

Many of the above species, and the wealth of small mammals and invertebrates which the brooks support, are potential prey for a range of other birds such as harriers, hawks, falcons and owls. Marsh harriers are scarce but, from November onwards, there are at least some prospects of a hen harrier. The Hanger, with its elevated views, is probably the best spot from which to watch for a kestrel, a merlin or, in October, a hobby. Ravens were noteworthy flyovers in October and December 2008. The scrub below the viewpoint is characteristic of the many places through which a sparrowhawk is likely to pass in its hunt for small birds. The spectacle of a peregrine, causing panic amongst the flocks or perched, well fed, in a tree, is a recurrent event. Far away, high in the sky, it is sometimes possible to spot a common buzzard. Early and late in the day, but not every year, barn owls hunt over the brooks. In those intermittent winters that are particularly good for short-eared owls, up to four can be watched quartering the meadows during the day. From time to time, little owls have been seen in the locality.

The trees and scrub stretching from Jupp's View, through the picnic area, around the Hanger, and onwards along the trail to Little Hanger, are part of another habitat with its own range of birds. Lesser spotted woodpeckers are as challenging to see here as anywhere but they use the trees in this area, as do great spotted woodpeckers. Green woodpeckers have a preference for the grass below the Hanger. November and December are the months in which to expect to find the largest numbers of fieldfares, often perched in the treetops. Blackbirds, song thrushes and redwings are more frequently found eating fruit in the bushes and hawthorn trees. Trunks and branches are occupied from time to time by foraging nuthatches and, more regularly, treecreepers. The call of a jay is almost certain to be heard, even if the bird responsible remains hidden. Commonly flitting around in the trees and, especially, the bushes are wrens, dunnocks, robins, goldcrests, long-tailed tits, blue tits, great tits, chaffinches, greenfinches and bullfinches. Rather less predicable are the few overwintering blackcaps and chiffchaffs, and also the occasional lesser redpolls. An unusual warbler sighting was the late sedge warbler near Nettley's in the middle of October. The picnic area has been the infrequent location for a firecrest.

Perhaps because of the variety of habitats, and perhaps because this part of the reserve is so well watched, a fair number of birds which are either difficult to see, scarce at the reserve or unusual at this season are recorded hereabouts. Out on the brooks grey partridges have been seen, and there have been October glimpses of wheatears and both grey and yellow wagtails. A ring ouzel was in the region between the Hanger and Little Hanger in mid-December 2001 and again late in November 2006. This was also once the location for a spotted flycatcher in October. Siskins have been seen from Nettley's and the Hanger in October and November, but not often. The Hanger area has been the site for a redstart and a pied flycatcher (both during October), a ring-necked parakeet, and bramblings in November and December. The path between Nettley's and Little Hanger has more than once been the place where a firecrest has appeared during the quarter. This stretch of the trail was where, in November and December 2005, sporadic views were to be had of a hawfinch, a forerunner of the regular sightings in the succeeding months and sequel to the stay of an individual near Little Hanger in November 2003.

One of the most reliable birds en route to West Mead is the stonechat. Often in pairs, they can be encountered almost anywhere, whether perched on posts and fence wires by the side of the trail, picking up food from the path, or on the tops of plants way out on the brooks. Bullfinches are also very dependable and although there are more of them (up to a dozen) than stonechats they spend much of their life deep in the bushes and brambles and, consequently, are more difficult to see. The part of the trail between Winpenny and West Mead is best for bullfinches, with the bushes near the latter hide being particularly favoured.

The low trees, hedges and undergrowth along the way are occupied by wrens, dunnocks and robins, sometimes identifiable only from their calls, sometimes emerging to feed in full view on the path. The same habitat also provides food and cover for many other species, of which regulars include goldcrests, long-tailed tits, blue tits, great tits, chaffinches and greenfinches. It is normal to find several yellowhammers, occasionally near Winpenny but more certainly at the West Mead end of the trail. Roving flocks of goldfinches, at times exceeding a hundred individuals, congregate on seed heads, search for food on the ground or pause high in the trees on their way to another feeding place. Early in October there may still be a few garden warblers, blackcaps, chiffchaffs, and willow warblers.

Numerous species spend time feeding in the adjacent fields and, in some cases, on the surface of the path itself. After suffering disturbance they can be found in nearby trees and bushes, to which they retreat until they feel confident enough to start looking for food again. Green woodpeckers behave in this fashion and are often much easier to see when on the path than in the long grass of the fields. Small numbers of skylarks and linnets and larger parties of meadow pipits should be seen from time to time, particularly in flight. Of the thrush family, fieldfares can assemble in flocks varying from a few up to a hundred or more but there are usually significantly fewer redwings. One or two blackbirds and song thrushes often feed close to the hedges near West Mead. Almost always, the fields are populated by at least a few jackdaws, magpies, rooks or carrion crows.

Deciduous trees always have the potential for woodpeckers and those near

Winpenny seem to be quite attractive to great spotted woodpeckers and in addition they are where, once in a blue moon, lesser spotted woodpeckers have appeared. There may also be woodpeckers in the trees near West Mead, and jays occasionally stray there from more thickly wooded places. The trees near Winpenny and West Mead are irregularly the location for small numbers of lesser redpolls.

Unsurprisingly, because both hides overlook much the same sort of habitat, many of the same birds are seen from both Winpenny and West Mead, but the latter hide usually gives closer views of a wider range of species.

Little egrets and grey herons are occasionally visible from Winpenny in low numbers. Hardly ever recorded on this southern side of the reserve are Bewick's swans but you can be almost certain of locating mute swans, although they may be quite distant. Whooper swans are very scarce winter visitors indeed, although there have been just one or two sightings on or over this part of the brooks. From time to time, feral and escaped wildfowl, like the black swan and barnacle and Egyptian geese recorded from here, crop up wherever there is suitable habitat.

The flocks of both greylag and Canada geese can run into hundreds, as can those of the wigeon that particularly like to graze on the riverbank. Teal, mallard, pintail and shoveler are seen from this hide but rarely in the same abundance likely from West Mead.

There is always the chance of a sparrowhawk or a kestrel. Other birds of prey are less frequent, the most probable being a buzzard or two high over the distant downs, a peregrine or, from November, a hen harrier. Early in October there is the outside hope of a hobby. An out of the ordinary Winpenny record is that of a red kite in December 2003.

Of the waders that occur in the winter, lapwings will be in the majority, congregating here as on all the areas of wet meadow. Ruff, snipe and black-tailed godwits are seen from Winpenny, although normally much more easily from West Mead. A jack snipe would be a notable sighting from either hide, as would another shy wetland bird, the water rail.

In those years when they are present, short-eared owls can often be seen well from Winpenny. Kingfishers are fickle in their choice of fishing spots but the ditches outside Winpenny are preferred at least as much as anywhere.

One advantage that Winpenny does have is its proximity to the river, so close views can be had of anything flying along its course, assuming that it is above the level of the floodbank. Two examples are the osprey in October 1999 and, extraordinarily, the lone juvenile gannets seen not only in November 1995 but again in November the following year.

Over the years, the extent of the water outside West Mead has varied according to the weather and to the management of the water control devices, and so the variety and abundance of species has fluctuated. When the water is reasonably deep, a little grebe is not unusual. Far from usual was the black-necked grebe, which dropped in for a couple of days in December 2005. More commonplace are the one or two cormorants that visit periodically. Whilst the water may not be deep enough for cormorants to dive they are sometimes able to swim just below the surface, with only the top of the back visible. Little egrets are irregular, although there have been up to five, but there is usually a grey heron to be seen.

Mid and South Brooks attract the full range of dabbling ducks, mostly not in quite the numbers seen on North Brooks, some of which come very close to the windows of West Mead. Wigeon and teal can be present in hundreds and there will probably be a gadwall or two. It would be amazing if there were not at least a few mallard and there are times when considerably more congregate on this part of the brooks. Although pintail and shoveler come here to feed, they are never as plentiful as on the other side of the reserve.

With the outside exception of a few pochard or tufted duck, this is not the place to expect diving ducks, except on those infrequent occasions of deep flooding, when the conditions attract more of both species. Flooding has the potential to draw in other birds such as the goldeneye that visited during one November.

As at Winpenny, sparrowhawks, kestrels and peregrines are the raptors that you will be most likely to encounter. Common buzzards are reasonably regular, though they may be high and distant. In October there is still the possibility of a hobby. A harrier will almost certainly be a hen harrier, single examples of which occur once in a while (normally not before November), rather than the much scarcer marsh harrier. The merlin, a winter visitor to the reserve, is infrequent here.

Several moorhens and coots are assured but you will need a slice of good fortune, or times of severe frost, to come across a water rail. There is no element of luck in finding lapwings because there will always be at least a few, and perhaps hundreds. Lapwings are sometimes accompanied by a small number of golden plovers. Snipe, some of which are often quite close to West Mead's windows, need to be looked for carefully since their highly effective camouflage gives them the ability to become all but invisible when standing motionless in the dead vegetation. Probably present, but virtually impossible to find, are jack snipe, a view of one counting as a rather exceptional event. A few ruff are also possible, as are dunlins. Curlews are definitely not an everyday sight, although they do pass through, and on a December day there was a record count of eight. The brooks here have seen a selection of other waders over the years but, at best, never more than sporadically, including the isolated appearances of curlew sandpipers and green sandpipers in October and, in November, black-tailed godwits and avocets.

Apart from the black-headed species, gulls are not very plentiful. There can be a few common gulls and, much more irregularly, the odd lesser black-backed, great black-backed and herring gull. An extraordinary seabird record is that of the little auk, which flew over in December 2000.

A few late migrants - sand martins, swallows, house martins and perhaps a yellow wagtail - on their way south in October reflect the end of autumn. In some winters the daytime scene is enhanced by one or two short-eared owls quartering the brooks. Barn owls are unlikely but have been seen from West Mead. A dark day could be enlivened by a kingfisher although, if one is intent on fishing this part of the reserve, the odds are that it will be closer to Winpenny. Careful scanning of the middle distance sometimes results in the glimpse of a reed bunting and, less often, a grey wagtail. You can be much more confident of finding members of the crow family foraging on the meadows. Carrion crows are usually in low numbers but mixed flocks of jackdaws and rooks can run into hundreds. Also potentially in hundreds are the starlings, which feed in the same places.

Over the years, this last division of the nature trail has not been without a selection of out-of-the-way birds. For more than two weeks from mid-September 1993 there were two black redstarts near Winpenny and twice a common redstart has been seen in the Redstart Corner area late in October. The Winpenny region has hosted whinchats in October and November, a wheatear twice in October, a few firecrests and the odd siskin. There has been a siskin, too, near West Mead, which has also been the place for some few and far between bramblings and, in October, spotted flycatchers. Another notable sight was the hawfinch, encountered on this section of the trail in mid-October 2006. The most highly desired bird at this part of the reserve has unquestionably been the great grey shrike. Of the very scarce sightings of this rare winter visitor, two have been between Redstart Corner and West Mead, one in December 2004 and the most recent in October 2005.

It is a short step from West Mead to Fattengates and the completion of your circuit of the nature trail. The walk back up the hill to Upperton's Barn gives, together with the courtyard and the car park, a final opportunity to add some additional species to your day's bird list.

Glossary of Terms

As far as possible, 'technical' terms have been avoided but some readers may find the following explanations of interest.

brooks (as in 'Pulborough Brooks'): see 'lowland wet grassland' below.

calls: relatively simple sounds, often consisting of a single note, produced by birds throughout the year, examples being alarm calls and contact notes.

drumming: in the context of this book, the loud drumming sound produced by woodpeckers (at the reserve, most frequently great spotted woodpeckers) striking their bills against tree branches, trunks and other resonant objects.

eclipse plumage: ducks, in common with other wildfowl, moult all their flight feathers at once in the late summer and autumn. In order to appear less conspicuous to predators whilst in this flightless and vulnerable state the drakes also moult their colourful breeding plumage, and then look very similar to the better camouflaged females.

feral: having been deliberately released, or escaped from captivity, and now living in a self-maintaining state in the wild.

migration: normally understood to mean the movements of populations of (in our case) birds between where they breed and where they spend the winter and vice versa. For example, swallows that breed at the reserve travel to Africa for the winter whilst Bewick's swans nest in Siberia and visit Pulborough Brooks during the winter.

moult: birds' feathers wear out and have, periodically, to be shed and replaced by new feathers in a process known as 'moulting'.

hirundine: one of the swallow family, represented at Pulborough Brooks by sand martins, house martins and swallows.

lowland wet grassland: periodically inundated pasture or meadow with ditches which maintain the water level. In this part of Sussex, such places are known as 'brooks'.

passage: the movement of birds, which do not breed or spend the winter at Pulborough Brooks, through the reserve while on migration.

RSPB: The Royal Society for the Protection of Birds is the largest wildlife conservation organisation in Europe with over one million members. It campaigns to protect wildlife and the environment and manages over 200 nature reserves throughout the UK, of which Pulborough Brooks is one.

songs: relatively long and complex series of sounds made, in most cases, mainly during the breeding season by, in most species, male birds. They are often appealing to the human ear.

twitcher: a birdwatcher whose prime purpose is to see as many rare birds as possible.

BIRDWATCHING AT PULBOROUGH BROOKS
THROUGH THE SEASONS

The pictures in the book have been provided by David and Janet Shaw.

Peregrines to cheetahs, swans to hippos - David and Janet just love to spend as much time as they can out in the country, taking stunning photographs of those rare moments that nature offers. They have had photographs and films used by the BBC, newspapers and magazines, and organisations such as the RSPB, NFU, Chichester Cathedral and DK Books. They are always very happy to take on a commission or help with a certain subject or picture when approached.

David and Janet would like to dedicate the pictures in this book to the memories of Natalie, John and Winnie, all of whom loved their wildlife.

Please visit their website at www.davidshawwildlife.co.uk